by
Bobby Gould
and
David Instone

Thomas Publications

T
P

First published in Great Britain in October, 2010
by Thomas Publications

ISBN 978-0-9550585-4-7

Thomas Publications
PO Box 17, Newport, Shropshire, TF10 7WT

Printed and bound by TJ International, Padstow, Cornwall

Contents

Acknowledgements

Ever since I reached 60, I have been very keen to write my autobiography, convinced as I am that my life has been full enough for such a story. But who should I pen it with? Who was prepared to set foot in my gobbledegook world as ghost writer? David Instone accepted the poisoned chalice.

During the two years we have worked on this project, we have had great fun, even if some of the early manuscript was handed back to David with the message that boring fact-based text really wasn't me. I'm glad to say he quickly bought into my pursuit of a more entertaining read, as well as a revealing one.

I have memorabilia by the cupboard full and, whenever he scrambled into my loft retreat – the area I lovingly call my bolthole – he was amazed by all the keepsakes I have gathered from my career. Each time we went up there to work, he uncovered another gem.

As 24 Carat Gould grew out of an initial interview for his excellent website (www.wolvesheroes.com), so did our army of helpers. We have been tireless in our efforts and I have been demanding in the standards expected of others. Eccentric I may be but I have never forgotten the six Ps that make up one of my football sayings: Proper Preparation Prevents P**s Poor Performance.

A thousand thank-yous are therefore extended to Liz Instone for her technical expertise, Tricia Mills for the stunning cover, Dave Armitage for his many design and marketing ideas and Dave Bagnall for the front-cover photograph. Also, I express my gratitude to my school friend Roy Deakin for his encouragement, Coventry City Former Players Association, journalists Ralph Ellis, Martin Smith, Phil Shaw, Don Veale, Rob Phillips and Adam Dent, the Press Association and to the two big local papers in my life, the Coventry Telegraph and Western Daily Press, both of whom I've leaned on for pictures in this book.

I was in set four in English at Caludon Castle, taken by Mr 'Teddy' Brown, and, at Stoke Council Junior School, I had to be taught by Mr Bennett not to put an extra 'r' in the middle of water. I therefore underline my admiration for how David Instone has put my many words, all 105,000 of them, in exactly the right order. I'm confident our friendship will continue to flourish.

Bob

Foreword

Bobby Moore, Sir Bobby Charlton, Bobby Gould...ask for the achievements and great feats of these three footballers and you would immediately remember the brilliance of two of them and maybe struggle with the third.

'World Cup Winner' is the ultimate accolade for Moore and Charlton among a glittering array of other honours. On the other hand, you perhaps need to be an 'anorak' or one of his closest pals to understand why the beautiful game should be just as proud to embrace Bobby Gould. Passion, determination and pride have always been the real hallmarks of my good friend.

In his professional football career, he has been on the books of nine clubs as a player and been manager or assistant manager of another 11. And that does not include his four-year tenure in charge of Wales.

It's a career spattered with highs and lows, a roller-coaster ride that could have come off the rails long before this extraordinary character stood in front of 100,000 people at the home of football, Wembley Stadium, holding aloft the FA Cup as his Wimbledon side created what I still believe to be the greatest shock in the history of this competition, denying mighty Liverpool a 1988 League and Cup double.

Lesser men would have lost belief and thrown in the towel long before this memorable achievement. That's not the Gould style. To be in Bob's company is revealing. He has an infectious enthusiasm for the game and tells fascinating and revealing stories that help remind you why football is the world's most popular sport.

That is what this autobiography is all about – the game of football. It's about both outstanding and less fortunate players, managers, coaches and officials, all seen through the eyes of a rare personality, someone who really does know the differences that exist between an Arsenal and a Cheltenham Town, the Bobbys Moore and Charlton and a Bobby Gould.

It's a story I proudly recommend you to read; the story of a Coventry lad who, with the unstinting support and love of his family, eventually followed in the footsteps of the other two legendary Bobbys to create his own special piece of history within football.

As my best pal and room-mate during his two and a half years at Arsenal, I know him better than most and the memory I have of us doing the washing up together in his Portishead home a few days after his FA Cup triumph, with the historic old trophy also included in the drying-up process, is one that I will never forget.

The full story of Bobby Gould and his life in and out of football is amusing, fascinating and serves as an inspiration to others who love the game.

When he asked me if I would write this foreword, I replied by saying that I'd have been disappointed if he hadn't asked.

Bob Wilson OBE

To Dad, who missed the second half, and our four wonderful grandchildren, Matt, Lou, Jess and Libby.

Don't cry because it's over. Smile because it happened.

Dead End Job

I can't remember the gentleman's name but he worked for Coventry Council and came to our school, Caludon Castle, in the spring of 1961 to give career advice. He sat me down in the common room next to the office that belonged to the Howard House master Mr Titt and asked what I wanted to do with my life when I left. I said: "Sir, I want to be a professional footballer." He didn't bat an eye-lid but I will never forget his reply: "Gould, it's a dead-end job."

Nearly 50 years and well over 20 appointments later, I'm still making a decent living from my 'dead-end job,' although by now it's mainly through talking about football on the radio for talkSPORT rather than playing or coaching it. In the meantime, I've been top scorer in the season my home-city club won promotion to the top division for the first time, won the FA Cup as a player and manager, scored in a League Cup final at Wembley, played in Europe, managed for nearly four years in international football, travelled the world, made a thousand friends and generally had a ball. Don't tell me you shouldn't be allowed to pursue your dream. I certainly wasn't going to let anyone deflect me from mine.

Our eldest son, who was not given the benefit of such 'advice,' has been to a World Cup as a player, found a good livelihood from the game for more than 20 years and is bringing up a family in a lovely part of the Southern Hemisphere. Our youngest is a former Army major and is now chief executive of Somerset County Cricket Club. So we haven't done too badly on the home front either.

Right, that's about as serious as I intend to be in this book. A couple of years ago, almost at the outset of this project, I threw a slab of text back at my ghost writer and told him the style wasn't 'me.' It was too heavy with statistics and dates. It didn't bounce along as I wanted it to, from anecdote to anecdote, skirmish to skirmish, club to club. But I'm delighted with it now. It's a fun read and I think anyone who opens these pages is guaranteed a good giggle.

I'm devoted to books and like them to entertain as well as enlighten me. When we were going on holiday early this summer, I was struggling to find anything that caught my eye for the beach but my ghost writer, who was starting to understand me by this stage, lent me a male-angst novel called Past And Presents, by the Daily Star's Midlands football reporter Dave Armitage. I couldn't put it down.

I will be flattered if anyone says that about my story but that's the effect I've been trying to achieve. I took 30 seconds to agree the financial arrangements with my publisher for this venture but we've deliberated for months and months over the text, all 100,000 words of it. You get one stab at an autobiography and I hope we've got it something like right.

It's stating the obvious to say that I never got remotely near being awarded a testimonial at any of my clubs. But, to make it easier to keep up while the text is being read, a concise list of my transfers and appointments appears at the back; so does a list of nicknames and who they relate to.

Inevitably, following almost half a century in dressing rooms and on team coaches, a certain amount of 'blokiness' will have crept in. My mates in the game would suspect something if there wasn't any swearing in these pages but, to younger and female readers, I offer the promise that it's only used in the context of necessary industrial language. To my mum and Jimmy Hill, I just say sorry and ask forgiveness.

I don't think I'm guilty of over-egging the story. Football may be a big business but it's also a game of high emotion. Is there anything like it for sparking debate in the pub or workplace? What else can quicken the pulse like our national sport? Those of us who make a livelihood from it are so, so lucky and it is something to be relished, whether that's in the playing, the managing, the coaching, the watching or even the reminiscing.

I assume the careers officer has long since been pushing up roses but he might have noted my fortunes if he remembered the young Robert Alfred Gould and realised I became the goal-hungry Bobby Gould. All I'd want him to know is that I've been blessed with a fabulous life and given it my best shot.

Crazy Gang Calling

The jobsworths on patrol outside White Hart Lane had never seen anything like it. They were used to doffing their caps at football's high and mighty and pointing out where gleaming luxury coaches should park when dropping off the tens of millions of pounds' worth of talent. But this was Wimbledon, rolling up for an FA Cup semi-final in a minibus.

We always did things differently. Sometimes it was by choice, sometimes out of financial necessity. There was no point pretending we had the resources to prepare like the Liverpools, Arsenals and Manchester Uniteds, even for massive games such as this. Wimbledon weren't a five-star club and the players didn't want to be treated that way. They were happier being seen as The Crazy Gang. It helped foster that famous team spirit.

After we had beaten Watford in the 1987-88 quarter-final in what one writer called a match straight from the Charles Hughes Manual on long-ball football, we decided we would prepare for the semi-final against Luton as if it were just a normal game at Tottenham or Arsenal. In other words, those lads like Vinnie Jones, John Fashanu, Eric Young, Lawrie Sanchez, Dennis Wise, our skipper Dave Beasant and our coach Don Howe, who all lived north of the Thames, would make their own way to the game. I would go with the rest from Plough Lane. We were comfortable that way.

We didn't even have an organised pre-match meal. We had the team meeting the day before and left the players to have a bit of brunch at home. Then we loaded the skip on to the navy and white VW at the ground, our kit man Syd Neal threw me the keys and we were on our way. I doubt there has been such an informal build-up to an FA Cup semi-final since the 1920s or 1930s.

The police outriders detailed to escort us were parked up on their motorcycles on one of the Thames bridges. They took some convincing that we were who they were waiting for as we drove up behind them but eventually they accepted my word and we headed for the busy streets of North London, with me at the wheel, and the likes of John Scales, Terry Phelan, Andy Thorn and Brian Gayle on board, along with Syd and his assistant Joe Dillon. My wife Marge was following in my red club Fiat Croma.

We had the same credibility problems at the ground, where the guy on the gate said: "That's not a team coach. It's not big enough and it's not coming in here." I shouted back: "If we're not allowed in, there won't be a game because half the players are on here and the other half won't have any kit to wear." It took five minutes for my persuasive charms to work, then we were shown to a huge parking space. The minibus made only a partial imprint on it and left enough room in the bay for a couple of other vehicles, so we did our bit for the car parking cause that day as well.

Our preparations may have seemed a bit Sunday morningish but all our personnel made it there in good time. Luton, I'm sure, did the conventional thing and the irony was that they were thrown into a spin when their club doctor was delayed in a motorway jam. Ray Harford told me some time afterwards that the doc was later than he wanted to be in administering a pain-killing injection to their talented midfielder Darron McDonough. By the time the needle was unwrapped, our lads were giving it the big build-up outside the dressing room with a chant that sounded like Yidahoi. In all the din and commotion, the injection apparently missed the spot.

The doc's nerves weren't helped by all accounts when he asked where the noise was coming from and was told it was from the opposition players. McDonough had to come off in the second half after the effects wore off and his ankle became more and more painful.

However unusual our schedule was, we didn't half play well at White Hart Lane. I had forgotten just how well until I pulled up a chair at home a few years ago, watched a recording of the game and felt very proud all over again. Luton had already won that season's League Cup by beating Arsenal at Wembley and they also reached the Simod Cup final. Like us, they were in the top half of what we simply called the First Division and Ray Harford had a more than decent side, with players like Ricky Hill, Steve Foster, Mal Donaghy, Danny Wilson, Brian Stein and Mick Harford.

Harford put them in front in the first half but Fash rolled in the equaliser from a penalty, then Corky crossed superbly for Wisey to slide in the winner in front of our fans. Wimbledon, still a non-League club 11 years earlier and in only their second season of top-flight football, were in the FA Cup final. "What a fairytale!" as Barry Davies put it on the TV.

It was at that point that we relaxed and realised there was no point becoming uptight. How else could we be really? We were going to Wembley to play Liverpool, who had beaten Nottingham Forest in the other semi-final and who had just won the League for a record 17th time. It wasn't exactly as if anyone thought we had a chance against them.

I had insisted on driving the minibus to the semi-final because I wanted something to do. I didn't want the players to sense any anxieties I might have – and I had a few despite having played in West Ham's 1975 semi-final win over Ipswich at Stamford Bridge. To be through to Wembley, though, lifted the tension and we set out to really enjoy ourselves.

The media afternoon a few days before the final didn't hold any of the demons it might have done and turned into a fun time. Once, that is, I'd put Eric Hall in his place. I could organise a press day like no-one else – a couple of benches, a plan where everyone was to sit and stand; bang, bang, some lively banter, finished, off home. Any player arriving late would be fined two weeks' wages. At Coventry, it ran even smoother because my secretary Jenny Poole was such a slick operator, too, and came out to help with the line-up.

My idea at Wimbledon was to have an open-house arrangement where the press could come in, float from one player to another doing interviews, have a cup of tea, a sandwich and a slice of cake and get everthing they wanted in one go. Things were going fine until one or two reporters complained that Eric, who was Wisey's agent, was denying them access to him. I was totally against the idea of individual deals and wanted any pounds, shillings and pence paid into the players' pool for the collective benefit.

I laid into Eric by saying: "Look, YOUR man belongs to MY team and this is Wimbledon's press day. Accept that or I'll have you escorted from the ground." We soon sorted it out and the convivial atmosphere was restored, helped by my good relationship with Fleet Street big hitters like Brian Woolnough, Nigel Clarke, Ian Ridley and Steve Curry. I'm sure Tony Stenson would have been there as well. 'Stengun' and me fought like cats when I discovered he and my predecessor Harry Bassett were as thick as thieves but we got over our teething problems and became good mates. They were all regular and willing visitors to Plough Lane because we were seen as front-page news as well as headline-makers on the back.

Organising the Cup Final suits was another enjoyable task. Peter Ridsdale was in charge of Top Man at the time and got us sorted. We had some great fun when we appeared on The Clothes Show and their cameras turned up at Plough Lane, especially as the top designer Jeff Banks made a great fuss of the wives, who were filmed as well after going to Top Shop for their gear. Fash went the extra yard as usual and had a waistcoat with his suit. We'd all have been surprised and disappointed if he hadn't done something different.

I was in a dilemma, though, and consulted my chief scout Ron Suart. I knew we all had to be identically dressed at Wembley for appearances' sake but I had my lucky FA Cup outfit to think about – the one I had worn for every game in the competition. I was so superstitious that I even wore the same socks, tie, belt and navy blue underpants for all the rounds.

I didn't want to leave that outfit in the wardrobe, so I compromised by dressing in my Top Man suit for our departure from the hotel while carrying a suit holder containing my Marks & Spencer blazer, shirt and trousers. I would put all that on at the stadium. My family know I want to be buried in that outfit, so I make sure I go on a run several times a week and try to stay in decent shape. That way, it should still fit me when the final whistle blows.

The squad latched on to one or two superstitions of their own in the Cup run, including having apple pie and ice cream as dessert in each hotel we stayed in as that's what we'd had before a couple of the earlier ties.

Many's the time I've wondered what Kenny Dalglish's preparations entailed other than going to pick up another Manager of the Year award and being constantly reminded of the inevitability of winning at Wembley. But I know for sure it won't have included one of my chores. We were always under-staffed at Wimbledon, so when the office people were looking round at each other wondering who was free to go and fetch some important boxes we needed from Wembley two or three weeks before the big day, I said I'd do it.

I didn't have that much to occupy me in the afternoons, so I jumped in the car and drove across London. That was the easy bit. Making the return journey with 22,000 Cup Final tickets in the back was a bit more nerve-racking. I suppose I could have made a detour to Stan Flashman's home and then kept going to Heathrow. I could have been in Marbella cracking open a San Miguel before anyone had missed me. Anyway, I was happy to muck in. That's what we all did.

The police insisted we left the minibus in the garage and used a coach for the ride up Wembley Way on Saturday, May 14. Fair enough. This was going to be the greatest experience of our football lives and we were happy to treat it as something very special. We booked in at the Cannizaro House Hotel on Wimbledon Common on the Friday and made sure they had some apple pie and ice cream in the fridge.

Not that I fancied eating anything after taking a call in my room early on match-day morning. It was Bob Wilson, my best mate in the game, telling me he thought the press coverage the players would soon be digesting with their tea and toast was disgraceful. The tabloids were laying into us again over our playing style and had clearly decided we were there just to make up the numbers.

I said: "Willo, it's 7.30am and I'm in for a long tiring day." But he was outraged and, when he gave me the gist of it all, I was as well, saying I'd ring the FA and the media and tell them that we'd present the Cup to Liverpool and then play them at cricket because obviously there was no point stepping on the same pitch to take them on at football.

We know our style wasn't sophisticated. Dave Bassett had developed a certain way of playing, the Wimbledon way if you like, and I saw no reason to change that when I was appointed as his successor. Our methods didn't please everyone but it would have been utter madness convincing ourselves we could outpass Liverpool, Everton, Arsenal and the other leading sides at that time. It was a case of being realistic.

Deep down, though, I thought we'd win at Wembley after the way we played in the semi-final and I joked in the media that Alan Hansen, Gary Gillespie and Gary Ablett should take some Aspirin along with them as there would be plenty of high balls landing in their penalty area. Gillespie and Nigel Spackman actually had their foreheads bandaged from the start after they were injured in the midweek, so they probably didn't fancy trying to combat our route-one style.

I'd said in my press conference and to the players that we could be relaxed, with all the pressure on Liverpool. The worst that can happen when you have been roundly written off is that you lose and go home quietly.

At the stadium, the first thing we did was tell our assistant kit man Joe Dillon to turn the clocks in our dressing room back two minutes. That meant we kept Liverpool waiting at every turn, whether it was for meeting the FA suits to have the protocol for the day explained to us, handing the team sheets in or, most importantly, assembling the players in the tunnel ready to walk out ten minutes before kick-off – or was that really only eight?

I felt good about the occasion and shook the hand of every one of Liverpool's players as we waited for the signal to head for the daylight and the din. But I had to put a rein on Kenny Dalglish when we finally emerged. He was striding out briskly, so I called: "Look Kenny, you might come here once or twice a season but this is probably going to be my only time……could you please slow down and let me savour the walk!"

During our Cup run, we had received letters and good-luck messages from all over the world, one landing on my desk from my former West Ham room-mate Bobby Ferguson. 'Fester' was by then living in Adelaide and asked me to give him a wave with my left hand as we emerged on to the pitch. I thought it was just for old time's sake. It was only later that I found out he had relieved a few mates in Australia of a pocketful of dollars after betting with them that I'd wave with my left hand.

Talking of luck, we couldn't believe ours when we had learned we would be meeting Princess Diana. She went along the Liverpool line first, then Lurch greeted her on our behalf as skipper and introduced her to our lads. I was last in line and bowed before uttering the words: "Afternoon, ma'am. You're looking a bit nervous. I've heard that you bite your fingernails when you're sitting on the edge of your seat." She flashed me that endearing coy look and replied: "Don't be so cheeky. You'll be the nervous one."

I don't know whether any of the lads made any inappropriate comments to her but if only I could have held their attention as well as she did. They were magical moments in a day we will never forget. But nothing beat the feeling a couple of hours later when the lads shook hands with her again and that shiny prize was all ours. The Crazy Gang had won the FA Cup.

A Coventry Boy

The FA Cup has always been big to me. Long before Coventry City won it in 1987 for the first and only time and Wimbledon followed up by doing the same 12 months later, there was something very special about it. Growing up in Coventry, I loved Cup ties at Highfield Road, even when my favourites were losing them. There was such excitement around watching a game when you knew the losers were knocked out and the winners went through to the next round.

But my links with the competition seem to run deeper than that. Of the dozens and dozens of winners' names now engraved on the base of the trophy, that of Wimbledon just happens to be next to Coventry's. Furthermore, my car registration number is R88 CUP in deference to my finest hour in management but my first vehicle – a £300 green Singer Hillman Chamois with a black stripe – came with the number FAC 658, decades before personalised plates were thought of. Was it written in the stars that the Cup would play such a big part in my career?

As a kid, I was entranced. I can look at a TV now and imagine it's the 12-inch screen that Dad, me, my brother Trevor and Granddad Dickie Gould, who had caught the bus over from Binley, all sat round to watch the 'Matthews Final' – the 1953 epic between Bolton and Blackpool. After that game, our kid and me played in the garden, one of us in the role of Blackpool keeper George Farm or his Bolton counterpart Stan Hanson, the other taking shots as Nat Lofthouse, Stanley Matthews or the hat-trick man Stan Mortensen.

I remember all the finals from then on, especially the one between Tottenham and Burnley because Bobby Smith was a favourite of mine. We were one of the first families in our street to have a telly, so several of my mates would come round as well.

The FA Cup's showpiece game was the only match televised for years and years, so it became a fixture of huge prestige. It was the one all football-mad kids dreamed of playing in – and I was certainly one of those. Am I the only man ever to win the Cup twice and not kick a ball in a final? Possibly. More of that later but what I am sure about is that an awful lot of graft went into my mission to reach a final. It's what I dedicated myself to from a very early age.

The only time I ever remember it raining in my childhood was on Monday mornings when I looked out of the window at Stoke Council Junior School. On Monday afternoons, Mr Bell and Mr Ackland would walk us for over half a mile in a long line to the Morris playing fields for football – but only if it was dry. After school and in the holidays, we never did anything but find a ball and play. And the sun always seemed to shine.

Wyken Wizards were my first side in the days when we played inter-park games without referees, linesmen, managers or kit. A dimpled Frido ball gave us hours of fun on Caludon Park and two of my mates, Kingsley Wood and his brother Peter, had access to another little pitch by their dad's allotment. It made good sense to keep in with them, not that I thought I would do so for as long as I have. When I was on my way to New Zealand to visit our son Jonathan in 2005, I tracked Kingsley down and we caught up on more than 40 years over a beer or two in a Los Angeles hotel near where he now lives.

As boyhood mates, often with others like Michael Oakes, Wally Beasley and Roy Deakin, we'd set off from Forknell Avenue, where we lived, and make a regular bee-line for the sloping area of grass next to the Devonshire Arms pub and the Wyken tip. From there, we could also keep an eye on Lyng Hall Girls' Comprehensive School. But it wasn't the hockey players there that we were interested in. It was the goals on their pitch. They had nets. We had never played in them before, so we took every chance we could to indulge ourselves when the groundsman wasn't around. It was a step closer to becoming another Matthews, Mortensen or Albert Dunlop, the Everton keeper we used to mimic by rolling our shorts up really brief.

Around the same time, our kid Trevor and me sampled the thrill of playing under 'floodlights' – having a kick-around in front of Billy Morton's butcher's shop on the corner of Honiton Road and Forknell Avenue. It made a change from the garden and being slaughtered by the neighbours for shooting against a black tin garage door in the entry, especially Mrs Edwards, who charged us sixpence a time if she had to throw the ball back from her garden. It was a drain on the meagre finances, so we sometimes resorted to wrapping Sellotape round a bundle of old socks and kicking that if we lost a ball altogether.

Dad, who was usually tinkering around on some mechanical job in his beloved garage, joined in with the complaints if we disturbed the guttering that was always loose. But the only time he ever hit me was when I owned up to cycling one-handed on the busy Walsgrave Road – one of those the Sky Blues travelled along during their tour with the FA Cup in 1987 – with the Frido under my arm. He wasn't having that and gave me a good hiding.

Dad used to play works football for Singer Motors as well as follow Coventry, who were then known as The Bantams or, during one special time, as the 'Old Five' because they seemed to put five past every side they played. Granddad Gould was a season ticket holder. When I was invited back for the last game at Highfield Road in 2004 with many other former players, I placed photographs of them both – and also pictures of our sons – in my suit pocket, so I could feel they were all there in spirit.

With Coventry beating Derby 6-2 to ensure they stayed up, it was a happy occasion and it was as if my Dad's brother Alan, who had died in an accident when he fell off a horse as a teenager, was the only male member of the family not 'present.' Straight after the final whistle, a chap approached me for my autograph and asked me to sign his programme: 'To Alan, Best Wishes.' Uncanny.

Granddad Gould, who had fought in the Boer War and once had a trial at Aston Villa, had the Christian names Alfred Ernest but was known as Dickie. My grandfather on Mum's side was Robert Morton, who was Scottish and had played for Blantyre Vics, the same junior club as Matt Busby. I was Christened Robert Alfred Gould so as to take a bit of both.

I didn't do as well with the naming of our sons. We called our first-born Jonathan Alan (initials J.A.G.) and chose Andrew as a middle name when Richard arrived at Paddington Hospital a couple of years later. The initials R.A.G. had been so lucky for me that I thought Richard should have them, too. The trouble was, in the post-natal euphoria, I became distracted when I found out the registrar was an Arsenal fan. I was playing for them at the time and we chatted at length over goings-on at Highbury, so much so that I fluffed my more important lines and we found ourselves bringing up two lads who had Alan as their middle name. And Marge has never let me forget it......

My mum, who was Christened Helen Gould, was from not far south of Glasgow, and, when my good pal Bob Wilson broke the mould in the 1970s by playing for Scotland despite being born in Chesterfield, I suppose I might have wondered whether the same door north of the border would open for me. Not that Dad, a proud Englishman, would have been too impressed. As it happened, the opportunity never came but Jonathan later played for the Tartan Army and went to the World Cup with them, although he in turn could have played for South Africa because Marge's father, George Page, was from Durban. In some ways, we have a complicated background, with our roots stretching to different countries, but I regard Coventry as my spiritual home and grew up feeling very proud of it.

We lived on the outskirts, on the flight path for the Luftwaffe pilots who devastated the city a few years before I was born. When the moon shone, they used Coombe Lake as a sighter to tell them they were three miles from their target area. I look back now and realise that not many people wanted to talk about what they lived through, including my dad, who was an auxiliary fireman. But I've learned that the hatches would be opened soon after the planes left the lake behind and headed over Wyken and Highfield Road, ready to unleash another night of terror.

Life, thankfully, was much more tranquil in my infancy. Mum worked the 6pm-10pm shift at GEC, the pinafore shift as they called it because of all the women, so Trevor and me spent a lot of time in the evenings with Dad. It was pure love. We bonded brilliantly, often in front of the telly marvelling at the martians in Quarter Mass. In the holidays and after school, I spent plenty of time with my grandparents and was very close to them all.

As an eight-year-old, I remember getting on a bus with Trevor or walking him the three miles – via the playing fields, of course – to my Scottish grandparents' house for lunch. They lived in Glencoe Road, right next to GEC. Granddad Bob was a miner who came down to Coventry to work in the pits and he spotted me quicker than I spotted him the day I was taken underground on a school trip when we were meant to be thinking of possible careers. "I hope you'll nae be working as a miner!" he told me in his gruff Glaswegian. The filth on his face meant that all I could recognise of him, apart from his accent, was his eyes. From that day, my desire to become a footballer grew even fiercer.

Dad often seemed to be on strike in the car industry and would fill his time off by potato picking. It was back-breaking work, as well as poorly paid, but Mum was brilliant at stretching the few bob it brought in and making sure there was still enough food on the table.

Granddad Gould was well known around the area for breeding bantams. He was also responsible for starting the massive collection of scrapbooks I have on my career. Any snippet bearing my name was cut out and stuck in, and the playing section of my football life is still neatly stored away in my 'bolthole' – the space in the loft I have converted into an office for when Marge red-cards me for more serious offences.

Despite my spells in solitary in the rafters, the Gould family have always been very 'together.' We're a happy, outgoing lot. Dad and me had a special relationship and he was brilliant with my early football development, always making sure I had the best boots – Adidas with screw-in studs. Mum would wash the white laces after every game. My boots were precious to me and I dreamt of using them to rattle in a few goals one day for my beloved Coventry City, especially in the FA Cup.

I became hooked from the age of five in the early 1950s. It didn't matter that the club were in the Third Division South, had no floodlights and were being knocked out of the Cup by Plymouth and Brighton. All their players were heroes to me, among them Roy Kirk, Alf Wood, Ray Sambrook, Lol Harvey, Tommy Capel, Ray Straw and Stuart Imlach, although the goalkeeper Reg Matthews (Coventry's first England international) was my favourite. I used to go and sit outside his house five minutes' walk from our home in Wyken to wait for his autograph.

Newport County, Millwall and Aldershot were typical opponents and Granddad would take his pigeons to the games in baskets and send them back to his brother (my Uncle Harry) in Walsgrave Road, bearing the score. It wasn't a service to rival Sky Sports but he mastered the art of tying notes to the birds' legs and was a busy man on the Spion Kop if the goals were raining in.

Attendances were only a few thousand, so I was trusted to go to matches on my own, or with my mate Terry Clarke, from the age of seven or eight. We lived a couple of miles from the ground and often chose to walk rather than catch the bus, so there was something to spare for some chips on the way home. A few years later, I took on a paper round; more matches, more chips.

It's a good job I could play football because I was never going to be an academic. Despite the efforts of Mr Bennett, a lovely man who once embarrassed me with a telling-off after I wrote a love letter to Susan Barrow, my first girlfriend, I failed my 11 Plus at Stoke Council Junior School. I went to the comprehensive, Caludon Castle, having fallen well short of the grade for Bablake and King Henry VIII Grammar. I never had any luck with those prestigious establishments. We tried to get Jonathan and Richard in there on a fee-paying basis many years later but were told the curriculum was too different to the one they were already on at their schools in the West Country.

All the houses at Caludon were named after knights. I was in Seagrave when I entered the school and Howard when I left. There were also Berkley Chester and Mowbray. Mr Vickery was my Seagrave house master and Mr Toman my group master. In Howard, my house master was Mr Titt. They were all good to me. Above them was a very disciplined headmaster, Mr Tilley, who wasn't afraid to rule with a rod of iron when needed.

We used to play school matches on Saturday mornings, then I'd go to Highfield Road or further afield in the afternoons. Hundreds of fans used to congregate at Pool Meadow station, where we would catch Red House Motor Services buses to games at Leicester, Birmingham, West Brom, Villa or Wolves, a chalk board showing which vehicles were going to which grounds.

I'd sometimes end up at Filbert Street to watch Leicester or at Molineux to drool over the great Wolves sides. I remember being there to see Stan Cullis's famous side beat Preston to lift one of their titles. But Coventry's away fixtures fell in such a way as to allow a few afternoons on that huge Spion Kop at St Andrew's as well. And no Saturday would be complete without a teatime dash to the Sewall Highway paper shop, where I would join a huge queue to buy the Pink and see what 'Nemo' had to say about that day's Bantams game. We hung on to every word in that paper. It was a massive part of our young lives.

I mentioned the scrapbooks. There were writing books, too, loads of them. Not so much for homework as for recording details of matches I played in. 'Won 4-2, scored two' and 'Drew 2-2, scored one' are typical entries but the page devoted to the final of the 1958-59 Birmingham and District Intermediate Trophy between Coventry Boys under-13s and South East Staffs remains blank, so I assume we lost and I struggled. What I do remember is that it was my first game at Highfield Road and I was determined it wouldn't be my last.

I had my first taste of touring when I went with the under-14s on a six-game trip around the Home Counties. We didn't do well but Ivor Wilkinson and Keith 'Nobby' Newbold, the coaches at Coventry Technical College, were brilliant. So were my football teachers at Caludon, Mr Buckingham and Mr Simpson; so passionate and committed. I owe them all big-time.

I progressed to the Coventry City B side and the St James under-16 team in 1961-62. 'Scored 9, 1 penalty' is underlined several times from the day I put Christ The King to the sword but there are also tell-tale signs of a highly competitive nature. 'Played inside-right, scored 2, tackled their full-back and he broke his leg' is the entry from the day I helped St James under-18s to victory over Chapel End Social at Hersall Common.

I was always leading scorer. All lads who make it as League strikers can say that of their teenage years and I scored 15 or 17 goals in one game for Ridgeley Rangers. Another day, I overshadowed Jimmy Hill when he lined up with us for a Coventry Colts game against Repton. As Coventry manager, his name was the one used in the headline in the Daily Telegraph's write-up of the game after he netted twice. Buried in the text is mention of the fact I scored three.

Despite all the goals, I didn't have that much confidence in my ability, certainly nothing like the belief and strength of character I acquired later. I probably never realised how good a player I was as a kid. Not even with the vote of confidence that came after Nan Gould wrote to the Evening Telegraph to complain that they had called me Brian instead of Bob. The paper apologised in print and their correspondent said: "I've a feeling we'll be hearing a lot more of this youngster in the future." It was such a thrill for me to see my name in that paper, even when they spelled it wrong.

After a big trial at their Elmdon training ground on the day I left school, Birmingham offered me terms. They also went for a keeper called Pat Durn but the thought of catching two or three buses each way was too daunting and, at 15, I certainly wasn't ready to leave home. I held out and was glad to be given an eight-week opportunity with Coventry. I scored plenty of goals in their B team, which was basically a fourth team made up of 15-year-olds, playing in a works league against sides of grown men. Many of our opponents had a week down the pit by way of preparation for match-day, so it was a tough environment.

It meant a lot to me when I scored a hat-trick against Binley because Granddad worked for the Miners' Welfare there. But not everybody appreciated it. The defender who was marking me said as I was celebrating one of my goals: "If you go past me again like that, I'll break your fuckin' leg." I vowed there and then to try to find an extra yard of pace.

At the end of the eight weeks, the club manager Billy Frith called me in and told me I wasn't good enough. He broke my heart. I went out on to the track running round Highfield Road and cried my heart out. Ronnie Rees, one of the groundstaff lads and later to play with me in Coventry's first team as well as being a future Welsh international, put his arm round me and said: "Gouldy, don't worry. You'll be back."

Love Is Blind

In one span of three and a half years early in my career, Dad missed only one of my matches – a midweek date at Plymouth. He never missed a home game I appeared in as a Football League player, yet he never saw me play professionally. He was blind from the age of 36.

We were coming back in the car once from a match at Arsenal and he asked me: "What did you do with that chance in the 27th minute?" I always marvelled at how much he knew about a match he couldn't see. He was kept informed by whoever took him, often my mum, my grandfather or later on Marge, but he also said: "If you shut your eyes while you're in the stand watching, you'd realise how much you can pick up by listening to other spectators."

Diabetes cost him his sight for the last 25 years of his life but he made light of his handicap and didn't do self-pity. When he was asked if he wanted a blind dog, he replied: "I'd rather have one that can see." He was so popular with his work-mates at the Rootes car assembly plant in Coventry, who nicknamed him Squash, that they insisted a job was still found for him there. They would pick him up in the morning, help him into his overalls and drop him home at night. He got on fine. He even noticed once, just by feeling, that the night shift had fixed some rubber rings on to the pistons the wrong way. The production line was held up for eight hours while the cars went round again.

Dad sometimes had one work-mate, Ray Turnbull, as his commentator at games and was a real boyo, always game for a laugh. Anyone who thinks I have a sense of humour should have met him. He was a funny man and his father was funnier still. On holiday once, Dad nagged and nagged Mum until she agreed to let him go water skiing. He stayed on his feet and, apparently, it's the only time in Malta that an entire beach has stood up and applauded.

From the time I turned 15, the already large part my grandparents played in my life became massive because we left our home in Forknell Avenue and moved in at 140 Clifford Bridge Road, right next door to Nan and Granddad Gould. There was logic to the decision. It was handy having them so close to help bring us up when Mum and Dad weren't there – and Dad was familiar enough with the lay-out of the house from his own upbringing to be able to find his way round safely after losing his sight in 1961.

I got in the habit of having a sleep before playing in night games and Nan Gould would wake me by knocking on the wall at four o'clock and serving me poached egg on toast. She would also fill me with words of wisdom. If the weather was wild and I was fretting about playing on a foul night, she'd say: "When the moon gets up, the wind will drop." It always did, so I now quote it to our grandkids.

Mum supported me as well by going to games but all that stopped when a car went into the back of her when she was driving my Singer Chamois to fetch Dad from work. I decided I was always useless anyway when she was there, so I banned her from matches – and she was never ever reinstated! Marge was on the scene by then and started doing the running around and commentary for Dad.

The reason I was given for my rejection by Billy Frith at Highfield Road was that I was too slow. I went straight to the Labour Exchange and got a job next door to the Coventry and North Warwick Hospital in Stoney Stanton Road at Daley & Son, a heating and ventilator engineers. I was earning some money and serving an apprenticeship to a lovely guy called Bill Blackmore, who joined in the two v two football matches we had in the lunch break.

When we took on a job in Hinckley, starting each day at eight o'clock, I cycled 12 miles each way and pocketed the pennies I was given to cover what they assumed was a return trip on a Midland Red bus. That was obviously the Scottish blood in me! Another job, at Binley School, gave me chance to spend ten minutes every morning with Granddad Gould, who I loved so much. He caught the bus from the Craven Arms to his job working on the jet engines at Anstey and often checked on my progress by asking how I was off for money. I thought he was enquiring whether I needed to borrow any and told him I had five bob left from my pay packet. But he said: "You couldn't lend it me until next Thursday, could you?" It was half a day's pay. I never tired of his sense of humour and he always paid me back.

Every Monday, I was packed off to the Technical College to study engineering and even worked Saturday mornings, so that was five and a half days of toil before going off to play in the afternoons for Ridgeley Rangers and, some time later, St James. While I was training as an engineer, Aston Villa called me back from a family holiday in Barry Island for a trial. They didn't want to risk taking me on and farmed me out instead to Hinckley Athletic for more experience. On one trip over there, we didn't even make it to the Leicestershire border before ending up in a ditch just outside Coventry. It was at that moment I realised Dad's eyes were going. He never drove again.

At the time, I was cycling to Hinckley anyway to carry out my heating and ventilator business chores, so it was awkward going back at night as well. Fortunately, I was still welcome to go for training two nights a week at Highfield Road with Arthur Cox, who worked us so hard we used to throw up over the wall when he finally allowed us a breather.

The lucky break I needed came with the sacking of Billy Frith over four years into his second spell as manager. Jimmy Hill took over and one of his first moves was to invite all the discarded lads back for a trial one Sunday morning at Shilton. It was another chance for anyone who had come to the club's attention in the recent past and then missed out.

Jimmy attended, along with his assistant Alan Dicks, and I caught his eye sufficiently to be asked back that afternoon. I said that was difficult, so he told me to report instead the following Sunday. I did well again and was informed straight after that of Coventry's intention to sign me.

Someone pointed out that I had actually been on the Highfield Road books before and been rejected. That brought the swift response from Jimmy: "In that case, he's coming back." Jimmy told me he would only take me on, though, if I explained why I had been reluctant to report back the previous weekend. I said Dad was losing his sight and was in hospital, and Sunday afternoons were my only opportunity to see him. Jimmy winked and said: "You and me are going to get on fine."

Bearded Wonder

There aren't many relationships in life like the one I had with Jimmy Hill. I would have run through a brick wall for him. He had this wonderful vision and Coventry's crowds shot up in no time. Attendances for games in the FA Cup – the competition that most set my young heart racing – were particularly spectacular and I recall there being more than 40,000 for a fifth-round victory against Sunderland, although the true figure was probably more than 50,000 because so many fans poured in for free after three gates were broken down. Then 30,000 queued in the rain for tickets for the visit of Manchester United at the next stage.

How I would have loved to be playing in those ties rather than just watching them as a hopeful groundstaff boy. To see your local club rise like that from a destitute state was tremendous and I lapped it all up, conscious as I was of my roots. I was bursting with pride for a city that was becoming famous for more than just a booming car industry, a ground-breaking shopping precinct, a new cathedral and a naked woman on a horse.

I had shed no tears when our forthright chairman Derrick Robins decided enough was enough with Billy Frith and showed him the door. Billy was a gentleman but I had felt unfairly treated when he broke my young heart. I thought I was worthy of further opportunity on the back of the goals I scored in the youth team. One of my problems was that there was a lad in my position called Dudley Roberts, who was a magnificent header of the ball, could also play at centre-half and had a big ally on the coaching staff – his dad Ted!

I'm still big pals with Dudley, who earned our respect in another way. We thought he was batting well above his average when he got together with 'Sky Blue Rose,' the lovely lady whose Scottish tones were heard on a recorded message when fans rang the club for ticket bulletins and other information. But it proved no mis-match. They are still married and living in Mansfield.

The union between Jimmy Hill and Coventry was another match made in heaven but it's a wonder he didn't turn tail after watching them play for the first time. They lost in the FA Cup at home to Kings Lynn. I was playing for Ridgeway that day, probably at the Memorial Park or Prior Deram Walk in Tile Hill, and couldn't believe it when I heard that a Southern League team had beaten my beloved club. I went home for confirmation of our 2-1 defeat and found it with the astonishing front-page headline in the Pink.

I was oblivious then to the way football clubs operated and only learned later that Jimmy was sounded out by Coventry a few days before the Kings Lynn tie. Apparently, he was at a Lord's Taverners function when he was introduced by the famous England spinner Jim Laker to Derrick Robins, a wonderful chairman who lived to be 90 and loved cricket as well as football.

The two clicked and, in no time, the club had a new manager – one who would completely transform the place. While I was evolving from hopeful kid to first-team regular, Jimmy wielded the enormous power he had by overhauling things off the pitch as well as those on it. He and Derrick were brilliant at spotting opportunities, such as hooking in junior fans by providing free crisps and pop for them when they went to collect players' autographs. As a groundstaff lad, one of my tasks was to shepherd the queues. A few years earlier, I would have been among the excited youngsters myself.

From developing Radio Sky Blue to chartering trains to away games, the duo didn't miss a trick. Their vision saw a totally new Highfield Road spring up after a fire in one of the stands and there were plans for restaurants and bowling alleys to be included in the designs. The 'Sky Blues' nickname only came into being when the club's shirts were given a different shade in about 1962. It was an important move in promoting the club's image.

Jimmy also became responsible for some of the best preparation facilities in the country by overseeing the development of the Ryton training complex. Before then, we would train on a field at Walsgrave or the village pitch at Shilton, where we played Midland Intermediate League games. George Curtis would come round at the end of each week to ask how many times we had taken our cars and give us five bob a journey as expenses.

The progress on all fronts was astonishing. JH, who initially filled his forward line with five free-transfer signings (Willie Humphries, Hubert Barr, Terry Bly, Jimmy Whitehouse and Bobby Laverick), even bought some aircraft seats for the extra comfort of the players on the team coach. And Ryton would become more special still after 1980 when The Beard, who was by then back as chairman, sold striker Ian Wallace to Nottingham Forest for £1.25m. The Sky Blue Connection buildings were built from the proceeds and became known as the Wallace Memorial.

Jimmy had the knack of making everyone feel special and involved – an important quality to me as one of the club's first apprentice professionals in a system that also soon produced Willie Carr, Jeff Blockley and our kid Trevor. He recognised the honesty in me and we never had a cross word.

I hit both goals when Coventry City A drew with Villa in the Midland Intermediate League, helped myself to a hat-trick against Wolves and braces when we faced Notts County and Walsall. I'm not saying it's a long while ago I was given my debut for the reserves but the team-sheet for one of my early games, at Portsmouth, referred to us wearing 'white knickers' rather than white shorts. We could have done with thermals as well because 1962-63 was one of the coldest winters on record, with something like 380 matches postponed.

Despite being a late call-up, I opened the scoring in a side also containing Dietmar Bruck, Ernie Machin and player-coach Alan Dicks. I gave the ball a right thwack and it ripped past the flailing John Milkins, one of Pompey's most famous keepers, into the top corner from 25 yards. It was a right rip-snorter. I was stunned and can still see it flying in. I didn't know I was capable of goals like that. The feeling of scoring for my home-city club, the one who had rejected me and then welcomed me back, was tremendous. I couldn't believe it and, even if it was only the reserves, it wrote my name in headlines in the Evening Telegraph.

I made a second Football Combination appearance when we went to Birmingham shortly afterwards but still found myself in awe of some of the characters in that dressing room. George Hudson, 'The Hud,' was now my big hero. He was the club's record buy at £21,000 from Peterborough, had a slick Elvis haircut and would strut in wearing a nicely tailored overcoat. His chest control was unbelievable. However awkwardly you knocked the ball in for him, he brought it down. He and George Kirby were the only players I ever remember confronting Jimmy Hill. George in particular clashed with him. They had both hit hat-tricks on their home debuts and were still good performers but Jimmy believed in me – and I was starting to as well.

Young and innocent though I was, those characteristics came with raw aggression. As much as I loved my Granny Gould, I would have kicked her out of the way if there was half a chance of a goal. And she knew it.

It was in place of 'The Hud,' who had a nose injury, that I made my debut in the first team. And the fact he was leading scorer at the time heaped a little more pressure on me for my big night at the Gay Meadow in a Third Division fixture on October 30, 1963. Arthur Rowley's Shrewsbury had lost 8-1 at our place the week before and around 2,000 Sky Blues fans made the journey along the A5 thinking we would win handsomely again. Among them were Granddad and Dad, who had their photo taken by the Telegraph coming out of 140 Clifford Bridge Road. They were so proud of 'Our Bob.'

We were top of the table but were thankful with our goalless draw and I was reassured to see familiar faces around me like George Curtis, John Sillett and, perhaps most poignantly, Ronnie Rees, who had assured me I'd be all right after Coventry sent me packing. I never stopped running all night and Jimmy Hill was kind in describing my debut as 'just wonderful.' I was also grateful to the Shrewsbury defender Peter Dolby, who congratulated me on my performance after I'd pulled him around at every opportunity.

Nemo (the pen name for Derek Henderson in the Evening Telegraph) wrote in his report that I played with 'great aplomb' – a description that sent me scurrying off to Jimmy's secretary, Joy, in search of clarification. Vocabulary isn't my strong point, never has been, and I had no idea whether he was being complimentary or insulting. Forty odd years on, I'm still likely to say 'polaroid' instead of paranoid and might talk of keeping my medals for 'prosperity' rather than posterity – the sort of gaffes that have led Radio 5Live's Alan Green to call me Mrs Malaprop. But I can promise you I'm trying hard to master my mother tongue. Our sons bought me a huge Collins Dictionary for the bolthole to help me over my difficulties.

No-one was prouder at my first-team arrival than my parents. A few days earlier, Trevor had scored a hat-trick from the right wing for Coventry Boys against North Oxfordshire as a 14-year-old and I had also gained a foot-in with the England Youth set-up, being invited for trials along with the likes of Howard Kendall, John Hollins, David Sadler, Ralph Coates and Harry Redknapp under the eye of both the coach Pat Welton and his boss Alf Ramsey, England's World Cup winning manager.

Things were moving along nicely but it might all have ended before it really began thanks to some banter with my hero Reg Matthews, of all people. He still trained with us despite having joined Derby and was busy with the 'verbals' from his peg in the away team dressing room, chasing me down the corridor at one point. As I reached out to push open the door, I somehow put my hand through the frosted window that had remained intact for years and years. I'll never know how it didn't sever my arm. Reg went white with fear as the blood poured and he sat in the toilet for half an hour, smoking a cigarette or two. I was scarred for decades but the trainer's room was right opposite and I was bandaged up thoroughly.

Another early episode might have left me on the back foot if I hadn't had an enlightened manager. Dudley Roberts, Micky Corlett, Peter Denton, Graham Saunders, Lester Staite and Micky Cartwright were also on the groundstaff at the time and we adopted a militant stance when the first team were flying near the top of Division Three South.

The weather was awful in 1962-63 and The Bearded Wonder was desperate to get games on while the team were winning. But we heard of the bonuses the first-team players were getting and felt hard done by that we were on £5.50 a week, without any extras for clearing ice and snow off the pitch, week after week, and covering it in straw as protection. We jumped in a lovely hot bath in the away team dressing room one freezing afternoon and refused to go back out to work after the groundsman, Ellick Smith, ordered us to.

Before we knew it, Jimmy's unmistakeable jaw came jutting into view through the steam and he looked round the eight or ten of us to find out who the leader of the revolt was. The lads kindly volunteered me as spokesman and I couldn't utter a word. I felt a bit vulnerable anyway stood there stark bollock naked and it didn't help when I started stuttering over my answer. Eventually, I blurted out that we considered ourselves worthy of extra money for doing so much additional work on the playing surface. Jimmy agreed immediately and promised us ten bob more in our pay packets, so we dried ourselves off that quickly that we were back at our spades and wheelbarrows before he reached his office.

My first League game behind me, it was back to the reserves before my next taste of the first team, this time at Highfield Road. It was only for a friendly but the fact it was against our local rivals Leicester in front of 13,500 made it competitive enough. The battles I had with Frank McLintock and Gordon Banks that night were another important lesson for me because Leicester were formidable opponents, having been to the FA Cup final in two of the previous three seasons.

Not in my wildest dreams could I have claimed to be worthy of a recall to our promotion challenge at this stage. The Hud scored 26 goals by the turn of the year and there were some spectacular victories, including a 6-3 success at QPR a couple of weeks after the side had hit six in the FA Cup at Trowbridge. We were nine points clear at the top in early January and promotion seemed a formality.

Then, from nowhere, we went 11 matches without a win and there was a clamour for me to be restored after I scored a hat-trick against Stoke in the Midland Intermediate League and two goals against Brentford Reserves in front of Jimmy a few days later. When he did bring me back, though, I was very ordinary in a draw at Wrexham and my return was brief.

The trip to North Wales brought us into opposition with Billy Myerscough, a former Aston Villa and Coventry forward who had left a big impression on me during my eight-week trial under Billy Frith. Myerscough was left out of the side once and had the guts to say what thousands of footballers down the years have thought: "Well, gaffer, I hope you win 1-0 tomorrow and it's by an own goal." Every player omitted from every team-sheet will have come to understand what Billy said that day. I certainly did.

The side finished strongly enough to take the title and ensure I wouldn't be needed again that season. The promotion race was a close-run thing, though, with us two points behind Crystal Palace and level with third-placed Watford after we let down 13,000 travelling fans – another amazing sign of our growing popularity – by losing at Peterborough in our penultimate fixture.

We faced Colchester at home in our final game and Jimmy sensed the players were on edge. I recall them being told to take sleeping tablets for the preceding two nights, then he took steps to relax them even more by having Jimmy Tarbuck in the dressing room to tell a few jokes. The ploy worked. We won 1-0, with The Hud scoring only his second goal of 1964.

Even so, we needed some help and our two rivals both surprisingly lost their last matches, the happy news of their misfortune being relayed to the crowd by the cricketer Godfrey Evans, who the club had drafted in as PA announcer. Our home games kicked off at 3.15pm because JH and Derrick thought the extra quarter of an hour was vital in tempting people who had to work in the car plants on a Saturday morning. So, not for the last time, a Coventry side were happy to play out time knowing they were safe if there was no more scoring. In this case, we were something like 0.175 of a goal better off than Palace and had the championship in the bag.

The celebrations went on around me as I had only played twice but it was good to know I would be performing at a higher level the next time I was named. And I made an impression back in the reserves towards the end of the season by scoring twice at Millwall and once against Reading.

I was learning so much – and not just about playing football. Pat Saward, who came from Ireland and played for Aston Villa before going to Brighton and Coventry, used to give us dress sense lessons on a Monday afternoon and show us how to coordinate our clothes. He was always immaculate and suave, and had the most wonderful shirts, suits and ties.

In 1964-65, three goals against Reading Reserves and two against Southend made me think my next chance might come sooner rather than later and The Beard obliged me with a call-up for the League Cup home game against Mansfield early in our Second Division campaign. The fact I scored my first senior goal and we won 3-2 made it a memorable home debut.

My first League goal soon followed at Portsmouth, where I had also netted my first in the Combination. Fratton Park was a lucky ground for me and always would be. Conscious of our pile-up of games, JH had had the vision to fly us down to the South Coast to save on travelling time but we had a scare on landing because the runway was on grass and was waterlogged.

Then, at 3.43pm on October 24, came my big moment. We were playing Manchester City at home and I fed Ernie Machin, who in turn found our wizard-on-the-wing Willie Humphries. His cross from the right was hard and low and I launched myself at it, two feet off the ground, to bullet a header past the keeper Alan Ogley. What a fantastic feeling – my first home League goal! Scoring in the first team was special at any time but to do so at Highfield Road was the dream ticket.

There was some family sadness, though, and not just because of the blindness that meant Dad couldn't fully appreciate the moment. I had also recently lost my Granddad Dickie, who was a chain smoker and had been found to be riddled with cancer when he was opened up. Nan set his bed up for him downstairs when he could no longer get about the house and I'd pop round every day to see him. Every day bar one, that is; and that was the day he died. I don't know whether I was late for training that morning but why do the most important things always go unsaid?

He would have been pleased with my progress. Even after we flopped at Charlton, it wasn't the 18-year-old Bobby Gould who was dropped, it was the £21,000 signing George Hudson, top scorer for the previous two seasons. In my young football life, I had been signed by Coventry City, discarded by them and then signed back. Now, as confirmation of my progress, I was handed the centre-forward shirt instead of the no 10 one.

Despite an 8-1 League Cup mauling at home to Leicester, it continued to be an exciting time for the club as a whole. JH knew the value of publicity and we were big news. The fans flocked to Highfield Road in such numbers that there were more than 12,000 present to see me hit the only goal of a Football Combination home game against QPR. We used to average 5,000 for reserve games and the place was alive. He had stimulated the whole city.

Players had names for JH in the dressing room because of his forceful character but he had a charisma like Jose Mourinho without being an outstanding coach. Alan Dicks, who was excellent with the youngsters, and Peter Hill took the practice sessions and JH only came out on a Thursday. At the end of a week, we trained in the afternoons because he thought that made more sense with our body clocks becoming used to kick-off time. We never went home until The Beard's team were leading, so if we fancied calling it a day, we made sure we slacked enough for his side to score. We played loads of five-a-sides and, when we practised set-pieces, he had numbers for our different routines – an idea I carried into management many years later.

Something else I recovered from my memory bank was a ploy brought in by Pat Saward, who was an assistant to Alan Dicks with the reserves. On the wall of the office they shared hung a chart bearing a list of players' names, each of them with a row of small coloured circles alongside – red to denote outstanding, green for good, blue for mediocre and yellow for poor.

A lot of one-to-one meetings with the lads would be held in there, so we would all be craning our necks to see how our performances were comparing. I adopted this system at Albion but the players there couldn't handle the chart being on show in the corridor. The lads in New Zealand, where I coached Jonathan's team a few seasons ago, loved it and it also became a huge thing at Wimbledon when Dennis Wise was sold on the back of my assessments. "Too many yellows," said the chairman Sam Hammam. "Sell him."

I could study a player's form over a long period of time, assess the dips and talk things through with him. Was his missus not happy? Had the preparation been right? Was he fully fit? I know Fabio Capello had something similar in mind this summer with his Index plan but what can you learn over three or four World Cup games? It was a bad idea and I have my suspicions that it was just a money-making idea.

It shouldn't be forgotten that JH was a disciplinarian as well. In our Second Division title-winning season, he got stuck big-time into Ian Gibson, a little Scottish midfielder who I had great telepathy with. Unkindly, the fixture list sent us to Brighton and Carlisle for successive games in the space of a few days and we went by rail from Sussex to Cumbria.

Gibbo had done well after costing the club £55,000 from Middlesbrough but became a bit of a Jack The Lad. On this never-ending train trip, his antics didn't go down with JH. Let's just say, he was demonstrating a flatulence habit by using a naked cigarette lighter flame as a prop. When he then had a poor first half at Brunton Park, JH absolutely tore into him. I'd never known a tirade like it. You didn't mess with The Beard. Gibbo was slapped on the transfer list, although he stayed and proceeded to score some of the goals that got us rolling on our long unbeaten run-in to lifting the championship.

We were always expected to work hard. But, as long as the time was right, there was opportunity for laughs as well and nobody proved that more than keeper Bill Glazier, who was as mad as a hatter. When we went to the West Indies to celebrate reaching the top flight, he thought he was in danger from the lizards running up the wall and tried to spear them with his knife and fork.

The fun wasn't always welcome. The youth coach Yannus Gerdof, who had been brought in from Hungary as a technical expert as another sign of JH's revolutionary thinking, wasn't too impressed when he went back one night to the digs he shared with Ernie Machin and said to his landlady: "What is this 'fuck' word? I hear it all the time." She was a religious old soul and hit him over the head with her frying pan.

The first-team squad bought a greyhound that they called 'Bearded Wonder' and raced at Coventry Dog Track. It was appropriate because JH loved animals. He once brought a horse down the corridor at Highfield Road for treatment from the physio Norman Pilgrim. Pulled hamstrings and tight groins were one thing, dodgy fetlocks and bruised hooves were something else altogether.

The Beard was a saviour to Coventry City. The club wouldn't have gone anywhere near as far up the League ladder without him. Derrick Robins was brilliant as chairman as well and you felt we hadn't finished climbing with our rise from the Third Division to the Second. And I wanted to stay part of it.

I scored my fourth senior goal of 1964-65 when we beat leaders Newcastle 5-4 in a fabulous match in January in which we almost threw away a four-goal lead. It was a healthy return because it was only my sixth game since we won promotion. But I was still a pup and was handled as such. My reward was a long spell in the reserves, although the term 'trainee hairdresser' that was given me by one paper was not an indication that I was seeking an alternative career.

I had by this time met Margery Page at a dance at the Locarno nightclub in Coventry and took the same healthy interest in her job that she showed towards mine. Her mum Jenny owned a string of hair salons in the Tile Hill area and, once she got over her initial reservations, I became a regular worker there in the afternoons. Jenny's first words to me were: "So you're the professional footballer, are you?" She didn't go as far as saying: "Your lot don't have a very good reputation round here." But the look she gave me, up and down, had me on my guard.

Jenny and George soon became a huge source of support to me, though, and bought season tickets in the City End, even though they must have come close to disowning me the day I made a clumsy grab at a woman's cleavage in one of the salons. I had learned to shampoo and take pins and rollers out and was happy to be photographed by the Evening Telegraph at work.

It was a story that resulted in the nickname 'Teasy Weasy' sticking to me for a while but it's a good job there were no cameras present when I dropped a curler down the front of one customer. In my haste to recover it, I had my hands somewhere Marge and Jenny definitely didn't think I should have. For once, I didn't argue. Even without action replays, I knew I had strayed into an offside position.

Wedded (And Promotion) Bliss

I was on a real high when Marge and I tied the knot in 1967. True to form, football came first and we had to bring our wedding forward from the original date, June 10 (two days before my 21st birthday), because the squad would by then be on tour in the West Indies as a reward for taking Coventry to the First Division for the first time. Much though I was in love, I wasn't going to miss that trip and wouldn't have been allowed to.

Jimmy Hill had promised when he took over that he would have the club in the top flight within five full seasons. He was true to his word and almost managed it in four. I was chaired off the pitch by our excited supporters after scoring in a victory away to Huddersfield on the last day of 1965-66 and can still hear them belting out the Sky Blue Song (adopted from the Eton Boating Song by a very influential Coventry City director called John Camkin) as they savoured seeing us sitting in second place in the table behind Manchester City. The trouble was that Southampton still had two away games to play and they used them to overhaul us by a single point and leave us disappointed in third spot.

With apologies to the writers of the Eton Boating Song:

Let's all sing together
Play Up Sky Blues
While We Sing Together
We Will Never Lose
Proud Posh Or Cobblers
Oysters Or Anyone
They Can't Defeat Us
We'll Fight 'till The Game Is Won

I was proud that, by the time I left, the names North End, Cobblers and Scunthorpe had been replaced in the song by Tottenham, Chelsea and United.

My impact was still more at reserve level than in the first team. I had scored 30 goals for them and the A team in 1964-65 and followed up with almost 20 in the junior sides the following season. But I managed five in the Second Division as well in the latter campaign and was kindly described by JH as 'twice the player' after Ray Pointer had been signed.

In addition, I had the ball in the net at 1-0 down when we visited Goodison Park in the FA Cup fifth round but it was disallowed for hands and Everton went on to win the competition. There were more than 60,000 there and I was up against England's Brian Labone, so it was an important afternoon in my education, although I was gutted we were out of the Cup.

We weren't to be denied in 1966-67. Everything clicked and we bombed along on the back of a tremendous team spirit that had been helped by an unusual trip in the summer of England's World Cup triumph. It wasn't the destination that was so off-beat – Austria and Switzerland certainly weren't so outlandish as Iceland, where we had been on my first senior tour the summer before. But most players would expect to fly to the Alpine nations rather than have to drive.

The Beard was always good for a publicity stunt. If we weren't hopping over walls for the photographers on Worthing sea front, we were splashing about with local youngsters in a municipal pool during pre-season training. We were a walking photo opportunity. He surpassed himself, though, when he fixed us up with a fleet of sky blue Rover 2000s from the Triumph factory in Coventry and we set off in convoy from the Council House for the Continent, George Curtis and me sharing the duties at the wheel of ours because John Burckitt hadn't passed his test. It must have been the only overseas trip when footballers have actually appreciated the scenery rather than lowered the blinds and got the cards out. Between all of us, we covered thousands of miles of Autobahn and mountain passes, and emerged with no bigger a mishap than a puncture.

Mind you, I had my mad moments, especially in a castle we stayed at in Germany. I woke up one night in a panic after drinking too much, looked up from the bed in my single room to see a tiny window high on the wall and ran down the corridor thinking I was locked in a prison. It was only when Mick

Kearns yelled at me to get back in bed that I regained my senses, also realising at this unhealthy hour that German beer was stronger than ours. I was virtually teetotal and promised myself then to treat those steins with more respect if I dabbled again.

Another day, in Vienna, we changed hotels and I frantically had to make plans for my regular love letter from Marge to be passed on. Johnny Key had different priorities. All he was interested in was where he could buy French fries. He lived on them and wasn't interested in five-star luxury. Inevitably, he was given the nickname Chips.

Although I scored a couple in a game against the Young Fellows Club of Zurich, results weren't good on the Rover Tour but we bonded superbly and hit the ground running in the season. I was on target at Plymouth and, as usual, at Portsmouth before the end of August and was full of pride a few weeks later when I looked down from the top of the division's goal charts and saw players like Derek Dougan, Ray Crawford and Kevin Hector in my wake.

We were particularly strong at home, where we lost only once in the League in 1966, and perhaps have to thank the Leofric Effect. As a player, that hotel in Coventry city centre played a big part in my life because it's where The Beard took us for eggs on toast before home games. We would assemble there in a big TV room after dropping in at Highfield Road in the morning for a walk round. We were encouraged to assess the pitch conditions, decide which end we would prefer to kick into first and even talk through one or two tactical manoeuvres. So we changed into our tracksuits before we went out – or at least most of us did. If there was the slightest breeze blowing, Brian Lewis would tuck his trousers into his socks and pull his tracksuit on over his 'civvies.'

We made our big push in early December, winning 3-1 at Wolves, who were the leaders, then hammering the new pacesetters Ipswich 5-0 at Highfield Road the following Friday – a win that meant we were right behind them. It was a night that left me with very happy memories.

The dressing room was always deathly quiet when The Beard went round making particular points to players. We hung on his every word. He stopped to say things to a couple of other lads, then pointed at me and said: "YOU. I fancy YOU for a hat-trick tonight." Ninety minutes later, I looked up at that scoreboard that stood on the Spion Kop as yet another sign of how far ahead of the game the club were. The digits 999 were up in lights because they put just a scorer's number up in those days, not his name, and I had bagged my first senior hat-trick. Barely half an hour had gone when I headed my third and, at the end, I just looked at JH in awe. How could he have known?

Remarkably, we didn't lose in the League after the game at Huddersfield in the middle of November and owed a lot to our mean defence. George Curtis, at centre-half, was a man not to meddle with. When we stopped over before a game at Southampton and went to watch Goldfinger at the pictures, I made the mistake of telling him on the walk back that he reminded me of Odd Job, one of the characters we'd just had a laugh at. I still have the bruise from where he belted me on the arm, then he locked me out of the room we were sharing. I was walking up and down the corridor for ages, throwing stones at the window. It was some time before he let me in and, even then, only after a grovelling apology.

He was always at your shoulder if you needed help, though, and I did after missing from three inches in the last minute of an FA Cup defeat against Newcastle. During the following week, I had a letter saying I was the worst player Coventry had ever signed. It continued in even more complimentary tones and ended with the remark: "You should think of committing suicide."

I cry easily, especially over family matters, and have been known to shed tears about football as well, like when I equalised late on for Arsenal in the 1969 League Cup final. I was very emotional about the letter and went to see JH. It made headlines in the Evening Telegraph. There was still sensitivity about me keeping The Hud out but it broke my heart when The Beard ended my ever-present record by leaving me out of the next match, at Bury.

Fortunately, I'm built to come out fighting rather than recoil into a shell and the first thing I wanted to do was prove the doubters wrong. I went on as substitute at Gigg Lane, had a goal disallowed and then came up with ten goals in ten appearances. I was helped hugely by the arrival of many messages of support from other fans and was eventually able to laugh the hate-mail episode off, even if it cut deeply. The letters – poison-pen and otherwise – form another part of my vast collection of keepsakes.

Excitement reached fever pitch in the spring with the First Division so close and I took my total into the 20s by the early spring. I thrived on having two great wingers in Ronnie Rees and Johnny Key, and lads like Gibbo and Ernie Machin were always breaking forward from midfield and popping up with a goal as well as keeping me well supplied. I was essentially playing as a lone forward in a 4-3-3 formation. I filled the Didier Drogba role and, fortunately, could run all day and night.

I don't think I realised at the time that I was up there with the top youngsters in the country. When I hit the only goal at home to Huddersfield in mid-April, I had 25 in the season at the age of barely 20. Alun Evans later went from Wolves to Liverpool as the first £100,000 teenager and I moved for £90,000 to Arsenal. Those fees were probably the equivalent of £4m-£5m now.

I was gutted to miss the run-in after breaking the scaphoid bone in my wrist at Cardiff. We came away with a 1-1 draw thanks to John Toshack putting a penalty wide late on and we were so close to promotion that JH was pictured pouring the champagne in the dressing room afterwards. He had his pipe lit but I can see from the way I'm holding a cup in my left hand and protecting my right that I wasn't very happy. I had just scored in six successive games and in nine out of ten, so the timing of the injury was awful.

I was in agony but somehow drove myself to the Coventry and North Warwick Hospital because we didn't have Sunday treatment at the club. I waited on my own for hours to be seen. What a difference from how today's players are treated. I was x-rayed and told by a specialist I would be in plaster for six weeks. I gave the bad news to Pilgers at Highfield Road the next day.

Several years later, at Luton, I broke my other scaphoid and recognised the problem straightaway. And the experiences did solve a long-running mystery. At Caludon Castle, I could never shin up the vertical ropes and it took all those years and two cases of misfortune to make me realise it was because I had weak scaphoids. The knowledge also came in useful much later. When Terry Gibson sustained the same injury at Wimbledon and came home from hospital in plaster, I told the physio to cut it off because it wouldn't help. Gibbo was going to get the PFA on my case but came round to trusting me. I'd missed out on those promotion games and didn't want him to miss out as well.

Promotion became a certainty a few days later when Blackburn, the only club who could stop us finishing in the top two with Wolves, were held by Bolton. As a way of making sure, it was a bit of an anti-climax but we more than made up for it a few days later – or at least the rest of the lads did.

I was especially upset to be in the dressing room in my club suit rather than our Sky Blue kit at the home game against Wolves that has gone down as one of the most famous days in Coventry's history; the 'Midlands Match of the Century' as JH called it. My emotions were all over the place. Delighted though I was with our win, I was gutted not to be out there and the lads knew it. They lifted me off my feet and held me up to the crowd when we sang the club song from the directors' box after the game, with The Beard conducting the tens of thousands celebrating on the pitch. It was wonderful.

We hit back from one behind to beat Wolves 3-1 in front of a crowd that smashed the club record gate out of sight. It was given as 51,000 odd but there were said to be many, many more. My seat in the stand allowed me to marvel at the precarious vantage points in use. Some fans had climbed on the roofs while others scaled high up the floodlight pylons and, as one writer put it, made themselves look like decorations on a Christmas tree. Many youngsters sat on the grass close to the touchlines. Quite what our friends in health and safety would have made of it, I've no idea and the pitch invasions after each of our goals caused the referee to make more than one threat to abandon the game.

That win blew the title race open and, with Wolves losing at Crystal Palace the following week, we were crowned champions after beating Millwall 3-1. I was thrilled by the prospect of playing at the top level but, as a boyhood Sky Blues fan, was so happy for the club as well; not least players like George Curtis, Ronnie Farmer, Mick Kearns and Brian Hill, who would soon be able to say they had played for Coventry City in all four divisions. For Brian, a lad from just down the road in Bedworth, it was extra special.

George and Mick couldn't believe their luck. Their joint testimonial game was staged just before the end of the season and 25,000 turned up to reward two stalwarts who had totalled almost a thousand games for the club. George's commitment and bravery were unquestioned. Late in the promotion season, he played game after game with 14 stitches in a knee wound.

We were sad the season had to end because it was one highlight and round of celebrations after another. But there had been another incentive for us to get over the finishing line. Derrick Robins, our terrific chairman, had promised us a mouth-watering end-of-season trip if we made it to the First Division. And, as a man of honour, he laid on a West Indies tour.

He was an outgoing character who ran a company called Banbury Buildings and drove a big Rolls Royce with the number plate DHR 1. Then he topped it by buying a sky blue one. He loved a good trip and ran a cricket team, the

Derrick Robins X1, who travelled the world. After buying a luxury house in Leamington Spa, he couldn't resist splashing out as well on the cricket club next door and he took us to play there once. I caught him on the boundary and he didn't speak to me for weeks.

We were thrilled to be off to the Caribbean, where cricket was the national sport, but Marge wasn't exactly doing somersaults. I would be on a beach with my team-mates on the June day we were due to be married in Coventry and still sunning myself on my 21st birthday. My mother-in-law wasn't very impressed either at having to do all the invitations again for an earlier date.

But they realised that such highs didn't come round very often and players have to enjoy them to the full when they do. My 25 goals made me the club's top scorer and it was a golden time. It was my big breakthrough year and I loved being part of a dressing room that was full of fun and had some great laughs.

Before a game at Middlesbrough, we stayed at the Saltburn Hotel, where the coach driver, Hughie Spencer, and me were handing out a rare pasting to George Curtis and John Sillett on the snooker table. Big mistake! They chased us down the corridor afterwards, caught Hughie and jammed a metal waste paper bin over his head. It stuck fast and a taxi had to be called to take him to hospital to have it removed. And young players today ask what we used to do before there were TVs in hotel bedrooms.

Hughie was a brilliant guy – and needed to be. He was always likely to have his balls grabbed or something put on his head while he was at the wheel. At other times, he had to get used to us invading his space at unexpected times. Once, we couldn't get back from a Football Combination game at Brighton because of bad weather and had to sleep on the coach. The same thing happened when a match at Millwall was called off after the fog came down suddenly. We'd been in the dressing room for ten minutes before someone realised our keeper Bob Wesson was still outside. He didn't know we'd all gone off. "I thought we must be playing well because I wasn't seeing anything of the ball," he said.

Life couldn't be better as Marge and I prepared for domestic bliss in the home that awaited us at 14 Grange Avenue, Kenilworth. We hadn't co-habited up to that time because couples didn't do that then. But we were very much in love and looking forward to setting up home together.

I'd like to say our meeting three and a half years earlier had been full of romantic gestures and intentions but it wasn't. I was with Eddie Kelly, a trialist from the north east and not to be confused with the Arsenal player of the same name a few years later. We were eyeing up the talent from the sidelines, in particular these two girls dancing round their handbags. My remark to Eddie was something that a centre-half might have said to his centre-forward at a corner: "I'll take the big 'un, you have the little 'un." The follow-up must have been okay because I took the "big 'un" to see a Doris Day film at the Gaumont the following evening and we're still together more than 45 years later.

In 1967, Marge had to make hasty new arrangements at St John's The Baptist Church in Berkswell and wait a few weeks for our honeymoon in the Canary Islands but she took the inconvenience in her stride, as usual. Footballers' wives don't have a straightforward life and she has dealt with more than her fair share of upheaval almost without complaint. I'm a very lucky man.

She looked radiant as she became my lawful wedded wife shortly before the squad's departure to the West Indies. Not that she was the only one I was answerable to. George Curtis was my best man and chided me for being photographed in the Birmingham Post while stopping right outside church to sign an autograph for a young fan. He reminded me I should have had eyes only for my bride. I did well to sign my name at all because my arm was still in plaster and the vicar helped us over another handicap. He played the organ with one finger because the organist didn't turn up.

Before we knew it, we – the Sky Blues squad, that is – were climbing aboard a BOAC jet heading for the sun and I remember swimming one-handed out to a raft in the Caribbean and having a great time. Travelling is one of the treats a footballer has and, as a lad who had never been further than Barry Island Cold Knapp on holiday, my head was spinning with the delights of Barbados, Trinidad and Bermuda. I could never have dreamt of going to places like that. It was a terrific education, although I also saw poverty for the first time in Port of Spain and was shocked to see people who had lost limbs begging on the street.

I scored one of the goals in our win in Bridgetown on my 21st birthday and the lads clubbed together to buy me 21 presents, which they presented at the hotel. We had a good drink as well, so much so that Brian Hill slept on the beach one night and a load of empty bottles were left in my bed. I fell in love with the West Indies and promised Marge I'd take her one day. That chance came sooner than expected thanks to the signing-on fee from my move to Arsenal and we headed for the same hotel, the Coral Reef Club.

Some of the fellow guests looked familiar from the year before and, in telling us by the pool how nice it was to see a couple of happy recently-weds, they made the point that they had had the company of a squad of raucous young footballers the year before. I felt myself sinking further and further down my sun-lounger as Marge's eyebrows went higher and higher.

With promotion won and my place in the first team at last cemented, I marched in to see JH to demand a pay rise. I had been on £20 a week in 1964, rising by £2 once I'd played five first-team games, up to £25 after ten, with another £2.50 increase for reaching 15 matches. You were always stretching yourself because it was hardly the sort of living that today's players enjoy and my 25 goals made me bold enough to tell the manager I wouldn't settle for a penny less than £40. He demanded that I remove myself from his office straightaway and prepared to be transfer-listed. Okay, so we did have a cross word after all……just one.

My tail was between my legs and I felt vulnerable. I was also mystified when nothing appeared in the paper in the next three days about my availability. Wasn't I even worth a couple of paragraphs underneath the county cricket scores? I went to see JH again and was told by his secretary Joy Bott to wait. Then I informed him that I wished to renegotiate. Almost immediately, he offered £32.50 and I said: "Done." Friends again.

There was nevertheless an unhappy follow-up. The Beard conducted this business knowing he was about to resign. A few weeks after our clash, and only two days before the start of the new season, he called us all together in the boardroom and dropped a bombshell by saying he was quitting. After five and a half years, he'd had enough of management and was going into TV.

He had unsuccessfully asked the board for a ten-year contract, had been offered only five and said he was no longer prepared to rely on the efforts of 11 players once or twice a week to keep him in a job. We were dumbstruck. I think we'd have been challenging for the League title in two or three years if JH had stayed. And I would never have left.

The fruits of Coventry City's rise weren't just reflected in the trappings of

Derrick Robins. JH's material possessions had improved, too. Having arrived at the club in a Sunbeam convertible with a ripped roof, he was now at the wheel of a sky blue Jaguar.

At least he was staying on until his successor was found but we started poorly in the top flight. We lost at Burnley, where John Tudor was preferred to me, and failed to win any of our first five League matches. But I scored a couple in a 3-3 draw at Nottingham Forest on an afternoon of decidedly mixed fortunes. I was delighted to mark my debut at that level by helping us get our first-ever point in Division One but I was on as substitute only because my great pal George Curtis had seen his leg broken by a wretched tackle in the first five minutes. JH was so incensed that he ran on the pitch.

For someone who had served the club so loyally and been such an inspirational captain, it was a desperate blow for him to miss so much of the season. He had hardly missed a match in eight or nine years and often used the phrase that football wasn't a game for cowards. He certainly never drew out of a challenge and we were sickened by his misfortune.

I also bagged a goal in a draw at Arsenal – did someone in Highbury's corridors of power make a mental note that day? – but it's fair to say there were a few teething troubles in the top flight. It was unsettling to know The Beard could be gone at any time. The board tried for Brian Clough but failed to prise him from Derby, then Malcolm Allison seemed to be on the brink of being installed until leaking the story of his impending appointment to a national newspaper and prompting Derrick Robins to back out.

I tore ligaments in my knee clattering into the West Brom keeper John Osborne in only our second win and had the best part of three months on the sidelines. I was in plaster from my thigh to my ankle and had to get lessons from big George in how to get round. Fortunately, I had just traded in my Singer for a sky blue Triumph Spitfire with a white top – an original sports car which meant my backside was almost on the floor when I was at the wheel. At least I could get in it, though. I would never have been able to stretch my leg enough to drive a conventional car.

There was an interesting spin-off to my immobilisation and I have to choose my words here so as not to offend our eldest son Jonathan. We told him long ago that he arrived on this earth more by accident than through any careful planning but he might want to skip the next few lines and spare himself the account of how my injury had unexpected side-effects in the bedroom department.

Amorous adventures had to be undertaken with a little more care than usual and, if I can just slip into horse racing parlance for a few moments, it's fair to say I failed to dismount in time due to the few pounds overweight I was carrying. The result: One bonny baby boy well ahead of schedule. But not to worry. He was loved to bits.

There were also bumps and lumps of a more conventional nature. Before being hurt against Albion, I gashed my head in a game, so the First Division was proving tough in more ways than one. Not that I was ever afraid of the rough and tumble. Aggression was very much part of my make-up and I gave as good as I got. I loved the combat.

Noel Cantwell was finally unveiled as our new manager, apparently following a recommendation from Matt Busby. By coincidence, he was also a PFA chairman, as Jimmy Hill had been, and had served as Matt's captain at Manchester United. He insisted on us calling him 'Chief.' We could have lived with 'Gaffer' or 'Boss,' even NC. But where did 'Chief' come from? I didn't really hit it off with him, although we came to respect each other plenty after going our separate ways.

It wasn't long after my return to fitness that I was linked with the first of my many moves. Interest hotted up round the time I followed up three goals against West Ham Reserves (in a game our kid Trevor also played in) with a first-team hat-trick against Burnley. It was my comeback match in the senior side and I was flying. I had seven goals in nine Division One games and the week of my two hat-tricks was also the one in which we learned Marge was expecting for the first time.

I scored against Arsenal again in the return at Highfield Road and Noel left me out of an FA Cup tie against Tranmere so I would be eligible to play for the Gunners later in the competition if necessary. Decision day was close but I wasn't convinced I wanted to go anywhere. Coventry were MY club and I didn't know whether I was ready for the bigger stage and the less intimate surroundings of London. Marge obviously agreed because, when we first drove into the capital together, she burst into tears.

Cantwell had at one point come out and insisted that even £100,000 wouldn't be enough to prise me from my home city but Arsenal, who had bid for me before my injury, wouldn't go away and returned with a second and third offer. Coventry were still struggling near the foot of the table and obviously saw the money as a way of strengthening elsewhere.

Bob Dennison, brought in from Middlesbrough as Cantwell's no 2, eventually drove me to Arsenal for talks and I was full of doubts as I walked in past the bust of Herbert Chapman in the foyer. And Marge knows my anxieties weren't just because I would be missing out on a place as a judge at a beauty contest in Coventry if I moved. Was I really good enough for this place after being discarded by Coventry as a kid? Was I an Arsenal-type player?

Maurice Setters, by then at Highfield Road, had told me to ask for £100 a week and a £4,500 signing-on fee, so I was rehearsing my lines over and over when Bertie Mee took me upstairs to meet the secretary Bob Wall and start the negotiations. I said: "I don't discuss wages with secretaries. Only managers." Bertie said: "Mr Wall handles every financial aspect of the club." Bob smiled and said: "Sit down young man, let's talk." I apologised. A good start…….

I later realised Mr Wall was 'Mr Arsenal' and didn't put up much of a fight, settling for £55 a week, albeit with a nice signing-on fee. Money has never been that important to me. As long as I earn or have enough to live comfortably, I'm happy. Apart from early on, when I had next to nothing and was trying to establish myself, the size of my wage packet has not been my motivation.

When it was agreed by everyone that I was going to Arsenal, the realisation hit me hard and I was in a state of shock. I just cried. The first person I saw outside Highfield Road was Hughie Spencer, who, as our coach driver for many years, had been like a second dad to me. He had been such an important man in my life and I was upset at the thought that I'd never be travelling with him again. I cuddled him. I was still a kid in many ways and it was as if I hadn't realised that my record of 40 goals in 82 League matches for the Sky Blues was bound to alert bigger clubs.

Big City, Big Frustration

My signing-on fee when I left Coventry on February 2, 1968, was more than half the cost of the house we subsequently bought in Barnet. But Arsenal soon reckoned I was being weighed down by more than just the £90,000 price tag that apparently made me Britain's tenth costliest player. They thought I was too heavy and ordered me to cut out the potatoes and bread.

Bertie Mee let it be known after I had been booked and then made a goal for George Graham on my debut at Manchester City that he was putting me on special training to boost the slimming effort. A few weeks later, after I had shed a stone and a half and found I was tiring in games, Don Howe told me to go back to my previous diet. Brilliant coach and manager or not, he and Bertie Mee didn't get everything right.

The other players proved they were sensitive to my waistline by giving me the nickname 'Bunter' but I had a shoulder to lean on as I tried to settle in London. Before Marge joined me, I shared a hotel with Martin Chivers, who had just joined Tottenham from Southampton for £125,000.

He was pleased for me when I got off the mark at the third attempt with an FA Cup winner at Swansea. My first League goal for Arsenal was another few weeks coming, in a win at Fulham. Both were headers. My first appearance on the score-sheet at Highbury followed against Leicester three weeks after that in another victory. Then I equalised in an FA Cup tie at Birmingham that we still lost. I was gutted to be out of the competition because I thought a club like Arsenal could take me to Wembley.

I was determined to use what many would see as a dream move to make me a better player and my settling-in process moved on apace with the arrival in the first team of a lanky, articulate lad who was too brave for his own good. Bob Wilson and I became more than just football mates and have remained firm family friends for decades. We roomed together all over the world and found we had the same dedication. There was one difference: he was well educated and I wasn't. True to his schoolteacher past, he even wore a jacket with leather elbow patches.

Arsenal had good players, like Jon Sammels, Geordie Armstrong and Frank McLintock, although I clashed a bit with two others, George Graham and Bob McNab. They didn't particularly rate me and a joke went round the camp that a medal would be struck for me if I could trap three consecutive passes successfully.

I regard Frank as one of the best skippers I've ever known, even if it was him who gave me that unflattering 'Bunter' nickname when I got off the train for a game at Sunderland and found I'd split the trousers of the new navy suits we had just been given, complete with embroidered gunner on the jacket lapel.

I learned Dave Sexton had wanted me at Arsenal some time before, when he was no 2 to Bertie Mee. He saw me as someone to play off George Graham and there was a representative from Highbury to see me bang in my Sky Blues hat-trick against Burnley. Dave had then gone off to Chelsea and been replaced by Don Howe, who was having a hard time getting the squad on-side because of his predecessor's popularity. Don didn't go out of his way to win friends. In training, we ran and ran and ran and I'll never forget one session at Highbury aimed at closing down the opposition. 'Hustle!' he yelled. 'Hustle every time they have the ball.' I'd never been worked like it and hadn't previously heard the word. Now I knew full well what it meant.

For a while, I lost some of my sharpness in the area and was dropped following a game against Newcastle. But my touch came back with a rush at the end of the season. As Arsenal finished ninth, I scored in my last four appearances – home and away against Sheffield Wednesday, plus one of the goals that helped us defeat a West Brom side who lifted the FA Cup a week later and another that contributed to us beating Leeds 4-3 and so deny them the title.

I carried my form into a tour of the Far East, where I became the first professional player ever to score in Japan. My fading copy of the Asahi News still shows the line 'Ace goal-getter Bobby Gould' under its back-page picture of me scoring the second of my two against the All Japan side in Tokyo. We then beat the same team 1-0 in Fukuoka and moved on to win 6-2 against Asian All Stars at Merdeka Stadium.

We met the King before the All Stars game and the Queen and Sultan of Selangor were present at one of the games. We also took in Kuala Lumpur, Vietnam and Hong Kong, so it was a memorable trip.

We were the first English professional club to visit Japan and, after flying over the North Pole on the way there and being given certificates to commemorate the fact, had a drama at 35,000ft on a Cathay Pacific flight later in the tour when we hit an air pocket so hard that one of the stewardesses fell and broke her arm. The incident occurred over Vietnam at a time when the Americans were still active there and the number of ashen faces on board reflected the worries about whether we were being fired at.

A few of the lads were much more at home on Japan's famous Bullet train but there were other wisecracks about the military on terra firma. We were wearing our club blazers, showing the gunner, and had more than one enquiry from the locals at the airports about which regiment we were in.

We didn't have to travel too far to have fun. Four of us – Peter Simpson, Geordie Armstrong, Geoff Barnett and me – went down to Cornwall once or twice for a few days' golf and took our families with us. The press caught up with us once teeing off at Bude and there was some surprise at the discovery that I played left-handed.

The Arsenal players were a lively bunch. For lunch on home match-days, we used South Herts Golf Club, where the legendary Dai Rees was the professional, and then burned rubber on the way to Highbury. It was like the Monte Carlo Rally as the competitive spirit bubbled over into a race to the ground.

I used to travel with John Radford, who was a neighbour of ours in Vincent Close, New Barnet. We shared lifts to training anyway as footballers' households only had one car then. Nabbers would be in there revving away, too, and Peter Simpson and Geordie Armstrong were a good double act. But Peter 'Snout' Storey always won. Over those ten miles of suburban roads, he would have given Jenson Button and Lewis Hamilton a good run.

I was seen as fair game to join in our version of the Wacky Races while I had my Spitfire but was then regarded as being too regal to take part when Dad did me a deal at a Rootes garage on Allesley Road at healthy discount and I bought a navy blue Humber Sceptre with a black vinyl roof and a gold stripe and leather seats. I was an Arsenal player after all! Others like Frank and

George were probably a cut above this daring nonsense as well but the sheer will-to-win in that team was unbelievable.

In the departure lounges on the Far East tour, armed with a tennis ball and miniature cricket bat, we staged 'Test Matches,' especially while we were delayed for hours in Hong Kong during a BOAC strike. Even in a fun knockabout like that, you didn't want to lose.

The togetherness on that trip, combined with the work Don Howe put us through, made Highbury a better place. We became a really solid team early in 1968-69 and were in the top six and not far off the pace. I scored a couple after going on as substitute in a win over Leicester and emerged from a quiet spell with a goal I dedicated to a man whose stern disciplinarian ways made Don look like a pussy cat.

As we got off the coach at Scunthorpe for a League Cup tie early that season, I was shocked to be greeted by Mr Bennett, one of my teachers at Stoke Council. I had long since forgiven him for humiliating me over my discovered love letter to Susan Barrow and also for making me stand in front of the class and explain why I had spelled water 'warter'. He knew I was a good lad despite my lapses and there was respect between us. Why else would he have travelled to see me after all those years?

Our good progress didn't stop the players tearing into each other every Monday at meetings in the Halfway House – a room just off the tunnel at the stadium. On a Saturday, the players' wives used the facility for a natter over tea and sandwiches. A couple of days later, the peace was shattered and the air was turned blue as we had our say on team matters. It wasn't just the natural leaders like George and Frank who vented their feelings, but even the more restrained ones like Willo, Ian 'Mary' Ure, 'Doggie' Court, Jon Sammels, Snout Storey, Stan (after the straight guy in Laurel and Hardy) Simpson and the wonderful Geordie Armstrong.

It was a set-up job by Don and Bertie. One of them would say something, then the players would join in and the place would explode in no time. George really tore into me once in there and accused me of thinking only about myself after I said before a game against Blackpool how much I needed a goal. In less than complimentary terms, he accused me of putting myself before the team.

No punches were ever thrown but tempers were extremely frayed and there was a lot of snarling. We really larruped each other verbally. Isn't there an

Army saying: "I'll meet you behind the kitchen door?" Apparently, it's where jackets would come off, rank would be forgotten and feuds settled. We were the same. Don would note where the sparks were flying and pick the teams for the subsequent training session accordingly, so differences could be sorted out on the pitch.

The air was always cleared. We didn't carry grievances around with us and we bonded so well because we could handle each other. Look at the success the club had soon after, especially with the double win of 1970-71. The philosophy of getting rid of tensions before they could fester was one I carried into my management career. I would stage organised fights in training, sometimes with me and one of the players pulling the boxing gloves on and all the others forming a baying circle and watching.

At Arsenal, we often trained on a shale surface at a college, where the sides were chosen specifically with the idea of creating maximum competition. It was in this environment that the coaching staff introduced a kid who was the best player, technically, I had ever seen. The ball fizzed about quicker than it did on grass and this lad learned to hit the ball so true and so early with barely a backlift. He was brilliant in the gym as well, a special talent. His name: Charlie George.

All the players recognised something special in Charlie and he became a right handful in training. He led a different life to most of us, though. While we were wondering where to play golf on an afternoon off, he would normally be heading to Wandsworth Jail. "Just off to spend some time with my mates," he would tell us. There were such characters at that club.

We all used to buy our carpets and curtains off the agent, Dennis Roach. I've still got receipts from 1968. Radders must have wondered whether he would need new windows as well, though, because more than once I had to throw stones up at his bedroom after he had overslept. He was one of life's biggest moaners but shouldn't have been because he met a lovely Dutch girl when the players had been put up by local families on a trip to Holland. He's still married to her.

By coincidence, one of my first trips with Arsenal was to Iceland, where I had also been with Coventry in the mid-1960s. I recall being greeted at the carousel by my best mate Bob Wilson because the Munich Air Crash was still fairly fresh in the memory and Arsenal often flew us on two separate planes.

Willo was all-action, in complete contrast to his deputy Geoff Barnett, who I was also an occasional room-mate to. I called him 'Lively.' All the lads had nicknames, although Ian Ure was always keen to shed his because of the famous actress he shared a surname with. His unusual habit was cleaning his teeth before games and we were forever pointing out we wanted him to clatter opposing centre-forwards, not kiss 'em.

With all due respect to Coventry, who I'd barely known as a top-flight club, the facilities at Arsenal were in a different league. Highbury was one of the first grounds to have a gym, plunge baths and underground heating in the dressing room. A boot man and washer lady were also employed. The set-up was high-class and the club were brilliant with Marge when she was pregnant with Jonathan.

Such off-field care helped my game. I kept up my record of scoring against my past or future clubs by netting the winner at Coventry and we had a Wembley final in our sights when our League Cup run took us into a two-leg semi-final against Tottenham. Don came up with a set-piece routine which worked a treat in the second leg at White Hart Lane. I was to clatter into Mike England as Geordie Armstrong swung over a free-kick aimed at one of the bigger guys – something I did just subtly enough for the referee to wave play on as John Radford headed home. So this was what it had come to.......I was being used as a decoy!

The final against Third Division Swindon seemed a foregone conclusion and probably would have been in normal circumstances. We won 5-0 at Sheffield Wednesday a couple of weeks earlier and were hot favourites. But the pitch was a disgrace after being churned up at the Horse of the Year show. We couldn't believe the FA would allow show jumping on there so close to showpiece matches. It's not only in recent seasons they have been accused of bizarre decisions.

Having been cup-tied for the previous season's final defeat against Leeds, I found it heartbreaking playing at Wembley for the first time in my career while it was in that state. Don Howe actually approached the referee at the end of normal time to say the game should be abandoned because the conditions were so bad.

On top of problems with cramp, we had illness in the camp and had a match called off the week before as a result. Stan Simpson shouldn't really have played and lasted only half the game and several of the other players, including Mary and possibly Nabbers, had flu as well. With the substitution already made, we were really struggling.

We hit the woodwork more than once, the Swindon keeper Peter Downsborough had the game of his life and their first goal was out of Fred Carno's Circus. But none of that gets away from the fact we were poor and our skipper Frank McLintock was in a state of distress afterwards. He was inconsolable. He was a serial Wembley loser after various trips there with Leicester, Arsenal and Scotland and must have feared he would never get his hands on a winners' medal.

My big day at Wembley started with me face-to-face in the tunnel with one of my former team-mates. Superstition dictated that I went out last, so there I was staring at the man bringing up the rear in the Swindon line, John Smith, who I had known as a young reserve at Coventry. I might not have stayed on the pitch long enough to congratulate him at the end, nor to score our equaliser, because the referee Bill Handley threatened me with one of Wembley's first sendings-off after I had roughed up Downsborough.

I was reprieved with a good talking-to and at least had something good to remember the afternoon by. We were trailing to a freakish in-off goal when I chased a through ball four minutes from the end and took a kick in the throat from Frank Burrows' size 12 boot on the way to scrambling the ball in after Downsborough had hit his clearance into my chest. I ran to the crowd, taking all the glory I could, then it just happened. I cried. Twenty-one years before Gazza's World Cup semi-final tears, I let all my emotions out. Me scoring at Wembley……..the theatre of all my boyhood dreams!

Just over half an hour later, there were more tears, this time Frank's after Swindon scored twice in extra-time to win 3-1. As our scorer, I took something from the occasion but I'd have been more distraught if I'd known then that I'd never play there again in a major match.

Don Rogers, who had been present when I went for England Youth trials back in 1963, swung it Swindon's way with two goals in the additional half hour and it is remembered as his final. If you look at film of the game, though, you'll see his kit is spotlessly white, even near the end on that heap of a pitch. He hardly had a kick for long spells.

The Daily Express called it 'the shame of Arsenal' and their writer Desmond

Hackett had threatened to eat his bowler hat if Swindon won – which is probably why he was inclined to have such a pop at us afterwards. We had made him look a pretty poor judge.

Fair play to Swindon but I didn't expect to still be hiding my head in shame over our defeat more than 40 years later. A few months ago, when I was on a talkSPORT visit to London, I was spotted in the station cafeteria by some Swindon fans on their way from a game at Colchester. They were merciless in reminding me of their big day and had another go on the train. The woman opposite blushed for me as I was being slaughtered.

My flirtation with trouble at the hands of referees didn't end with the 1969 League Cup final. A few weeks later, Gary Sprake decked me with a left hook in the first five minutes of our home game against Leeds. The first I saw of it was when I sat down to watch that night's Match of the Day. Jimmy Hill said Sprake hadn't hit me. Thanks JH! Well, somebody did because my gums were bleeding and I was still seeing stars when Ken Burns got his book out and took both our names.

Sprake said I called him a 'Welsh so and so' and I could have chosen a better day to let rip. Ken Burns was also Welsh and I remember him saying: "It's okay, Gareth. I heard what he said." Justice of a kind was done when the papers slated Sprake the next day but I was accused of having a nibble at him with a stray boot to his most sensitive area by way of provocation. As if!

We lost 2-1 and it was the most brutal game I ever played in. But all the matches against Leeds were gigantic. As a forward, I would have Jack Charlton and Norman Hunter for company and the full-backs Paul Reaney and Terry Cooper weren't above joining in any shenanigans. If the need arose, Billy Bremner, with his dirty socks and his various other gimmicks, would drop back to keep an extra eye out.

Don't expect me to say I was delighted when Leeds were crowned champions a few weeks later. Facing them was one of those occasions when you had to pack the boxing gloves in your kit bag. If you weren't prepared to give as good as you got, you may as well have stayed in the tunnel.

I didn't mind mixing it and hated bloody goalkeepers. Although strikers were allowed to challenge them then much more than they are today, I resented the fact that they could use their hands and even wore gloves. No wonder a few of the pictures in my collection – okay, quite a lot actually – show me raising a knee into their ribs, or leading with my elbow. It would have been rude not to warn them I was around. They must have detested me. I even had a go at my best mate Willo when I went back to Highbury as a Wolves player. I couldn't help myself. I was a different person on the pitch.

Eric Martin, of Southampton, wrote in a book that he feared me more than anyone else but I can assure him he wasn't singled out for special treatment. I saw it as a challenge to unsettle any keeper in the first five minutes and leave him on edge for the rest of the game. I wouldn't have been half as effective now with referees giving them so much protection and waving cards at every turn.

I once knocked seven lumps out of Carlisle's Alan Ross at Highfield Road. I absolutely battered him. Eventually, he snapped and took some retaliation by whacking me on the chin and decking me. He didn't even wait for the referee to point to the tunnel. He just started the long walk in his own time but stopped over my prostrate body to say: "It's worth it. I loved doing that."

It's ironic that my best mate is a goalkeeper and we had a son who became an international in that position. And it's equally strange that I never needed any persuading to have a go in goal myself. Many strikers love throwing themselves round in the mud in training but my involvement spilled over into matches. Soon after I left West Brom, I took over Ray Cashley's green jersey against them for Bristol City and kept them out for the best part of an hour in a 1-1 draw in which I'd earlier scored the equaliser.

And my glove-work helped Nottingham Forest win the European Cup. Peter Shilton is generally acclaimed over such matters, so I'll explain. On the last day of 1976-77, Wolves were leading Bolton 1-0 with a few minutes left when Gary Pierce was carried off. It was a case of 'send for Gouldy' again as I went in and, in front of thousands of our fans at the open end of Burnden Park, we successfully rebuffed the last few waves of intense pressure. We were already up as champions but our win meant Bolton narrowly missed out to Forest in the chase for the final promotion place. So, if I'd thrown one in, Forest wouldn't have gone up and therefore couldn't have won the League Championship the season later or the European Cup 12 months after that. No wonder Cloughie planted a kiss on my cheek at the City Ground when I took Wimbledon there in the late 1980s.

I wasn't blessed with great natural ability in my 'day job' of chasing goals but had spirit and courage in abundance. Charlton, Hunter, Chopper Harris...... I wasn't scared of any of them. I'd try to give as good as I got. Playing for West Brom once against Liverpool, I was whacked up the arse by Tommy Smith as we chased a ball down the line from Ray Wilson and took revenge by landing my studs in a much more sensitive part of his anatomy. "Smithy, if you're going to kick me, I'm going to kick you back," I yelled. "That's 1-1." The referee Pat Partridge was not amused and ran over, saying: "No, it's not, it's 2-0 to me. You're both booked."

Sometimes, trouble followed me round. I battered Alan Stephenson once in a Crystal Palace-Coventry game in which I scored the winner and cut his eye when we met again in a West Ham-Arsenal match. I was having a quiet drink in the players' bar with Willo and Nabbers afterwards when I suddenly felt this whack to the back of my head and turned round to see a woman brandishing a handbag, wearing a crazed expression and blaming me for ruining her husband's looks.

She hadn't finished there. I was with Marge at a Christmas party at Mike Bailey's house in London in the late 1980s when a voice piped up: "You don't remember me, do you?" I went pale and many a player might have been having flashbacks of John Terry proportions. But it was only her again. I cowered and set myself to sway out of the way of a swinging handbag but fortunately she came this time in peace rather than on another revenge mission. "You obviously knew more about him than I did when you thumped him," the former Mrs Stephenson said. "We've split up."

Arsenal's fourth place in 1968-69, albeit a long way behind Leeds, was a ticket into the Fairs Cup but my fortunes had gone into a dip. I didn't score in the last 12 matches of the season, including an outing with Young England against England at Stamford Bridge the night before the Cup Final, and was under pressure for my place alongside Radders from Ray Kennedy as well as the mercurial Charlie George.

It didn't take long the following season for me to become unsettled. It hurt to be left out while the side were making excellent progress in Europe and I had to look back to Highfield Road for a pick-me-up. 'Our kid' Trevor made his first-team debut at home to West Brom, although Willie Carr's name was the one on everyone's lips after he scored a hat-trick from midfield.

It came to my attention that Crystal Palace had enquired about me. When I went on the transfer list along with Terry Neill and David Court, nothing much happened and I said to Bertie Mee: "You couldn't sell a boiled egg." At least the decision to put me up for sale brought a positive response in another sense – I scored four in a friendly against the Cypriot side Omonia. I would have preferred it to be in the Fairs Cup against Sporting Lisbon or Ajax but I showed I wasn't a spent force.

Eventually, Villa, whose manager Tommy Docherty had signed my old mate George Curtis, expressed an interest as well. I fancied a move back to the Midlands with a young and growing family and thought £50,000-60,000 would be enough to tempt Bertie. I wasn't amused to learn that The Doc had offered only £5,000.

Arsenal went on to conquer Europe that season, beating Anderlecht in the final, but my impact was elsewhere, far from the spotlight. I was scoring hatfuls in the reserves, including four against West Ham at Highbury as part of a haul of 35 for the season, and felt short-changed by my exclusion from the first team.

Before one Football Combination match at Peterborough, Harry Miller from the Daily Mirror rang me to say: "Play well tonight.......you're being watched." I was so keen to see who by that I walked on to the pitch backwards to scour the faces in the directors' box. The interested party was Bill McGarry of Wolves, who I immediately clapped eyes on. Harry rang me back the next day to say Bill had been impressed at how I had rolled up my sleeves and got over my disappointment.

I joined Wolves for £55,000 on June 2, 1970, but might have linked up instead with their most famous-ever manager because Stan Cullis wanted to take me to Birmingham. Talk about clubs being like London buses and three coming at once after a long wait. I left Arsenal with a heavy heart because I knew the seeds of success were being sewn there. But I was unhappy at not playing and history shows that I wasn't one to hang around where I wasn't wanted.

Advances With Wolves

One of Bill McGarry's friends apparently rang him up and said "Don't be such an idiot" when he was about to sign me. It's a good job I'm thick-skinned and had belief in my ability because it's obvious that a lot didn't. Maybe the doubters agreed with Bill Shankly's view. He said once: "That Bobby Gould couldn't trap a bag of cement."

It didn't bother me, either, that many of my new team-mates didn't like Bill McGarry, who had us suppressing fits of laughter once when he told Gerry Taylor before a match at Highbury: "When you're concentrating properly, son, and you're fully on your game, you could keep Manley Statthews quiet." He was my type of manager, even if he had his moods, moments and malapropisms.

My transfer talks at Molineux had given me the chance to iron out some family issues. A few days earlier, we stormed away from my in-laws' house in Balsall Common, with Marge in tears, after a row over how we were feeding Richard while he had croup. It was fortunate that my journey home after agreeing terms with Wolves took me past Birmingham because I was able to drop in, say sorry and make sure we were all friends again.

Bill McGarry could fly off the handle as well. He had a three-legged dog called Lucky and used to bring him into Molineux and then leave him for the groundsman to take him walkies. It was as if the poor beast knew when we had lost. There was nothing like a bad result to bring the gaffer's aggressive side out and, as I had done in the presence of the formidable Mrs Stephenson, Lucky seemed to fret when Bill was stamping round after a defeat.

Hopefully, he was well out of sight early in 1970-71 because we made an awful start. We lost everywhere on a tour of Holland and Germany and couldn't stop the rot when we played a return at home to Hanover, although I scored my first goal. Then we kicked off with three League defeats. I had to shoulder my share of the blame after fluffing several chances in our opening defeat at Newcastle. I was dropped in double-quick time, then recalled at Coventry and shot my mouth off in the press about it being a grudge match because I hadn't got on with Noel Cantwell. I didn't score but made the only goal for Hughie Curran.

It proved something of a false dawn because we were soon losing again and you could have cut the air with a knife when a crisis meeting was called following our humbling at Oxford in the League Cup – a game in which we had Derek Dougan playing at centre-half.

Bill's face was red with anger and he looked round for suggestions as to where it was going wrong. Eventually, Jimmy McCalliog put his hand up and said in his soft Scottish accent: "Gaffer, you've stopped us having tea, toast and preserves before games." McGarry responded: "Preserves? You can have as much tea, toast and preserves as you fuckin' want as long as you start winning!" The lads cracked up; once we knew it was safe to do so.

At home games, Bill usually sat on the front row of the directors' box with our chairman John Ireland and it was a sure sign we were in for a bollocking if he stood up during the play and came down to join Sammy Chung in the dug-out. His temper was legendary and we'd all disappear to the far side of the pitch so we couldn't hear him. We must have been the most lop-sided team in the country!

Soon after, we were losing at half-time and Bill stormed through the door, pointed at me and the Doog and raged: "If I had a radar on you two, I wouldn't have had a fuckin' beep out of it." We won well in the end and he came in afterwards, winked and added: "That's motivation for you!" Of our next 24 games after Oxford, we lost only four and one of those was against Morton in a home second leg in the Texaco Cup after we had won 3-0 at their place.

Danny Hegan made his debut the same day as me and was a very good player. He was also a born comedian. Anyone who thinks I'm nuts should meet him because he's the sort of bloke you only have to look at and you laugh. On the last night of the pre-season tour, he had one drink too many, as he was inclined to do, and threw up at the back of the coach. The contents of his stomach, which were very much alcohol-based, trickled down the aisle and settled at Bill's feet. Don't ask me why but when a group of blokes are cooped up together for a week or two, that sort of event seems hilarious.

There had been speculation that Doog was going to be sold to Sheffield Wednesday but he got his act together as well and we hit it off. I went there thinking he would help my career, especially with the great providers we had like Dave Wagstaffe, who we called Nijinsky, 'Manny' Bailey and Kenny Hibbitt. Our game was all geared to driving runs from midfield and crosses, crosses, crosses. Doog was the target for most of those but Hughie Curran was excellent in the air as well and I was the man anticipating the knock-downs.

Starting from the day of my first Wolves goal, at Ipswich, I scored 15 times in 18 matches and even helped the youthful John Richards on his way. I was taken off at home to Huddersfield and he went on and hit his first League goal. That was my part in his emergence. At least I had netted in the same game and in the process we broke our eight-month wait for a victory at Molineux.

My goal-scoring run came at a time when Hughie was absolutely on fire and was the sort I'd dreamed of. It was a golden time for the club, if you'll pardon the pun, as Hibby also went into the side and got off the mark in my absence in a tremendous draw at Chelsea. McGarry told me he'd kick my backside if he saw me in our half of the field and I obeyed his orders.

From mid-September, I netted 12 times in 11 appearances – more than I'd managed in Arsenal's first team in 20 months – and was ribbed mercilessly by the lads for turning up game after game in my threadbare lucky blue suit. But I was nervous about changes in routine when I was in form.

At Coventry, I always used to borrow Dave Clements' comb to straighten my hair. And I once horrified my mum by retrieving some shoes she had put in the dustbin. They had holes in them and the heels were worn but I was on a good trot at the time and wanted to stick with them. I had lucky suits, lucky ties (at Arsenal, I always wore a maroon one with blue stripes that I'd pinched off our Trevor), even lucky underpants. No detail was overlooked.

I always felt I had goals in me. What I didn't expect was the chant Wolves fans came up with to mark my contribution to our surge. 'E For B' – short for 'eggs for breakfast' – was a popular catchphrase from a TV advert of the time in which a young lad chanted 'E for B and Georgie Best.' Molineux's North Bank seized the moment and responded with 'E for B and Bobby Gould.' That's even though I was strictly a Weetabix and toast man, with plenty of Jimmy Mac's preserves, of course.

I roomed with Manny and he was a funny bloke, nothing like the dour individual he might have seemed from a distance. He wasn't too impressed with my snoring, nor was he too extravagant when it came to opening his wallet. We did well to get that party out of him at Charlton many years later. I took a leaf out of his prudent-housekeeping book and, for 30 years, we have sent each other the same Christmas card. Every December, there's a panic to work out who has got it and to find a small corner of space to put a suitably cryptic message on. He's also high on my list for the 'round robin' I send out each January or February – the long hand-written letter I despatch to friends I rarely see, updating them with family and professional news.

Not only was Mike a terrific skipper, he was an outstanding player. It was wonderful for Doog and me to know he was going to find Waggy with all those passes. A stream of crosses – the sort we worked on endlessly in training – was bound to follow. Nectar!

I still have the match ball from when I hit a hat-trick against Manchester United. It was nice to snatch some of the attention away from George Best because my memory of facing him is being in many a players' bar after a game and watching a load of female heads turn as he walked in. We overshadowed him that day, Charlton and Law as well, and beat them 3-2.

I followed up in the same month by netting twice against Manchester City as we reeled off six League victories in a row. I was very happy at Molineux and we were well settled in a house in Sutton Coldfield, around half-way between Wolverhampton and our parents in Coventry.

I recall an early demonstration of Billy Bonds' common sense when I bagged one of the two goals we scored in the last six minutes to draw at West Ham. The referee was accidentally bowled over at one point when he got too close to the action and, as the crowd showed him all the mercy you would expect, Bonzo brought some order to proceedings by grabbing the whistle and blowing it to stop play. Not quite in the same league as when Hibby once wrote his own name into the book following a foul at Manchester City but it raised a laugh.

I wasn't prepared to tolerate anything standing in my way, not even my best mate. I still spoke once or twice a week to Bob Wilson and there was a fair amount of press interest when we went to face Arsenal in the December. I didn't score, nor did I disappoint Willo. I clattered into him at one point and left him winded, just to remind him I still loved keepers. Marge was sat next

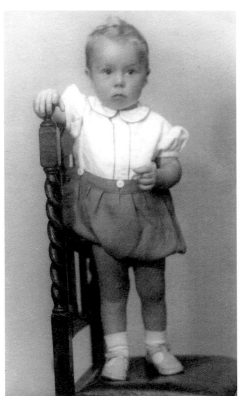
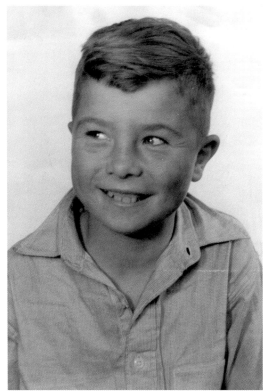

Early pictures from the Coventry City 'Academy.' Above left: At home in the days when chairs were more fun when they were being stood on than used as seating. Top right: Is that a footballer in the making or a budding film star? Below: No prizes for guessing who the skipper is, sat next to the headmaster Mr Tilley, in this team shot from Caludon Castle more than 50 years ago. It was a time that holds such happy memories for me, even though I was no academic.

For once (above), it's not me giving the keeper a hard time. It's Alan Turner, who also played in Sky Blues' first team. I'm the forward backing up in this Coventry v Aston Villa youth game at Shilton. Left: A keepsake from my League debut. Below: Waiting for slips at home to Manchester City on the day I scored my first League goal.

Above: A useful dress rehearsal for the 'Midlands Match of the Century' and the promotion celebrations that followed. The travelling fans thought we might be going up after I'd scored in this victory at Huddersfield at the end of 1965-66. Southampton spoiled the fun but Jimmy Hill had us in the mood to make sure 12 months later, using his imagination (below) on the pre-season alpine tour. In the same natty shorts on the left is Alan Dicks while John Sillett is sat on the back, leaning on the shoulders of George Curtis. I clashed big-time with Dicks and Schnoz years later.

Can't think why some of my best mates are goalkeepers! From left above, Blackburn's John Barton, Huddersfield's John Oldfield and Liverpool's Tommy Lawrence find getting up close and personal with me a dubious pleasure. Left: Birmingham's Jim Herriott is on the receiving end of another full-blooded challenge. Below: Not a keeper in sight as I celebrate a Coventry goal against Charlton in front of that huge open bank at The Valley during the second half of our promotion season..

These poison-pens force Gould out

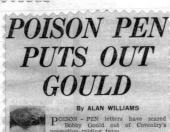

This is a sample of the anonymous letters—with misspellings—that have been hounding Gould.

COVENTRY CITY'S top scorer, 20-year-old Bobby Gould, has been virtually hounded out of today's team to play at Bury by a stream of abusive letters sent by anonymous Sky Blue fans.

One letter, received by Gould after Coventry's home Cup defeat by Newcastle last Saturday, told him he should "commit suicide."

Gould, a product of Coventry's youth squad, has scored 15 goals this season. But against Newcastle he missed three great chances and the fans booed him as he walked off.

After manager Jimmy Hill saw the player yesterday he decided that Gould was too depressed and shocked by the letters to play at Bury.

Said Hill angrily: "I have had to leave him out for his own good. He is only 20, and this vicious campaign has hit him very hard. This sort of behaviour by supporters can ruin young players.

"I was going to give him another chance to regain his form at Bury," said Hill, "I was prepared to back his great guts and character to win the game."

Gould has been replaced in the first team by reserve Johnny Tudor and will travel as substitute.

Gould, spending the evening with his parents, said last night: "I know that I have not been playing too well, but these letters have really hurt me.

"The fans pay their money and I suppose they have a right to criticise, but these letters go beyond the line. I shall fight back into the team and show these cranks how wrong they are."

'I WILL PLAY'

Despite being made the scapegoat by the Coventry supporters, Gould has no thoughts

POISON PEN PUTS OUT GOULD

By ALAN WILLIAMS

POISON - PEN letters have scared Bobby Gould out of Coventry's promotion-raiding team.

Gould, 20-year-old centre forward, said yesterday : "One of the letters advised me to commit suicide."

He added : "I know I have not been playing well and I missed a couple of goals in the Cup tie against Newcastle.

"But I never thought this poison-pen business would happen to me. It has shaken me up ; my confidence has been hit.

"I have no intention of asking for a transfer. I will show I can fight back and prove the cranks wrong."

Gould, whose 15 goals have helped Coventry into a two-point lead at the head of the Second

IT'S 9-9-9—BUT NO AID FOR IPSWICH

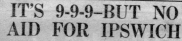

The electric scoreboard records the 999 emergency for Ipswich created by the goalscoring efforts of Bobby Gould, who hit a 33-minute "hat-trick" last night. No-one answered the call, and later John Key and Ian Gibson turned the crisis into a disaster for the East Anglians with further goals.

Contrasting memories from my scrapbook library; the time I was dropped after a poison pen letter and the night I obeyed JH with a hat-trick against Ipswich. Left: A goal against Carlisle and, below, one v Huddersfield just before promotion was won. Derek Parkin, later a Wolves pal, is on the far post, the keeper is John Oldfield and the defender in front of me is Chris Cattlin, who later joined Coventry.

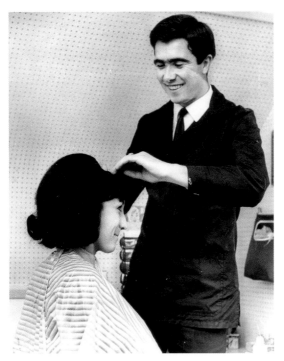

Above: Keeping my hands strictly at head height on the day the cameras recorded my 'other' life. But things weren't always so respectable. Top right: Marriage to Marge just after a promotion-winning season in which I'd top-scored for the Sky Blues. Below: Whooping it up with Brian Lewis and Ernie Machin at Nottingham Forest on the day I scored my first top-flight goals.

Another red-letter day (above), this time against Burnley in the First Division in December, 1967, soon after my return to the side following injury. Ian Gibson was first on the scene to help me celebrate the last of my three goals on an afternoon when we ran out 5-1 victors and recorded our first League win in nearly three months. Right: With Christmas rapidly approaching, I was pictured at home with Marge and the Puma boots I wore when I scored my second hat-trick in a week. I had also netted three just before against West Ham Reserves. It was a happy time but I was to leave Coventry a few weeks later for Arsenal - and my next Football League treble would be as a Wolves player at home to Manchester United.

Was this the day that sowed the seeds for my move from the Sky Blues to Arsenal? Early in our first top-flight season, we drew 1-1 at Highbury - a fixture in which I rounded goalkeeper Jim Furnell and fired us into the lead (above). It was an effort that clearly thrilled my huge fan club on Highbury's North Bank (right) but maybe Bertie Mee had a few reservations about me after I had proved less impressive from this second-half opportunity (below), which Furnell dealt with. I always seemed to score goals against former clubs and those I later joined, and netted in the return against the Gunners before I was left out of Coventry's FA Cup tie against Tranmere when my new manager Noel Cantwell obviously sensed that a sale was close. It was that competition, though, that brought me my first Gunners goal a few weeks later.

to Megs Wilson in the crowd, had to apologise for her husband's robust behaviour and was interested to see that one of the Fleet Street reporters based his match report round what the two wives said to each other in the stand.

My 1970-71 goal tally included five as we won the cup. Okay, it was the Texaco Cup, not the FA Cup, but we grew to enjoy those trips over the Scottish border and the one westwards to face Derry City. When I say 'enjoyed', I do so with certain qualifications in the latter case. There was a big anti-British thing in Belfast at the time and a Derry fan raced past our bench during the game and smacked one of our young substitutes in the face.

That was child's play compared with what occurred when we went to Linfield for a pre-season friendly. I was sharing sleeping quarters with The Doog and didn't earn any marks for subtlety when I shouted "Don't shoot, it's Derek Dougan!" as the two of us returned to our room after a walk. Just as I said it, a bomb exploded at the back of our hotel and the newspaper office went up. When McGarry called us together for a meeting downstairs, he was as white as a sheet. And Derek, whatever he might have told us later, was shitting himself. I made no such pretence but some good came out of the trip. We won 4-0 and I scored a hat-trick.

I liked the Texaco Cup and was delighted to score a couple away to Morton in a game watched by my Granddad Bob Morton. Yep, they had the same name. I had also been there with Coventry and he joined me in the players' bar after Wolves' visit and got so engrossed in conversation with the lads that he missed his last train back into Glasgow. Bill McGarry must have mellowed with our victory because he agreed to him having a lift into the city and even gave him a seat at the front.

It was the tie at Dundee that started us off on our goal-filled winning run in the League and we chalked up some big victories in the competition either side of Christmas, although we stumbled over the finishing line by losing at Molineux in the second leg of the final against Hearts after winning 3-1 at their place. We bonded really well in the process and also finished fourth in the League. It was a terrific season; a case of work hard, play hard.

As much as McGarry put us through it, he also knew how to allow us to unwind. Wednesday was golf day at somewhere like South Staffs or Brocton Hall. Derek Dougan hated it. Attendance was compulsory and it wasn't a bad idea to make sure you were around the tee to make a complimentary remark when the gaffer drove off first. If he duffed his shot, the giggles were stifled behind hands.

I used to love floating round the dressing room, getting on with everybody......The Tea Set compromising The Doog, John Holsgrove, Squeak Parkin and The Reverend (Les Wilson), who ordered tea together everywhere we went, the other older lads like Manny and Waggy, and the younger group such as John McAlle, Hibby and John Richards. The Doog could be difficult but he was a cult figure because of his crowd-pleasing personality and his knack of timing his runs and leaps perfectly.

He was a contradiction of a player. He couldn't kick the ball 15 yards and his shooting certainly wasn't great. No-one was better, though, at finding the 'honey-pot' position when crosses went in – the area between the centre-half and full-back that I've nagged my strikers to get into down the years. And he was a strong runner, always up near the front on the many stamina work-outs we were put through. He learned to be sharp from a standing start as well. McGarry never gave us a warm-up and always expected a good first-lap time as we did our circuits of Molineux.

Whatever the methods, we sparkled in the League as well as in the Texaco Cup. Although we were well beaten in the return against Arsenal and I again fired blanks in the return against Coventry, I hit a brace as we saw off West Ham shortly afterwards and knocked in one of the four that defeated Albion at The Hawthorns in our next League game. A bit of food for thought perhaps as both clubs were to sign me over the next year or two.

We secured Wolves' highest finish since the Cullis glory years and were falling over ourselves scoring goals, with Hughie and me in the 20s and Doog in the teens. The competition was so fierce that I played on for three games with a foot injury because I was scared of telling Bill and losing my place. Our midfield was full of goals as well and we were an exciting side, so who would have thought that such a free-scoring attack, one that had fired the club into Europe for the first time in over a decade, was about to be broken up?

There was one fly in the ointment as far as I was concerned – one that sprouted deadly feet and a predator's brain that was too much for many. At Arsenal, a young Charlie George challenged me. In Wolverhampton, it was the up-and-coming Richards. He made it clear he was after my shirt and, once he had a foot in the door, it became obvious he wasn't going to go away.

If we weren't doing the pass-and-cross drills at Castlecroft, we were either running up and down that massive South Bank in training or having shooting practice in the old Social Club next to the ground. And it was in that gym that I remember thinking what a good finisher Richie looked. He also had a first touch that left mine looking Second Division by comparison.

I shot myself in the foot by swearing at McGarry when he took me off against Southampton. He didn't pick me for the last three League games of the season, although he recalled me for the return home leg of the Texaco final, which we lost 1-0.

It was obvious John couldn't be held back indefinitely. The writing was on the wall when McGarry said to me early the following season: "I'm leaving you out." The conversation continued: "You can't leave me out gaffer." "Well, when did you last score?" "Six games ago." "Exactly, you'll get me the sack." I liked his honesty, even if it spelled bad news this time.

Over the years, we stayed close enough for him to visit me at my various clubs for a cuppa when he was over from Africa, but we were about to part. My demotion was an endorsement for Richie because I had top-scored with 24 goals in my first season there, yet here was the gaffer saying he thought the young pretender was better.

Hughie was jettisoned as well as the Dougan-Richards partnership started to blossom. I recognised the signals and sensed that another chapter would soon be closing. Apparently, I had unsuccessfully been offered as bait with The Reverend for Bristol City's Chris Garland, and Leicester also seemed to be hovering. As a goalscorer, I often attracted interest.

It was strange considering the big impact I had made only a few months earlier that I was surplus to requirements – and it was a bit galling, too. Having missed Arsenal's run to the Fairs Cup final, I regretted the thought that I'd be leaving Wolves just as they were setting off on their run to the 1971-72 final of the competition's successor, the EUFA Cup (quickly renamed the UEFA Cup). But you've probably got the picture by now: I never wanted to stay beyond my sell-by date.

Tough Times – And Howe!

I remember Marge and me agreeing that, if there was one manager who would never sign me, it was Don Howe. I had a right pop at him when Arsenal hadn't given me more of a run despite my 35 goals in the reserves in one season and his ears were probably still throbbing. It wasn't as though I had expected Bertie Mee and him to make me an automatic choice but I was angry and frustrated they didn't give me a better chance.

My frustration with them had boiled over to such an extent that I thought Bill McGarry was winding me up when he called me into his cramped Molineux office and told me that West Brom, who were by now managed by Don, had put an offer in for me early in 1971-72. So did I want to link up again with my former coach from Highbury?

Albion had been a free-scoring side for many years with players like Jeff Astle, Tony Brown and Bobby Hope on board and emerged as a major force in the cups in the second half of the 1960s. Maybe *they* could take me to the FA Cup final. But the goals had dried up under their change of style following the departure of their manager Alan Ashman, whose successor reckoned there was someone nine miles down the A41 who could address the problem.

Once more, I was attracted to a rival club where my prospects of first-team football were greater. I said I'd go if the money was the same and my contract was the same length. They were, so I was on the move yet again, and Bob Wilson rang to pass on his congratulations. It was a case of another sizeable transfer fee and another five per cent being squirreled away for a rainy day. And that's an apt turn of phrase because, very soon, it was monsoon time.

In my first game, at home to Ipswich, I was marked by a former Wolves team-mate, Derek Jefferson, and the side finally came up with a goal thanks to Bomber Brown's penalty. But we lost 2-1 and I had my name taken – didn't I always on my debut? In my first away game, Derby had 24 corners and we had none and, although we somehow escaped with a draw, I already sensed we were up against it.

I was paired for the first time with Big Jeff when we went to Crystal Palace. He had had an appendicitis operation and his return coincided with my first goal as we ended our long wait for a win. But you couldn't say Don Howe's methods were expansive by any means and we were about to go into a sharp nosedive.

We lost seven games in a row up to Christmas, slumped to the bottom of the First Division and looked every inch a relegation side. The players were struggling to adapt to Don following the more carefree style of Ashman, the FA Cup-winning manager who the club sacked while he was on holiday in Greece. The lads were being driven much harder in training and it's fair to say there was a bit of a dressing-room backlash.

You couldn't meet a nicer guy than the keeper John Osborne and even he was riled enough to moan: "He has only gone and stopped our table tennis in the afternoons." Another day, the Spring Road training ground was waterlogged and we thought we'd be sent home early but Don built 'fences' on the track by lying brooms over two spread-out buckets and had us racing round and jumping them like horses. We didn't know whether we were preparing for Aintree or Anfield. Jeff and Colin Suggett loved a flutter on the gee-gees but hated this drill and were two laps behind everybody else.

Don had wanted me in to shake the place up and break down the resentment towards him. He remembered from Arsenal what a good trainer I was. I just wanted to make as much of myself as I could as a professional footballer and he would have recalled me pounding up and down Highbury's North Bank with a smile on my face when others were chuntering at the demands put on them. I found it very hard not to be cheerful because rarely did I feel down.

I suspect a few of the Albion lads thought I was a spy, 'planted' in the dressing room to pass back to Don what they were saying about him. I wasn't. I'd never split on my mates and in some ways I was anti-management. I did detect one fly in the ointment, though, and I'll come back to him shortly.

There were a few other excellent players at The Hawthorns like Doug Fraser, Hopey and John Kaye, who were ageing together. Graham Williams had just taken up a coaching role at Don's side and Jeff, the darling of the fans, was having chronic problems with his knee. There was still ability in the side with Bomber, Asa Hartford and Len Cantello while John Wile and Alistair Robertson were formidable defenders. But it wasn't a happy camp.

When we were struggling, especially for goals, we played Manchester City and Mike Doyle asked me during a break in play: "Why did you come here?" I said: "Because they were the ones to come in for me." I might also have said: "And because Malcolm Allison would never have me near Maine Road."

Thankfully, the tide turned spectacularly. At Christmas, despite victories and no goals against in the first two games of 1971-72 (before I arrived), we had a princely 11 points, admittedly when only two were on offer for a win. From then on, we played like a top-six side to finish a full ten points clear of the danger line, although we fell at the first hurdle in the Cup at home to Coventry. It was a huge turnaround.

The Wolves games typified our season. They scored after 31 seconds at The Hawthorns, where my late goal couldn't stop us losing 3-2 during our nightmare trot, but we were flying when we went there after Easter. We won thanks to Bomber Brown's strike in 55 seconds and took almost three times as many points in the second half of the season as the first.

In the previous season's Black Country derby, I had been pictured with Yorky Kaye, each of us trying to grab the other round the throat – probably after I had lunged in on the keeper Jim Cumbes. On the day I signed at The Hawthorns, though, we were pictured together in the foyer, all smiles and relaxed. How relationships change in football….

Like the team, I came good after Christmas. We beat Liverpool in front of 43,000 on Boxing Day – our first home victory since August – and my superstition habit kicked in when I decided to wear the same suit, shirt and tie for games from then on. We won again when I notched to help us come from two down at Ipswich the following Saturday, just before Don took us over to Jersey for a few days. He loved a trip.

I got another when Albion recorded their usual home win over Manchester United and ended the season with 13 goals, all but one (a strike in a Wolves shirt against Spurs on kick-off day in August) for the Baggies. I was in a particularly hot spell when we signed off for the summer with our survival secured in comfort. I netted in a 4-0 win against Chelsea, scored twice when we lost at Newcastle and flashed a great volley past Gordon Banks in a draw at Stoke.

We went on an end-of-season tour of Yugoslavia and I scored in all three games despite the shock of seeing a revolver drawn by a local when we went out for a beer or two in Sarajevo. It was probably the quickest exit a group of footballers have ever made from a nightclub. There was certainly no need for the lights to be flashed or someone to shout 'Last orders.' It was more likely to be a case of last rites.

Graham Smith, a keeper Don had signed from Colchester, took a liking to the wine and was running in and out of all our bedrooms on that trip. I turned a blind eye to his excesses and went with him into a business called Professional Footballers Investment Services. Even in the early 1970s, we had approaching 400 players on our books, including Bobby Robson and George Graham, and I owe a huge debt of thanks to one of our other two partners, John Hazell. He was also from Colchester, became my financial adviser and died around ten years ago while writing his autobiography. The fourth member of the group was a fellow called Mike Duley.

It was never worth putting your passport back in the drawer with Don. He took us to Sweden the other side of our summer break and, once more, everything I tried flew in. Another goal away to Feyenoord and one on yet another jaunt, this time to Scotland to face Hibernian, had me straining at the leash for the new season to start. But you've guessed it: When it mattered, I couldn't hit a cow's arse with a banjo.

We managed one goal in our first five matches and the die was cast for another season of struggle. My late winner past Wolves keeper Lofty Parkes at The Hawthorns was a rare highlight but only the goals of Bomber Brown gave us even half a chance of survival. He was my room-mate and said there was always a job for me at his and Irene's house in Walsall if I hit on hard times. That's how tidy he thought I was. I'm available now if he still needs me – but afternoons only. I push the hoover round our home every day after breakfast.

I hardly missed a game for Albion in almost a year and a half but a rival to my place had surfaced with the signing of Alistair Brown from Leicester. And I don't think George Wright did me any favours. George was the physio but had an input on the coaching side as well, having followed Don up from Arsenal. He had the ear of the manager and didn't have the highest regard for me as a player. He could have expressed his views a bit more subtly, though.

Before I knew it, he was driving me down to the West Country for talks with Bristol City – or at least trying to. We broke down at Cheltenham.

I had grown to like the Albion lads. Wiley was a fine character and there was never a dull moment with Big Jeff around. Without fail, he would have us in fits of laughter by conning the officials when they came in to inspect the players' studs before a game. He would hold up his right boot and then turn round, lean against the wall with his hands and offer the same foot. They never twigged!

I was satisfied I'd given Albion value for money. I had scored 19 goals, at better than one in every three games, in a low-scoring team. And I carried out one more important task: I made room for Willie Johnston at The Hawthorns. As a Wolves player 18 months or so earlier, I had met him and his Glasgow Rangers team-mates when we stayed in the same hotel near Stockholm on a summer tour. Now, my last Albion game, a draw against Liverpool, was his debut after he came down from Rangers in a club record deal. He was a brilliant winger and I was sorry not to have stayed around long enough to get on the end of his crosses. In fact, it was more a case of me setting him up because he and his family moved into our house in Sutton Coldfield when I left.

Dicksy And The Bath-Time Blues

I was only 26 and Bristol City represented my fifth stopping-off point. But I was thankful there had been comparatively little upheaval to date for Marge and our growing household. Richard had arrived as a second 'Paddington Bear' while I was still at Arsenal, and all we had basically done to keep Pickfords in business was leave the Midlands once and return there once. Now, though, my move to the West Country meant we had to sell up again and go house-hunting.

Domestically, it was the best thing we ever did. We uprooted to Portishead and have had a home there for 38 years. In fact, when we moved a couple of hundred yards round the corner to our present abode in 1981, we were sufficiently tired of uprooting to give it the name 'Evermore' and decided that was the place we would always return to. We fell in love with those four walls and the lovely garden beyond them and knew we'd never sell it. There might be callings that would require spells in rented accommodation but I would take jobs only on the proviso that we kept that property and I would lay my head under its roof on as many nights as possible.

Happy though we were domestically, I knew within weeks on a football level that I'd made a mistake joining Bristol City. When I was a teenager, I had known Alan Dicks as a player-coach at Coventry and we'd rubbed along together very well. Reuniting with him, as with Don Howe, was a case of signing for someone I knew and I had a reputation for being a bouncy character round the dressing room. But I had been round the block since my Highfield Road days, spent a few years in the First Division and changed a bit, and Dicksy probably thought I had become too big for my boots.

At £60,000, I was the most expensive signing ever made by a Bristol club and maybe I was guilty of believing my own publicity. It was big news when I moved there and, as I walked into the ground to sign, I bumped into their top scorer John Galley, a big Yorkshire lad who had learned his trade at Wolves well before I got there. I said: "I think we'll be quite a partnership." He replied: "I doubt it. I'm just off to sign for Nottingham Forest."

That was a disappointment but I enjoyed the company of the lads John was leaving behind, like Gerry Sweeney, David Rodgers and the keeper Ray Cashley. And it was nice to link up again with my old Wolves mate, The Reverend Les Wilson, although we were destined to play only a handful of matches together.

I got off to a good start by scoring a beauty at Preston in my second game and quickly made an impression on the dressing room. After being known as Teasy Weasy, Bunter or plain Gouldy at my previous clubs, I now answered to 'Snip'. But, bargain signing or not, there was conflict between the management and me from the early days.

John Sillett, who had also been at Coventry, was Dicks' assistant and it wasn't long before he had me round the throat, threatening to knock my head off. There was a misunderstanding when I threw the ball at an opponent and dished out some verbals. Our bench thought I had uttered an expletive in their direction. Schnoz couldn't wait to get me in the dressing room and get a grip of me, which he did, literally. Once the air had started to pass through my windpipe again, I reassured him my venom was aimed at the officials and he kindly let me slide gently down the wall back to the floor.

Schnoz, so called because his big hooter made him look like the singer and pianist Jimmy 'Schnozzola' Durante, had been one of the senior players at Coventry when I was a youngster and he probably remembered me as one of the quieter, more conscientious lads. He thought I still needed bringing down a peg or two, though, and was making it his business to do it. There were further ructions when I got blocked off at a free-kick in a Watney Cup game against Peterborough and the player I was marking, Chris Turner, scored as a result. It was another cue for Schnoz to hang me on the back of the door. And that was a game I scored two in!

Despite the flashpoints I endured, we did all right in 1972-73. We were very strong at home in the second half of the season, putting Swindon, Brighton, Portsmouth and Aston Villa away with two or three goals to spare. We also drew at Burnley, who finished as Second Division champions. We came in fifth but only two teams went up then and runners-up QPR were well ahead of us.

I had initially been handed Galley's no 9 shirt and filled it reasonably well.

My tally of ten in the few months I had there wasn't spectacular but it left me second behind Gerry Gow in the club charts and I fancied myself to become a force after five or six years in the top flight. I again found Portsmouth lucky opponents by netting home and away against them in the FA Cup third round and was delighted to put a couple of chances away against Villa. Inevitably, though, that was at Ashton Gate. I could never score at Villa Park.

I also took flight with the Robins when they went to America at the end of the season. Eating at a McDonald's wasn't my only 'first' on that trip. I also made my debut on astro-turf, scoring against Cincinnati Comets, while the other match was at a baseball stadium in Baltimore, with the pitcher's mound clearly visible on the pitch. The PA man also sounded a loud trumpet fanfare every time our hosts attacked – something that had us looking round for the approaching cavalry the first couple of times.

The tour was a step too far for Schnoz. Our plane was just reversing from the gate at Heathrow when he stood up and rushed down the aisle, his fear of flying having got the better of him. He said he couldn't face the trip at any price and was allowed to disembark before his luggage was retrieved for him.

As usual, I had plenty of eventful meetings at home with my former clubs. We were beaten at Wolves in the fourth round of the FA Cup but I scored a couple against Coventry in the League Cup the following season and had the last laugh on my old Albion mates. They were relegated in 1973 and were soon at our place, where Ray Cashley dislocated his shoulder and handed the green jersey to me.

I was in goal well before half-time and enjoyed frustrating Bomber Brown and Co. He and I had both scored early in the game, then he pinged a shot past me, only to be denied by an offside flag. Finally, with my work almost done, I stubbed my toe taking a goal-kick in the last minute and had to rush out of my area to block-tackle him to make sure it stayed at 1-1. If Don Howe thought I had some eccentric ways as a striker, he now knew they were nothing compared with my madcap goalkeeping.

That was a rare highlight, though, in what was generally a rough time. And things came to a head when we made the long trip to Humberside early in the autumn. Hull had a full-back called Roger De Vries who was fast enough to catch pigeons and I was busy in the first half yelling at Keith Fear to track back with him. At half-time, Alan Dicks lambasted me for acting like a First Division superstar and I'd just about had enough. I bent down, undid my laces and hurled my boots at the skip, the lads watching as my footwear bounced off it and landed at the gaffer's feet.

Needless to say, my services were not required in the second half, so I jumped in the bath. But no sooner had the lads gone out again than I felt some hands on my shoulders and realised Dicksy had taken the plunge as well, fully clothed. He was grappling with me as Schnoz this time acted as peace-maker by wading in to pull us apart. I knew it was the end for me at Ashton Gate.

I didn't bother going out to watch the second half of our defeat and instead walked down the road from Boothferry Park in search of a telephone box. "Start packing, love," I said to a mystified Marge, explaining to her why I was on the blower rather than on the pitch. She was upset at my news and I concluded by giving her the relevant information in the only way I thought I could. "I'm finished here," I added. "We're on the move again."

If there was any chance at all of us kissing and making up – that's Dicksy and me, not Marge and myself – it was soon snuffed out. We were staying over and the lads went out to drown their sorrows. But I was at my lowest ebb and soon made my way back to the Eden Hotel with Trevor Tainton, alias 'Wuzzy Woo.' The club were always looking to cut costs and I wasn't happy about spending a night in the camp-bed I'd landed myself with, even less so when my room-mate Gerry Gow returned from the night out and playfully tipped it up at such an angle that my knees were in front of my face.

There was a hell of an atmosphere in the foyer the next morning after it transpired one of the directors had been disturbed by the lads staggering back in the early hours. Not a word was spoken. There had been complaints from other guests as well and the night porter had reported the commotion.

Dicksy was scowling at everyone and promising to read us the riot act back at Ashton Gate. He didn't disappoint and slapped a £25 fine on us all – almost a third of a week's wages. Straightaway, I put my hand up and said I wasn't paying because I was fast asleep at the time. I badgered Wuzzy Woo by saying: "And you can get your hand up because you were in bed as well." The FA sided with us but the story broke in the press and I told the manager I had to go. It was the first time I'd asked for a move.

Funnily enough, the fall-out was followed by a little scoring flurry. I netted against the Baggies before pulling my goalkeeper gloves on, then scored in a win at Millwall and bagged a couple in the League Cup draw with Coventry. I was in double figures for the season and our leading scorer. I had even tucked away a penalty against Luton by the time the Ashton Gate phones turned hot.

Dicksy still wanted to get shut and took a call from Norwich about me because Ron Saunders was looking for a replacement for David Cross, who was being sent to Coventry – in another way. I found out when I went for talks that, if I wanted to put serious distance between myself and Bristol City, I couldn't do any better than ply my trade in Norfolk. Talk about long haul!

I travelled on three trains, including a tube, and it seemed like 1am when I checked in at my hotel. Thank goodness there was a warm welcome from none other than The Reverend, who was there after moving to Carrow Road a few weeks earlier. Ron Saunders had a hard-man reputation but I was convinced I could play for him, having already worked well with Bill McGarry.

We agreed terms of nearly £100 a week, with all my removal costs paid, and I had the transfer forms in my pocket. Then Ron stunned me by saying: "There's just one problem. I might be getting the sack. The chairman and me aren't getting on very well, so let's see what happens in our next game." It may have seemed a funny way of conducting negotiations but Ron was good to me. He was honest enough to suggest I held fire, however desperate he might have been for a striker.

I went home and told Marge what a horrific journey it was; a seriously long way. The decision, though, was taken out of my hands. Norwich lost 3-0 at home to Everton and Saunders resigned. They were not a pretty sight on that night's Match of the Day. The phone rang next morning and I was greeted by a posh voice requesting that we had a chat. "Leave it out, Willo," I said. "Stop taking the piss." Then, after an awkward silence, I heard the follow-up words: "It's Arthur South, chairman of Norwich City. We need to talk, dear boy."

The Canaries still wanted to add me to the perch but I told them I couldn't fly the nest without knowing who my manager would be. And, while my head was still spinning, Ron Saunders rang to say sorry for what had happened. He didn't need to. The news he gave me at the same time was just what I wanted to hear: West Ham were also interested. Five weeks after the hell of Hull, I planned to be there in a shot.

Happy With The Hammers

So keen was Dicksy to see the back of me that he had John Sillett drive me across to London, with the transfer forms bulging in my pocket. He had put pressure on me to go to Norwich and would have been surprised if he could have seen me whistling and singing as I went back into the dressing room after telling him a move to Norfolk definitely wasn't on my agenda.

At that stage, I was one step ahead of him in knowing West Ham wanted me. But that changed in a flash and his secretary Annie chased me down the corridor to say I was required back in the manager's office straightaway. When I walked in, I said: "Alan, I've done nothing in the last 30 seconds that you could possibly reprimand me for." I was staggered to see him sat with his head in his hands. In the moments I had been away, Ron Greenwood had been on the phone asking for my services and agreed to pay the full £80,000.

Much as Schnoz and him wanted to see me out, they found it hard to stomach that not one, but two clubs were trying to take me out of the Second Division – where Bristol City were then playing – and back to the top flight. Dicksy formally told me West Ham had been on the phone and I pointed a finger at him and said: "That's great, I'm definitely going there."

There was more merriment and raised eyebrows among the other players when they heard about the new development. But why was it that I always seemed to be wanted more elsewhere than by the club I was at? I had, after all, scored at the rate of a goal every other game in my 40-odd matches for City.

Ron Greenwood had done his homework by ringing Ron Saunders to ask how I'd interviewed and this time I let it be known where I was heading. Everyone was happy. West Ham were getting their man, I was joining a fine club only half the travelling distance from Bristol as Norwich, and Dicks was washing his hands of me and making a £20,000 profit at the same time.

My talks with Greenwood were at White Hart Lane, where he was watching a youth-team game, and we got on superbly. He quickly realised I wasn't really motivated by money. In fact, when I asked for a quick break in our talks to ring Marge and say how well we were getting on, she was surprised to learn that we hadn't even talked wages.

It was only the next day when I went back that I reminded Ron there was still the small matter of agreement on finances. I told him I'd been on £80 a week at Bristol and he said: "I think we pay our players £150. Are you happy with that?" I was more than happy. I was cock-a-hoop. And I was getting a £4,000 signing-on fee.

There were two problems – first, of course, the small matter of adapting to working life more than 100 miles away. We were still fairly new to our home in Riverleaze, Portishead, and I dreaded uprooting the family again. We nevertheless found a fabulous place in Chigwell, where many of the West Ham players lived. We would have gone but couldn't sell our place.

It was November, 1973, the time of the miners' strike and the three-day week, and money was tight, so I commuted for two years. That meant my routine changed big time and one of the newspaper photographers spent a morning with me to illustrate my unusual timetable.

I was up at 5.30am and the snapper showed me saying hello to the milkman before I got on the first train from Bristol at 5.55. We pulled into Paddington at 7.45 and I was picked up from the tube station by Trevor Brooking ready to do the last few miles to the training ground at Chadwell Heath, near Romford, by car. Fortunately, I still had more than enough energy left to then put my heart and soul into my work.

The Brookings were kind enough to let me stop over for one night, which was an even nicer gesture as they were newly-weds. I promptly repaid their hospitality by pulling the curtains down in my bedroom. Hard though I found it to believe, 'Boogaloo' – so-called because of his likeness to a baseball star West Ham had seen on a trip to the States a few years earlier – was as inadequate as I was at DIY. As a result, poor Helga had to come and fix the problem while we did all we could to help her: namely, keep well out of the way. There was no way I could go back after that.

My other headache concerned playing styles. Not even my staunchest fan could say I was a natural choice for a club with the reputation for pure football and I couldn't get it out of my head that it was sacrilege for them to sign a player who Bill Shankly, remember, reckoned couldn't trap a bag of cement.

West Ham were my sixth club in just over five years and the move wasn't such great news for one member of the family. My young second cousin Lorna, from Coventry, followed my career so avidly that she insisted on having her bedroom redecorated in the colours of my new club every time I was transferred. Sales of paint and wallpaper in unusual colours like gold and black, and claret and blue soared but one coat could barely have dried before the brush had to come out again.

Would you believe it but my debut was against Arsenal? I didn't score but, if I'd been able to face former clubs every week, I'd have been one of the highest scorers of all time. I'd escaped George Curtis's bruising marking to hit the winner at Highfield Road when I first went back with Arsenal (as captain for the day) and I eroded a bit more of the goodwill the fans there still had for me when I equalised late on to salvage a draw for West Ham in 1974-75. On top of that, I remember netting at least twice for West Ham against Wolves.

Things skipped along okay for me at Upton Park. Manchester City, who had just appointed Ron Saunders as manager, were our opponents when we recorded our first win with me in the side and the goals started to flow as well. My first for the Hammers came at Birmingham, in my fourth game, and my first at home followed against Norwich four games later after I'd also netted in a 4-2 win at Chelsea on Boxing Day. I instinctively knew I'd get one in our high-scoring victory over the Canaries. A couple of weeks earlier, though, I would never have expected Ted MacDougall to grab a couple at the other end. He had just moved to Carrow Road after initially partnering me in the Hammers attack.

It was all change. Graham Paddon and Mick McGiven made their West Ham debuts around the same time as me and this was the season Bobby Moore finally called it a day there and moved to Fulham. And obviously not everything worked out perfectly because we ended up surviving by just a point as Manchester United, of all teams, went down.

Four weeks into my time at Upton Park, Ron Greenwood remarked that my first touch wasn't that good. I wondered why it had taken him so long to notice. I had seriously worried West Ham were going against the grain by signing a player whose strength was definitely not joining in with clever link-ups. I thrived on scoring goals, so it wasn't promising for me when many of our training sessions were small-sided games played without posts. It was pass, pass, pass. With me, it was control, tackle, stumble.

The laughs came thick and fast, though. The physio Rob Jenkins, whose dad had performed the same duties years before, was a legend and had more than just bandages and sponges by way of getting the lads out on the pitch. Before my debut against Arsenal, I could smell alcohol in the corridor and eventually traced it back to the fridge in Rob's room next to the dressing room. He had two bottles of brandy in there that Mooro, Bonzo and Frank Lampard used to have a sip of before games. It was their way of dealing with the stresses of the build-up.

West Ham always had the reputation as a fine football side but had players who could look after themselves as well. Lampard would put me in a headlock if he thought I was pushing my luck while no-one was too keen to tangle with Bonzo. Maybe it was the smell of alcohol on their breath that kept opponents and even referees at arm's length.

Frank was a valuable ally to Rob Jenkins, who was the most nervous flier I've ever known, although Snout Storey and Schnoz pushed him close and Ryan Giggs is much happier with his feet on firm ground. Rob would always have to sit next to Frank for reassurance and his face was as white as a sheet when we disembarked.

Despite my goals, I was taking some stick from the crowd and can't say I blamed them. I thought I'd be packing my bags again sharpish after being dropped early in my stay there and hearing that Portsmouth were in for me. They would be. I never failed against them. But John Lyall told me to get my head down and work. That tended to be at Football Combination level because I was barely seen in the first team between the January and April as I became the fish out of water I had fretted about being.

Ron didn't like to hear us use the word 'steel' when talking about our play but Billy Jennings was obsessed with something made out of the stuff. He combed his hair in front of the mirror on the wall of the dressing room so often that we nicknamed him Jilly. He was often in the headlines as well because we really hit on something after his arrival in the summer of 1974 was followed by the signing of Keith Robson.

Things started to take off in the September – the month Ron retreated to a role 'upstairs' as general manager after more than a decade in charge. Tate &

Lyall took over the team and you couldn't hope to meet two lovelier men, so it was a smooth transition.

I put myself in the frame with a hat-trick against Swindon Reserves, then my return to favour in the League Cup replay at home to Tranmere Rovers owed much to Billy Bonds' generosity. Jilly was cup-tied and Bonzo could have had a hat-trick himself when we were awarded a second penalty near the end, with both of us having scored twice. Bonzo had stuck the first one away but kindly lobbed me the ball when the referee pointed to the spot again.

I could hear John Lyall yelling from the dug-out: "Don't let him take it. Don't let him take it." It was hardly the biggest vote of confidence I'd heard but I quickly grabbed the ball, jogged backwards to the end of my run and sidefooted my shot in. Tate & Lyall had a big smile on his face as I turned to acknowledge him but it was thanks to Bonzo that I have that match ball in my bolthole. He was a great fella, a real legend.

My treble was a big turning point for me. I hit a brace against Leicester in our next game when we ran up another six, then we won 3-0 against Birmingham and humped Burnley five. I was seething at Turf Moor because I was in the no 9 shirt and didn't score but Ron, who we knew as Daffy Duck because of the way he walked, put his arm round me, said 'great win' and paid me the biggest compliment he could have done. He said I was starting to look like a West Ham player. After years of charging here, bustling there and baring my fangs at defenders, I was improving technically.

I was passing the ball better because I appreciated what the club were all about. I was named the Daily Mirror's Player of the Month for September and even looked the part when I was used wide on the right. At the age of 28, I was maturing as a player and was never the same Bobby Gould again, although the words 'shy and retiring' were rarely used to describe my personality, on or off the pitch.

Unfortunately, it didn't take long for the bubble to burst. After my eight goals in a week, I remained a regular until the second half of the season, then Peter Osgood did me with a woeful tackle in our 2-1 win at Southampton on FA Cup third-round day. He went over the top and left me in a heap. The referee Gordon Hill told me to get up and I'd be okay. I'm glad he thought so because I was in bloody agony and very worried. But I somehow managed to play on for 20 minutes and actually scored with a diving header to increase our lead.

To get from the pitch to the dressing rooms at The Dell, you used to have to walk up some steps and I was virtually crawling up them at half-time, going so slowly that even the officials overtook me on the way in. I was replaced by Patsy Holland and was found to have broken my left leg. With living in Bristol, I had travelled by rail to the game and was a pathetic sight again as I struggled to the platform for my train to Temple Meads.

Before I left the ground, I informed Daffy that I'd see Osgood to let him know my feelings. But I was told: "Bobby, we don't do that sort of thing at West Ham." I couldn't bite my tongue completely, though, and went for him in the papers instead. That got me a severe reprimand from Ron on the Monday. I didn't bump into Ossie for 14 years until we were both on the top table at a dinner at Highbury. I raised the subject of the tackle and he said it was born out of frustration.

Fortunately, my break wasn't a bad one and I was back in contention in a month and a half. Back in the squad, that is, because I just couldn't get back into the starting 11 again after marking my comeback with a goal as substitute at Molineux. Well, I would, wouldn't I?

A cutting in my scrapbook says I endured 26 matches on the substitutes' bench, including 15 in succession without going on. I went to see Rob Jenkins and the doc about anti-woodworm injections but the remedy was only partially successful. I'm still getting the splinters out. The effects were all the more uncomfortable as we were heading towards Wembley at the time and what I believed would be my last chance of FA Cup final glory.

The lads laid one of my old ghosts to rest by putting Swindon away in a fourth-round replay at the County Ground in my absence and we also dealt with QPR at a time when an unusual pattern was developing. This was long before managers ever thought of resting players in the Cup or not playing their strongest side in all games but I became a regular again in the League side and didn't play much in the Cup run, even when I was available.

The name of Alan Taylor wasn't exactly hot on fans' lips by the time we were drawn at Arsenal in the quarter-finals. Why should it have been? 'Sparrow' had been signed from Rochdale and didn't make his debut until December, 1974, but I sensed my place was in danger when he was preferred to me at Highbury and used his extra pace to net twice in our victory.

I was recalled at Keith Robson's expense for the semi-final against Ipswich at Villa Park and was useless in a wide left role, feeling sheepish when I was rightly taken off and replaced by Patsy. I was retained for the replay at Stamford Bridge and at least contributed this time by heading down Boogaloo's cross in the build-up to our first goal as we booked a big May date with Fulham. But it was Sparrow – so called because of his spindly legs – who took all the plaudits again by scoring twice. The no 9 shirt was now his and John Lyall seemed to be backing him over me. Maybe he was more of a shock weapon because he wasn't as well known to defenders.

Uncharacteristically, I became negative. I was transfixed by the uncertainty over my place and grew apprehensive as to whether I would be selected at Wembley. I just couldn't settle and play normally. I was putrid in a League game at Ipswich, where we were thumped 4-1 only three weeks after beating them in the Cup, and I had no complaints when Tate & Lyall told me he was playing Patsy wide on the right instead.

It should have been a carefree time. We were on our way to a comfortable mid-table finish in John's first season in charge and I would come in second behind Jilly Jennings in the club's goal charts with 13 – ahead of the likes of Taylor and Keith Robson. And there was extra family pride, with our kid reaching the FA Trophy semi-final with Southern League Bedford Town at a time when we were being measured up for our Cup Final suits.

I have fond memories of another feature of the build-up. David Essex, who had been with West Ham as a youngster, was the star turn at our pre-Wembley photo shoot and four of us were pictured holding him as he lay across our arms. He was an obvious pick as the professional behind our Cup Final record and nursed us through a full-blooded rendition of "I'm Forever Blowing Bubbles"– a song I still know all the words to.

David grew up kicking a ball round the same street as Frank Lampard Snr, who reckoned he might have made it in the game if he hadn't chosen a musical career instead. He was also a good Hammers fan and made sure we all enjoyed our time in the studio. We climbed the charts rapidly and were disappointed to just miss out on an appearance on Top of the Pops.

We were an emerging side in the wake of the departure of Mooro, Geoff Hurst and Martin Peters and had promising young players who would go on to have excellent careers. Mervyn Day, in particular, had a tremendous season and became a firm favourite of the crowd.

Much of the countdown to the game was centred on the fact Bobby was now skipper of our Second Division opponents and would be facing the club he had played almost 650 matches for. What a legend he was. When we were at Upton Park together, he said he never realised until he played and trained with me how much passion and commitment I had. They were lovely words and have remained with me. Bobby left in the spring of 1974 and was one up on us before Wembley because we had lost at Craven Cottage in the League Cup earlier in the season with Alan Mullery and him in the side.

I defied Daffy's orders on Cup Final day. Whenever I was a substitute for West Ham, I wore a spare goalkeeper's green jersey over my no 12 shirt but Ron told me to walk out, like the others, in just my claret and blue shirt. So I grabbed Merv The Swerve's spare top when Ron wasn't looking and there are two of us walking out in that long line, wearing green.

I had a theory about Fulham's blond keeper Peter Mellor and said in the paper that I thought he was vulnerable, especially on crosses. So it proved. Both of our two goals came when the ball didn't stick in his hands.

My enjoyment of the day was somewhat muted and I got it into my head that the best I could hope for was to be sent on as substitute for the final few minutes if we had Fulham in our pockets in good time. With ten minutes left, we were leading through a couple of goals by Sparrow – who else? – and I remember having a coughing bout on the bench, trying to catch John and Ron's eye. But they were having none of it.

When the whistle went and everyone was hugging each other in celebration, it was a very low moment in my life. Of course I was delighted for the club, the supporters and my team-mates that we had won the Cup but I felt so sad that this should have been the happiest day of my playing career. Instead, I hadn't kicked a ball. Am I the only man to collect a winners' medal as a player and a manager and not get on the pitch in either final?

It's going too far to say I felt cheated. John picked a team who won comfortably enough and Sparrow had become a hero with his big goals when they really mattered. But, for someone who was such a team player, I had become selfish and self-pitying about my own exclusion and they aren't traits I'm proud of 35 years on. As the cliché goes, playing in a final is every footballer's dream and I'd missed out, possibly for good. So I have a winner's medal, which means plenty, but I didn't have the appearance I craved.

West Ham didn't look after the wives and children as well as they might have done, sticking them in the lower tier of the stadium on benches. And, after we had done the lap of honour and were near the tunnel, I shouted that we should go and see our families once more before disappearing. It was then that Sparrow and me ran over to them holding the Cup. That was my proudest moment of the day, as I gave Marge and six-year-old Jonathan a fond wave. Richard was only five and was being baby-sat in Bristol by our lifetime friend Susie Avery.

Back at our hotel, the Grosvenor, the club put a banquet on for us but Stan Flashman got in on the act by treating us to a celebration do down the road at the Hilton. I had got match tickets for Gordon Parr, a 1960s Bristol City player and by now a great pal, and his wife Sheila, and we managed to smuggle them into Stan's do as well before they crashed out by squeezing into Jonathan's single bed while he jumped in with us. It's what you do for mates.

I was thrilled to have Jonathan on the open-top bus with me as we did our tour of the streets around Upton Park the following day. But when Marge and I were making up a bed back home in Portishead, I was suddenly hit by a deep depression. I burst uncontrollably into tears and couldn't accept that I had been to Wembley with an FA Cup-winning team and not played there.

To cap it all, Trevor's club Bedford lost to Scarborough in their semi-final and missed out on Wembley altogether. I did at least have European football to look forward to and we racked up the air miles over the summer as the club put us in the mood for criss-crossing the Continent. For the second successive close season, we went on tour to Norway, where I notched a couple of goals.

We were back at Wembley before we knew it, for the Charity Shield against Derby, who beat us comfortably on a stiflingly hot day. Playing in that game was a very poor consolation for missing the Cup Final and, would you believe it, I was subbed. Having longed for John Lyall to throw me on three months earlier, I had the shepherd's crook and headed petulantly straight for the tunnel rather than the bench.

Jilly Jennings was already in the bath after being taken off and, after a while, we looked at each other and said: "We've fucked up here, haven't we?" The penny had dropped by then that we were in no fit state to go up and collect our medals, even if they were losers' ones. I still had some growing up to do and that bit of nonsense taught me a lesson.

We were off to a flier in the League, though, with Sparrow scoring twice against Liverpool in the first week and two more against Burnley in our opening home game. I had netted a cracker at Stoke in an opening-day victory and, after nine League matches, we were unbeaten and second in the table following a win at Wolves. Unfortunately, I had been back on the sidelines after pulling up with a hamstring injury at Anfield.

We also put Bristol City out of the League Cup by winning at Ashton Gate. I don't suppose Alan Dicks was too chuffed at that but I wasn't in the best of moods either. Even when I had recovered, I was becoming more and more frustrated at not playing enough first-team football – and at having only a brief taste of our Cup Winners Cup adventure.

My previous taste of European competition, with Arsenal, had been limited to a game against Glentoran, and the first two excursions with West Ham in 1975 were to destinations you don't find in the holiday brochures. I was out injured when we comfortably beat Reipas Lahti of Finland but included when we set off to face Ararat Yerevan of Russia.

The trip didn't get off to a promising start. As soon as we disembarked the plane, an officer with a stick whacked one of the lads across the hand for trying to take a photo. Rob Jenkins, our physio, was as white as a ghost. It wasn't the after-care of the 'ground crew' that upset him – it was just his fear of flying showing itself again. Even with the help of some of his famous Dutch courage, it needed the attention of Frank Lampard Snr to calm him down via one of those uncompromising headlocks.

Rob came to the fore, though, at meal-time. The club had decided not to sample the delights of the local cuisine and had packed all our food as well as taking along a chef. The night porter at the hotel couldn't believe his eyes when we unwrapped a cold meat salad just after our late-evening arrival. And he was positively drooling when the 'afters' came out......a bundle of chocolate éclairs. He was delighted to be offered one of them and looked like the girl in the Cadbury's Flake advert, clearly finding eating it an almost orgasmic experience.

Trevor Brooking was in a room with me and pulled back his bedclothes to discover a nest of cockroaches. Fortunately, there was a stern-looking woman sitting in the corridor on each floor to deal with such matters and she simply entered the room and swept them out of the way. It was another task Boogaloo and myself were not up to. We hadn't quite finished with the lady's services at that. She also came in useful with fetching some soaked toilet paper to ram into the sink because the hotel seemed to see plugs for the hand basin as optional extras.

Unlike with the Coral Reef Club in Barbados, I felt no urge to rush back there with Marge but we came through relatively unscathed. We drew 1-1, safely negotiated the return and earned a tie against Den Haag in the next round. But it was an assignment I didn't hang around to see.

I suppose the writing was on the wall. I was in and out of the side in the shadow of Billy Jennings, Patsy Holland, who had the no 11 shirt for the final, and Sparrow, and the club allowed me to train at times with Bristol Rovers, who were then managed by Gary Megson's father Don.

My stay at Upton Park was drawing towards a close but there was just time for me to knock one in at the back post and help us to two points against Manchester United at the end of October. In the process, I had some fisticuffs with Martin Buchan, who thought I'd unfairly gone in on the keeper. No, not me…..it must have been a case of mistaken identity!

Departure day was December 4, 1975, and the Hammers went into a right nosedive in the New Year to finish 18th, although they reached the European final and lost to Anderlecht. By then, I was on familiar ground after my phone was warmed up by a familiar voice. Bill McGarry was in trouble with Wolves and I wanted to go and do him a favour when he asked me back.

Ups And Downs At Molineux

I had a respectable 19 goals to my credit in 58 West Ham games, quite a few of them as substitute, and was sorry I couldn't have gone there when I was 21. Jimmy Hill later revealed they had enquired about me when I was a youngster at Coventry and, with West Ham's philosophy and my passion, I would really have improved. In fact I think I would have played for England, maybe alongside my good pal Geoff Hurst.

But the commuting was a problem for me in the mid-1970s and it always slightly rankled that the club wouldn't sort us out with a bridging loan so we could buy that dream property in Chigwell. It was a rejection I hadn't expected because Arsenal had put us in a lovely club house in New Barnet when I joined them, then Wolves did likewise for us at 34 Dunchurch Crescent, Sutton Coldfield – a house we stayed in when I made the short move to Albion.

Back at Wolves, I was pitched into a struggling side after signing for them in a Southport hotel. They were up there for a mid-season break. I was advised against the move by one of the players I sounded out and found Bill McGarry different to the man I had remembered from four years earlier. He had lost some of his aggression and toughness but I still respected him and very much wanted to lift him and the club out of relegation danger.

Manny Bailey was still there, so were Frank Munro and Lofty Parkes, although all three were approaching the end, at Molineux at least. John Richards remained a fine player despite having had knee problems and Kenny Hibbitt, John McAlle and Derek Parkin were good for another few years while others like Alan Sunderland, Geoff Palmer and Steve Daley had come through during my time out of the Midlands and Willie Carr, who I'd known as a kid at Coventry, had been bought.

With a battering ram of a forward in Steve Kindon – would there be room for the two of us in the same team? – I thought we had enough to stay up. The early signs weren't good, though. My first three games all ended in defeat to ensure us a difficult Christmas and it wasn't until my seventh match – a draw at home to Leeds – that I scored for the first time. At least we had started winning by then, taking both points thanks to Willie's penalty in a big basement game at Birmingham and despatching Arsenal well in the FA Cup after a few days' special training at Southport.

I'd like to say my winner at home to Ipswich in the next round was a case of outstanding vision and accuracy because Bill had had me in his office in the morning and reminded me that Paul Cooper was on the short side and likely to struggle when the ball was in the air. He ordered me to get in as many crosses as possible and I admit the one I aimed at the back post at the North Bank end from well out on the left wing was just that – a centre. But it dropped in through Cooper's hands for the only goal of the game. Ipswich must have been sick of the sight of me. I always seemed to do well against them.

I had become fairly familiar with playing wide following my stint out on the right at West Ham and it was at Upton Park that my left foot improved considerably. No longer was it just a swinger. Maybe the goal that put us in the fifth round of the FA Cup wasn't such a fluke after all.

Two more goals came my way in a League defeat at QPR but that was my lot for the season. I had nearly a month out of the side from early March and was to start only one more game, with a few substitute appearances thrown in. It was ironic, considering our struggles, that I allowed myself to dream again about playing in the FA Cup final. JR went on as a substitute to score three against Charlton in the fifth round and Lofty was magnificent as we held on at Old Trafford and took Manchester United back to see how they could cope in front of 45,000 at Molineux in a quarter-final replay. Unfortunately, the answer was 'pretty well', although they had to hit back for their victory after we'd gone two up early on.

My own season tailed off disappointingly. After playing in a 0-0 draw back at West Ham, I was on substitute duty for the rest of the season, including games at Arsenal and Coventry, and went on for the final 20 minutes at home to Liverpool on the night our fate at the foot of the table was confirmed.

None of us liked having a relegation on our CV. It was the first time in a career already stretching more than a decade that I had suffered the drop and it was a horrible feeling, not helped by the fact Liverpool's players were celebrating the winning of another title a few yards down the corridor. Kindo gave us hope with an early goal but the flickering light was put out in the second half.

I was upset when Bill McGarry paid the penalty by being sacked. We were in our pre-Evermore phase and had put our house in Portishead up for sale while we had one built in Balsall Common, where Marge was from. That's a signal of the intention I had of being at Molineux for a long while but the lads were joking that I'd soon be on the move again. When Bill's assistant Sammy Chung was appointed as his successor, they pushed me to the front of the photos the press took because they thought I'd be on the way out soon.

I'd known Sammy for a long time as well, of course, didn't mind getting my hands dirty in the Second Division and scored four in the first game. Okay, it was only a tour match up in the wilds of Sweden but we were determined to make it a short stay out of the top flight. Manny's stay on tour became a shorter one than for the rest of us when he was allowed to fly home after his house was broken into.

We seemed to travel for hours and hours on that trip just to get to games. It was like playing every game at Newcastle or Plymouth. On the way back from one match, Willie and Hibby worked their way through a bottle of Scotch and, with each extra glass, lambasted Sammy a bit more for his inability to find games closer to where we were staying. The following May, we flew back to Scandinavia and did it all over again, this time for an end-of-season trek round Norway. More big wins, pine forests and long games of cards......

In between the trips, we delivered big-time. We had 50 goals on the board by Christmas week and five of us – Hibby, Alan Sunderland, JR, Steve Daley and me – ended with double-figure totals. I was on fire early on and helped myself to braces against Nottingham Forest, Charlton and at Hereford, where we scored six just three days before being hit for six by Southampton at Molineux. It was a spectacular turnaround in fortunes.

I had ten goals to my name by mid-December – not bad considering I'd started only 12 matches – and was having a ball, with Daley on the left hand side of a diamond and me in the hole behind Sundy and Kindo. Sundy had a terrific football brain, so, with that ingredient and Kindo's movement, I was able to get into some lovely spaces and wreak my havoc.

We weren't as successful on the home front. The property in Portishead did not sell, so we were still living down there and I was obviously looking forward to cutting out some M5 time and playing against Bristol Rovers over Christmas. But I did my bloody hamstring doing some sprinting by the sea front on the morning of the game and ruled myself out. The side muddled by without me at Eastville. They only won five that day.

Things were never the same for me at Wolves again. I still have the large lump from the injury and was disappointed the club didn't manage the problem better. All the travelling up and down the motorway didn't help, although I had some treatment as well at Rovers, and it took weeks and weeks before I could play again. But I didn't start another competitive game for the club and had to be content with a few substitute appearances as Richie returned from injury problems of his own and took my place all over again.

We clinched promotion with three matches to spare thanks to a draw at Plymouth and, like at Coventry ten years earlier, I felt a bit cheated at not being part of the games that got us over the finishing line. I did go on in the draw with Chelsea that secured the title for us and the second promotion place for them, and I made that unusual late entrance when I took over in goal from Gary Pierce on an exciting last day at Bolton. But I was reading familiar signs.

McGarry had left some great kids like Sunderland and Daley and I couldn't see myself holding down a regular place in the First Division. My work in the Midlands, as a player, was nearly done but there was still time for a return to a familiar beat. It didn't seem five minutes since we had unpacked our bags after returning from the end-of-season trip to Norway, where I scored three goals in three sub outings, before Sammy had us on yet another jaunt across the sea, this time to Sweden.

I scored a couple over there but was unused on the bench on the opening day of 1977-78 at Bristol City, where we beat my old club 3-2 in an amazing match of four penalties. Poor Piercey had been an ever-present in the promotion season, only to then hurt his wrist over the summer saving a shot from Kevin Beattie in the filming of an ATV programme. He hardly played for the club again as Lofty Parkes came back in goal.

In my quest to avoid becoming a forgotten man at Molineux, I stayed in the groove by netting a few for the reserves in the Central League and hit six against a Universities XI at Lilleshall a few weeks later in what proved to be my last game for the club. It was amazing to think that I hadn't started a senior match for them since scoring the winner against Bolton the previous December but I was still in demand. Portsmouth, Preston, Blackburn, Bristol Rovers and even John Sillett at Hereford were after me.

Sammy Chung was a lovely guy but I feel he let his ego get the better of him. Maybe he thought this management lark was easier than it was after he had led us in some style to the championship. He changed a little in his ways when he was in charge and loved plonking himself in the front seat on the coach that Bill McGarry used to occupy.

He soon found the top flight much tougher to crack and I was not going to have the chance to try to help. Wolves had been great for me over my two spells there and I became very fond of Molineux but it was time for me to bail out again. Sammy probably guessed a parting of the ways was imminent when he offered me a new contract with a measly £10-per-appearance rise. I gave the matter all due consideration, weighed up the pros and cons and then told him to stick it up his arse.

Ship-Shape And Bristol Fashion

I had been allowed to train at Bristol Rovers in my final months at Molineux and I suppose it was a cast-iron guarantee that I would join them some day. More and more, my heart lay in the city, where we were happy to see our lads growing up, and I was delighted when Don Megson's offer was accepted and Wolves recouped the £10,000 they had paid for me 18 months earlier.

I hadn't scored as much as a fluky in-off with my backside on a debut for any of my previous six clubs but joined Rovers on the Friday and came up with a hat-trick in the first 25 minutes of my first game the following day. I had to feel, though, for the visiting manager Jim Smith because he was one of the other managers who had been in for me. If only he had known the story behind my emergence as a hero in the blue half of Bristol.

Jimmy Hill had drummed it into us from the age of 17 that we shouldn't indulge our primeval passions after a Wednesday. To you and me, that means no sex. But, having commuted for four years and finally having the chance for a lie-in on match-day morning, I found myself having a kiss, a cuddle and a little bit more with Marge a few hours before I was to make my Rovers debut. So that's where I had been going wrong!

I arrived at Eastville weighed down with the usual telegrams, including several from Wolves, and Marge was in the stand to witness my every move. Among my team-mates was Lee Hendrie's dad, Paul. Apparently, I was only the third player in Rovers history to score three goals on his debut and there was a lot of back-slapping, not least because the club had won only one of their first 12 League and League Cup matches of the season.

It was a dream start for me considering I hadn't played a full first-team game for ten months, and people were saying afterwards we had turned the corner. If we had, it was into a cul-de-sac because we were slaughtered 9-0 at Tottenham in my second game. Colin Lee (on his debut) scored four, Ian

Moores three and Glenn Hoddle and Peter Taylor also wreaked havoc. Spurs had only just arrived in the Second Division and, not surprisingly, were there for only one season.

Our side had several new faces around the time of my arrival, one of them an 18-year-old called Glyn Jones in goal. The score would have been well into double figures if he hadn't made a few good saves. Actually, I'll take some of the credit as well for a subtle tactical adjustment. I remember our centre-half Graham Day bounding past me when we won a corner with the score at nine. I said to him: "Where the fuck are you going?" He said: "I'm going up to try to help us pull one back." My response was: "If I were you, I'd get back to the other end and try to keep their total under ten." Cruelly, Glyn was back at White Hart Lane just over a week later but had a much happier time of it second time round as he helped the reserves to a 1-1 draw.

Martin Thomas, the senior keeper, soon reclaimed his place and the first team bounced back with a 0-0 draw against Southampton. Then we copped another right good hiding at Sunderland a couple of weeks later. Talk about up-and-down results. We didn't perform well on the bigger stages. In the League at least, we were more comfortable playing in front of our loyal crowds of below 10,000.

I don't know whether I was lucky or unlucky as the Spurs hangover lingered. The lads envied me being able to get off a predictably quiet coach almost as soon as we joined the M4 because I was flying from Heathrow to Norway to negotiate going back there in the summer for a coaching position with Ålesund up near the Arctic Circle. I was on the same flight as Emlyn Hughes, who was a guest at a cup final over there, and I I turned up at the chairman's house to find Norwegian television showing the highlights of Tottenham 9 Rovers 0. For a second time, I had to suffer the embarrassment of fluffing three chances from inside the six-yard area. Has any other player ever had such contrasting fortunes in his first two matches?

The decision for me to branch out into coaching wasn't taken on impulse. I had done my preliminary badge in 1969 under the eye of John Lyall while I was still at Arsenal, then went to Lilleshall for a fortnight two years later. It was a great time, as good as any in my football life. Terry Venables and Eddie McCreadie were also in the group and we couldn't get enough of it; all of us eager to learn as much as we could about a game we were totally in love with.

My chance to pull on a tracksuit and grab a clipboard had come with the move to Eastville but my player-coach duties were increased quicker than I expected. Don Megson, who had been given the freedom to spend a bit of money to try to compete with Bristol City's lofty placing in the top flight, left in the November to take up a position with Portland Timbers in the North American Soccer League. Bobby Campbell, Rovers' trainer since the early 1960s, was appointed in his place, with me assisting him. It was a step on the management ladder and I took to it well. The lads loved my training methods, even if we were so impoverished that we had to use a local park.

I liked Bobby but he wasn't as comfortable with my methods as the squad were. I'm sure he saw me as a threat to his job and he was trying to edge me out. Perhaps he wasn't very impressed from the time I was suffering from cystitis and scored against Crystal Palace. I ran past our startled bench and hared up the tunnel to the toilet. The gaffer was banging on the door ordering me back out but had to wait......and wait and wait. I couldn't pee for love nor money!

The laughs didn't end there. He was resourceful enough to have us training in hotels when the need arose. I remember running up and down corridors on a lovely carpet by way of a work-out when we stayed overnight before one match, then we went a step further by jogging up and down the stairs. It was a bit of an eye-opener for the other guests.

After I'd left, the squad were apparently heading for a game at Newcastle, became seriously snowed in at the hotel and trained by running among the other guests down the corridors. Word has it they also helped organise various activities to keep children amused when their parents tired of finding things for them to do – and even went trudging off in search of bread and milk when the delivery vans couldn't get in.

Bobby obviously knew I was going to manage sooner or later and he didn't want it to be at his expense. I was still scoring regularly enough, though, to be of value to his team. Because as many of my games for Rovers were wide on the right as up front, my record of 13 goals in 40 games was decent and I was able to watch the emergence of a feisty young Welsh lad in midfield called Tony Pulis, who could handle himself. He wasn't involved in that historic game at Tottenham, so he was given permission to go to a wedding instead and was chirping in the dressing room on the Monday about how well things had obviously gone in his absence. We put him down a peg or two again by reminding him what a poor player he must have been if he couldn't get in a side hammered 9-0.

Paul Randall, whose place I had taken on my debut, was hot property up front and Dave Staniforth and David Williams also contributed a few goals. I even scored another couple of penalties, one of them away to Millwall in a win in a game that was staged at Portsmouth because of crowd disorder at The Den. My Fratton Park knack was obviously still with me.

I also netted the decider in the Cup at Sunderland and we then put out the 1976 holders Southampton and held Ipswich in the snow at Eastville before being humped good and proper in the replay. The goal I had ruled out in the first game for offside, when the ball ricocheted to me off one of their players, is still spoken of by Rovers supporters as a great injustice.

Scoring wasn't our problem. Without matching the massive output of the famous Bruce Bannister-Alan Warboys partnership of a few years earlier, we found goals fairly easy to come by. Unfortunately, we found it even easier to concede them and it was just as well 'Punky' Randall kept it going brilliantly with something like 13 goals in 14 League appearances.

We were always struggling in the League and the battle for survival went to the last day, when we survived by a point thanks to Randall's winner at Hull and Blackpool's defeat at Brighton. Punky had bagged a couple against Stoke in our last home game and later moved to the Victoria Ground. We didn't begrudge him the opportunity because it was his goals that kept us in the Second Division.

No sooner had we finished the season in 18th place than I was packing my bags again on an adventure of an altogether different kind – one that was to pave the way for the second half of my career.

Fun Among The Fjords

It was Bristol Rovers who first added the word 'coach' to my long-time tag of 'player.' But, as my main preoccupation then was still scoring goals, I look back now and regard my first steps in management as having come much further afield.

All those summer slogs round Scandinavia did more than build up my pre-season stamina and match fitness. They also paved the way for two successive summers in Norway that left us with some of our happiest memories from my five decades or so in the game.

Ålesund was just a small dot on the map up near the Arctic Circle when I scored a couple of goals there for West Ham a few weeks after our 1975 FA Cup final victory. But I also stored away at the back of my mind the message from John Lyall that they were looking for an English coach to run their team of part-timers in Norway's third division.

I made the appropriate introductions before we moved on for our next game in Bergen and had some joy from my decision to stay in touch with the people in charge of the club when they invited me over as their coach in the summer of 1978. By coincidence, the Hammers were in the area again and I actually played against them in one of their pre-season friendlies. In another warm-up game, I scored four against a side called Stryn.

I was still registered with Bristol Rovers, though, so I couldn't play any competitive games for Ålesund. Nonetheless, I threw myself into my work with them and remain very grateful for the grounding the job gave me. And I'm happy to say that, more than 30 years on, we still have good friends in Norway and stay in contact with them.

I trained the players from 4pm until 8pm after they had done their day jobs and we got on so well that I extended my coaching work to take in kids' sessions and even keep-fit work-outs for the wives and girlfriends. That was a natural progression for me because there was a lovely family atmosphere to the football over there, although the will to win was still very evident come match-day.

Marge and the boys trailed over to Norway two or three weeks after me and had some drama of their own at the airport. Ipswich Town's players, who had won the FA Cup a few weeks earlier, were in the terminal building at the same time and Jonathan was so busy gawping at them that he didn't notice a pillar and gave himself a nasty blow on the forehead. The first person to rush to help was Bobby Robson, who saw the incident and impressed Marge no end with his willingness to aid a damsel in distress.

Ålesund often went by boat, rather than air, to away games, which not only meant a scenic trip across the fjords but also gave us an extra few minutes for recreation. If the ferry was late in, the fishing rods would come out and the lads would be busy trying to catch something for the dinner table.

All sorts went with us on our travels. The wives and children often came as well, so pushchairs and picnic mats would be squeezed in alongside the skip containing the kit. The families sat at one end of the coach and the players at the other, the Norwegians' love of the outdoor life seeing to it that no opportunity for a swim or a forest walk was passed up.

We were provided with a flat and a car and even had a reminder of England when we bumped into the Wolves players while they were on a summer visit over there under their new manager John Barnwell. We had a training camp of our own and headed into the mountains – again with the women and kids in tow – after I had popped over to Menorca for a few days with Marge and the boys.

The Norwegians were used to roughing it and loved catering for themselves in little chalets in the woods. But they insisted on pandering to our creature comforts, so they put us four in bed and breakfast accommodation. We all got on famously, so much so that a get-together was arranged for mid-summer's day and a big group of us sat around singing along to Beatles classics as our goalkeeper strummed away on his guitar.

The Gould family performed a passable imitation of the hillbillies when we went over to Norway for the second time. We didn't bother with the air miles this time and instead had our yellow Ford Escort crammed to bursting with food, clothes, various belongings and even a curriculum for the lads to continue

99

their schooling under my tutelage. We sailed from Newcastle to Bergen and I was as sick as a dog. Where was Bobby Robson when *I* needed him?

I got Ålesund promoted from the third division to the second and am proud that they are now full-time and in the top division. More than that, they have this season been playing in Europe. My skipper, a big midfielder by the name of Reidar Vagnes who was easily good enough to have had a professional career in England, has stayed in the game and been over to stay with us more than once and brought his son with him.

It was a brilliant education for me and I honed a few of the organisational skills I later prided myself on by arranging a trip over here for about 50 of them – for youth teams as well as the senior squad. I found guest houses for them all, hired coaches to meet them at the airport and fixed up games for them in the West Country. They paid for themselves and just loved the experience.

The impression we left at Ålesund was obviously a good one because they arranged a reunion three years ago, around three decades on, and paid for Marge and me to go over. Reidar, or 'Big Man' as I called him, was at the airport to meet us and insisted on picking us up from the hotel an hour or two later when we really would have preferred to chill out and have an early night.

He drove us out for dinner and, when we walked in, we were dumbstruck.... there were all those faces we hadn't seen for 30 years. What a great night we had. I have very fond memories of the Ålesund people and hope they realise that my two summers over there played a big part in shaping my coaching and management career.

We were sad when my time in Norway came to an end and were given a wonderful send-off. About 30 players and staff lined up on the quay-side as our boat pulled out and they belted out a rendition of the club song 'Ålesund, Ålesund, Super Club!' It was an incredibly emotional experience, enough to draw a few tears from us as I prepared for the remnants of my playing career in England.

That, for a little while longer, was at Bristol Rovers. I scored against Fulham and Oldham following our return but my thoughts were turning more and more to the bootroom. I had by now been invited on to a coaching course at Bisham Abbey with the likes of Dario Gradi and Roger Hynd and became a 'fag' to my big hero Geoff Hurst, fetching his tea and cleaning his boots. He told me there and then that, if he was ever given a manager's job, he would take me as his no 2. My horizons were expanding and it was clear I wasn't going to be at Eastville for more than a few months.

It took a phone call from an old friend of mine for Bobby Campbell to be granted his wish. Mike Bailey was by now Hereford's manager after returning from a playing stint in the USA and had an ace up his sleeve when he dangled the job as player and assistant manager at Edgar Street before my eyes. For the first time in my life, I was being offered a club car. I was immediately tempted, the fee already agreed at £10,000.

I took it – the job and the Renault – but the irony was that I broke down on the way to Cardiff on one of my first scouting assignments. It was the only time I set off for a match and didn't make it. Even more bizarrely, I can stand at our back windows or in the garden and see the city of Cardiff across the Severn estuary.

Manny was a forceful, driving captain at Wolves and a good mate but soon reminded me of the more volatile side to his nature. In his anger at the way we were playing, he once hurled a pot of tea at the magnetic board we used for moving around pieces to illustrate formations and patterns of play. As a player, I was on the end of his temper as well but guess who had to get on his hands and knees to splash through the debris and pick everything up?

I obviously wasn't one of those players intent on bowing out at the top. Hereford were in the Fourth Division and it was hardly a stage for graceful departures. But I didn't mind the muck and nettles. And I had glimpsed some potential there a couple of weeks earlier when I went on as substitute for a Bristol Rovers side who were thrashed 4-0 at Edgar Street in the League Cup.

My introduction was much happier because I scored twice against Crewe in my second game and would bag another brace, this time against Scunthorpe, later in the season. On a personal note, I was pleased enough with my tally of 15 goals, all but two of them with Hereford, but I was now having to think more of others, be there for Manny and set the right example.

I proved I could still handle myself when I caught Peter Jackson of Barnsley with my elbow and broke his nose accidentally on purpose. He has never failed to remind me of the incident and all I can say in my defence is that Mick McCarthy was at his side kicking lumps out of me and I was hardly going to take him on in my twilight years. Peter was more my match.

I copped for one as well when we faced Portsmouth in the last game of the season. My ankle was badly cut and swollen, so the physio Pete Isaacs took me to hospital. They insisted on giving me an injection, although I'm allergic to tetanus, and my foot was right to the floor on the accelerator pedal to make sure I got home before the inevitable reaction came. Fortunately, the Renault did its job this time – then I flaked out in my bed for 48 hours.

There were nice little perks to the job as well as we finished comfortably in mid-table in 1978-79. My coaching role meant I was welcome in the boardroom for a cuppa, so I was getting my feet under the table in the management sense and starting to make my way. There were certain compensations after all at having to accept I'd soon be turning my back on running out on cold Tuesday nights at Halifax and Hartlepool.

My last League goal came in a 1-1 draw at Port Vale on May 1, 1979, and the only times I netted the following season were in my last two appearances in Hereford's Reserves, against QPR and then Swindon at Edgar Street. Almost 20 years on from being discarded by Coventry and then given my big second chance, I was at journey's end as regards scoring goals for a living. Very soon, the 'player' bit would disappear from my player-coach title and I would sink and swim on the strength of how well I could teach others everything I'd learned along the way.

I might have been changing roles but my club-hopping was showing no sign of slowing. Manny Bailey's frustration at Hereford led to him jumping ship and returning to his first club Charlton and I dared to wonder whether I would have the manager's plate nailed to my door sooner than I expected. I was interviewed for the post but lost out to Frank Lord.

It wasn't a big blow and the silver lining to the cloud soon materialised when the phone rang again. I couldn't believe who was on the other end – but how would I tell Marge that we would be selling our home in the West Country, looking for new schools for our sons and seeing a lot more of London again?

A Bridge Too Far

I was thrilled to bits when Geoff Hurst asked me to go and work with him at Stamford Bridge. He had proved to be a man of his word and taken a big step towards ensuring he became a lifelong friend in addition to the personal all-time hero he already was to me. I was just preparing for a Hereford reserve game when he called and said: "Get in your car, Gouldy. You're my no 2 at Chelsea." What a step-up!

I went over to meet him while he was staying over before a game at Cardiff and soon discovered the club needed some straightening out. It wasn't only that monstrosity of a new stand that was casting a shadow over Chelsea. They were in the Second Division and on their uppers. But joining such a big club was another stride in the right direction for me.

Apart from when I stood in the crowd the day Sir Geoff scored his World Cup final hat-trick, our paths hadn't crossed much as players because he had left West Ham for Stoke by the time I pitched up there. Now, he was keen to make an impression as successor to Danny Blanchflower at the Bridge and I was desperate to succeed with him as he handed me a three-year contract.

We had bonded well on the coaching course at Bisham and he recognised that I worked extra hard to come off in management because I had been limited as a player. I sweated blood to bridge that gap and, alongside a national icon such as Geoff, the gap sometimes seemed more like the Cheddar Gorge. He saw the honest trier in me, though, and couldn't fail to have noticed how determined I was to succeed with him.

He was brilliant when he joined in training sessions; the best player there. We had a lot of two-touch five-a-sides, with the ball not allowed to go above head height. His awareness and the angles he made with his body to kill a pass and make one of his own were something I envied. He knew this job was his big opportunity after he had cut his managerial teeth at Telford.

Moving to London wasn't such a big step, domestically, as it had been when I left Coventry for Arsenal. I was obviously much more worldly and, although we now had the two lads in tow, we were amazed at how much green there still was in such a big city. We settled on Camberley in Surrey as our base, although we lived for a while just off the Kings Road in a guest-house with the parents of one of the main secretaries at Chelsea who was Ray Wilkins' girlfriend and wife-to-be.

Life at work was more of an eye-opener. The architect of that huge stand was obviously blind to football. It was gigantic and all top-show. The dressing rooms were poor, there was no gym and the manager's office was a disgrace. As for mine, cubby hole would be a more apt description. The club were deep in financial trouble and the stand was nearly the straw that broke the camel's back.

The directors certainly came to regret installing phones in the lifts that carried the well-heeled customers up to the best seats and the corporate hospitality areas. Most of the waiters were foreign and soon realised how to make a quick call home for nothing. That hardly helped the overdraft.

Hard as it is to believe by the standards of today's Chelsea, we didn't even have our own training ground. We used pitches at the Police Academy near Hampton Court, where the groundsman wandered out one wet day with a sandwich board bearing the message 'Pitch Unfit For Play.' That was it, end of session and the cue for us to go and find new facilities under the flight path out of Heathrow. Terry, Lampard, Drogba and Co wouldn't have been impressed.

I soon developed a lot of respect for the Chelsea fans. Some of their supporters might have had a reputation for causing trouble but, by and large, I found them very loyal and there were some good people working there. Brian Mears was a lovely man and great company, but not the leader he needed to be as chairman. Geoff would have a meeting with him and be given a decision to an important question and, by the time he reached his office, Brian would be ringing to say he had changed his mind.

I had to smile when I read in Brian's memoirs how he negotiated with Manchester City's Peter Swales over our signing of Colin Viljeon. He apparently had to queue with the punters to use the pay phone because he was on a day out at Cheltenham races.

A lot of the players had come through the ranks, so we thought we were set fair. What a good lad Ray Wilkins was – and a terrific player. 'Butch', as he was then better known, had his brother Graham in a squad who also contained Droy, Fillery, Langley, Walker, Borota, Rofe, Lee, Britton, Rhoades-Brown and others; players we thought we could do something with.

Before Christmas, we had three victories against my former clubs – West Ham twice and Bristol Rovers – and won 7-3 at Orient. Clive Walker and Tommy Langley were sublime against Orient. We played excellent football and the lads were coming in with a spring in their step, relishing Geoff's training sessions and admiring how he showed the way with his exceptional touches. I'd like to say my imprint was on the side as well but the lads were playing in the style Geoff wanted. The credit was all his.

I had lots to learn but my enthusiasm, passion and organisation were out of the top drawer. I was happy to be playing the supporting role because I loved Geoff to bits, still do, and wouldn't say a word against him. He was so revered everywhere we went. He flew to America at the end of the season and even people in a football backwater like Florida would swim up to him while he chilled out and ask: "You're Geoff Hurst, aren't you?"

Having missed out on promotion to Birmingham on goal difference in our first season, we were playing superbly again by the time we reached the middle of December in our second. We had lost once in something like 16 League matches and hit six against Newcastle and won 4-0 at Wrexham. Then we took maximum points at Cambridge with a goal by Colin Lee, who I remembered well from that infamous Spurs v Rovers game and who was looking like money well spent as a £250,000 capture. We were second, one point behind West Ham, then we just ran out of steam for some reason.

We lost at Grimsby on the 13th and won only three of the remaining 20 matches, amazingly failing to score in 17 of them. It said everything about how good our start was and how badly we fell away that Lee still finished as the division's top marksman with 15 goals, although he scored only one after December.

From being right on the heels of the leaders, we couldn't buy a goal for long spells. We had Peter Rhoades-Brown flying down one wing and a lad called Phil Driver with pace to burn on the other, so the ammunition was there. There were also the likes of Langley, Walker and Lee to supply the finishing touches but, somehow, we just couldn't get it out of the players. People said it was amazing that Geoff and I, two renowned goalscorers for many years, were at the helm of a team who couldn't hit a barn door. And they were right. It was crazy.

Maybe we weren't experienced enough in management terms. We hadn't gained that knowledge you need to know how to handle the difficult times and make the necessary changes. First and foremost, we should have spent more time on finishing drills in training. We weren't reacting well enough to the pressure and I was certainly feeling the strain. When the Daily Express said the supporters wouldn't be happy to hear that I was doing the coaching for a few days while Geoff was away, I tried to sue them. In keeping with everything else I tried that season, I failed. It was the first time in my career I'd felt got at by the press.

While we were struggling desperately to break teams down, I badgered Hursty into giving me a game again. I thought I could still do it, so he gave me a run at Ipswich in the reserve team that Brian Eastick ran. After 20 minutes, I was breathing through my backside. I kept making runs and looking for the ball to be knocked down the channels but the emphasis was on total football and keeping possession. Each time I set off on a gallop, the ball would be played square from one defender to another and I'd have to come back and start again. I was three inches shorter by the time I crawled off the pitch.

We took that passing mentality into games and were fine while the pitches were good. When they became heavy, though, we floundered and failed to score in five matches in December and in any of our last nine games of the season. We nosedived in the table. At the same time, Howard Wilkinson was having an increasing influence as coach to Jimmy Sirrel at Notts County and they clinched promotion at our place by winning on the last Saturday of the season. We were weaving pretty patterns and losing. They were going much more direct and winning. Mmmm, food for thought......

We pulled in only 11,500 for a game against Cardiff at the Bridge in April and, as the fans understandably turned, the media larruped us. Geoff went into a board meeting after a 2-0 home defeat against Luton and asked Brian Mears to back him or sack him. The expression on his face when he came out told me which option they had gone for. Like Bobby Moore, Bobby Charlton and Nobby Stiles, I don't think management ever sat comfortably with him.

I was finished at Chelsea as well. I knew I was too inexperienced to be considered for the role as his successor. Besides, we had worked as a pair and I would have felt disloyal stepping into his shoes. I did actually take over for two games and the players responded brilliantly, so that was one up the Express. We went to Swansea for our last game of 1980-81 and I told the lads to forget all the defeats, the missed chances, the fans' anger, the board's impatience and the stigma of our spectacular collapse, and just play for themselves and the sake of their careers. We lost 3-0.

I still had two years left on my contract and did well to get £15,000 of the £30,000 I was due. The club were in such a mess financially that the Mears family sold up to Ken Bates for £1. That was about as much as he would have needed to feed the meter for an hour if he'd had his way and erected those electrified fences he wanted to keep the hooligan element off the pitch.

It was the first time I had ever been out of work, so I went to Camberley Jobcentre and was asked by the girl behind the counter what I did. When I said 'football coach,' she frowned and said: "Oh, we don't have many vacancies in that line around here."

But at least I had some money in my pocket for a nice holiday. We went off to Spain, where I read in the Express (well, I'm not one to bear a grudge) that Dave Bassett at Wimbledon was looking for an experienced striker. When I rang him, he said: "Yes, Gouldy, who are you recommending to me?" He dropped the phone laughing when I told him.

In The Hot Seat

I was still only 35 and, by today's vastly superior nutritional and fitness standards, could well have been good for another year or two pounding away at the head of someone's attack. Three decades ago, though, you were very much yesterday's news at that age as a player. That said, Harry Bassett recovered his composure sufficiently after his fit of the giggles down the phone to tell me to report for pre-season training at Wimbledon and he would assess things.

What wasn't as welcome was the news I was banned from the first-team dressing room. The likes of Dave Beasant, Wally Downs, Alan Cork and Brian Gayle gave me the nickname 'Moroccan Mole,' partly because I was sporting a heck of a tan after my fortnight on the Costas but also because they suspected I was being 'planted' by Harry as another set of eyes and ears. They kicked me out and told me to change with the reserves. The Crazy Gang culture had already taken root and they weren't ready to welcome a stranger they had reservations about.

To get over the resistance, I had to work extra hard on the banter at our training ground in Richardson Evans Park, a public expanse just off Wimbledon Common. I loved the craic with the other players, always have done, and soon broke down a few of the barriers as my outlook was broadened by the methods of Harry and his coach Alan Gillett.

Whereas Geoff Hurst had lived and died by passing the ball, weaving patterns and making sure our football was easy on the eye, my new gaffer was all for practising set-pieces and hitting long balls into the corners. There was clearly more than one way to skin a cat and I was happy to support Harry in every way I could. I was still reasonably fit and ready to graft, so I could see myself getting on all right at Plough Lane; more so as my relationship with the rest of the squad improved in no time.

Wimbledon had just won promotion from the Fourth Division and were paying me a princely £20 a week, which they increased to £60 by awarding me a short-term contract. I had been on £250 a week at Chelsea, so the belt was being tightened a bit but my love for the game was undiminished and it didn't take long for that realisation to dawn on the people who mattered at my new club.

I played in a friendly at Southend and in a couple of reserve matches and Sam Hammam, the Dons' chairman, was impressed with my desire and passion. There was even the likelihood of a run in the first team because Corky broke his leg early on. Then everything was turned on its head when Aldershot called and offered me £150 a week to go in as player-coach under Len Walker. I told Harry I'd stay at Wimbledon for £80 plus expenses because I'd fallen in love with the place but they couldn't meet even those modest demands. So Aldershot it was and I had to say cheerio to the lads I'd grown so fond of in the space of a few weeks. Brief though my association was with the players, at least I'd allayed their initial suspicions about me.

The garrison town of Aldershot was just down the road from where we lived in Camberley, so it was ideal on that score. And I was happy enough there, even if I was on the substitutes' bench every game and still wanted to play. I liked the coaching and was visualising a future there when the news broke that Terry Cooper had had the tin-tack at Bristol Rovers after a heavy home defeat against Swindon – a big no-no in the eyes of supporters.

I had a call from Eastville to ask if I was interested and decided to pay at the turnstiles, with my cloth cap on and collar turned up, to watch Rovers play under the temporary management of the chief scout Ron Gingell at Oxford. I'm not sure how necessary my disguise was. There was a buzz round the West Country anyway that I was the wanted man and it wasn't long before I was being interviewed for the job and then offered it.

I had turned Rovers down while I was at Chelsea and they had since gone down from the Second Division to the Third. But I was so proud to be a Football League manager, especially when we beat Huddersfield 3-2 at home in my first game, on October 24, 1981. Nevertheless, when I walked in the office afterwards and shut the door behind me, I burst into tears.

I felt so emotional and happy to have started with a victory but Marge was elsewhere in the ground and, after 20 years of celebrating victories and cursing defeats in a crowded, sweaty dressing room, it really hit home that I had got no-one to share the moment with. It had taken me only 90 minutes to realise what a lonely job management can be.

More tears were shed after I opened a good-luck telegram from Bunner Williams, a childhood mate who I had met on most of the six or seven family holidays we had at Barry Island. A few days after he kindly got in touch, I heard he had died suddenly, so my first trip as a League manager was a very sad one, to his funeral at Newbridge in the Welsh valleys.

We were like second brothers because we were the same age and had great fun together on the big dipper near the Glani-Mor holiday camp. We looked forward hugely to meeting up each year and became such good pals that we stayed in touch throughout my playing career and into my time as a manager.

My Rovers reign nearly became the shortest in football history because I threatened to quit within 48 hours when I found out most of the players were on more than me. Terry Cooper had persuaded the directors to push the boat out and was able to offer his signings decent money. Some of the lads were on £400 a week and I had shaken on £250 for myself.

I didn't think the club had given me the full picture and I wasn't going to settle for less than what I regarded as a fair wage, so I rang the financial director Martin Flook at midnight from the hotel next to the training ground and told him the board would have my resignation letter the following morning. Barmy Bobby or not, it wasn't an idle threat. I would have walked.

Surely they knew I'd soon find out what the top earners were on. Every manager needs to know the pay structure. The board panicked a little at the thought of me going and thankfully the matter was soon sorted out with a pay rise for me in double-quick time. We got back down to business and our working relationship was good from then on.

The reins had been pulled in following relegation, with TC forced to switch from buying established players like Bob Lee to grooming his own. We were both fortunate that there was a terrific crop on the way up – lads like Gary Mabbutt, Geraint Williams, Ian Holloway, Keith Curle, Tim Parkin and a striker out of the Western League called Archie Stephens, who scored in my first game.

We lost at Doncaster in my second match, then won two home games in a row and had a victory over City at Eastville in Christmas week before completing the double over them in April. Any manager who oversees a couple of wins in the Bristol derby has bought himself some time. We took some tankings as well, though, so it was no surprise we finished in mid-table.

I thought I needed another guiding hand to help extract the best from the up-and-coming lads and brought Tony Pulis back from a spell in Hong Kong as my youth coach. In his playing days, Tony couldn't run but possessed a lot of my traits. He was very determined and had pride, discipline and ambition. I liked his organisational skills and his spotless appearance. He knew where he wanted to go in the game. He was also a good sounding board when I encountered some initial resistance from those players who were loyal to my predecessor.

Even before I took the club for a few extra bob in my pay packet, there was no money to spend on the squad but I was thrilled to be in control and puffed my chest out each time I sat at my desk at the start of a day. As well as my office at Eastville, I had one at the training ground at Hambrook three miles away and soon put the telephones in them both to good use.

Desperate to learn everything I could about my new profession, I rang five top managers and asked them to each give me one piece of advice. Ron Saunders said discipline in the camp was important and told me not to be soft on anyone, Bob Paisley urged me to choose a system, hang my hat on it and not let anyone talk me into anything else and John Lyall insisted it was vital the players enjoyed their training and looked forward to going back in the next day. But my brain still had spare capacity for another couple of nuggets of information.

From Lawrie McMenemy, there was a different tack. He reckoned I should keep the press room cabinet well stocked with Scotch – five bottles before the game, five at half-time and ten at the end – 'so the bastards won't know what they are writing.' Then I took a deep breath, flicked through my book for a number for Nottingham Forest and asked the girl on the switchboard if she could put me through to Brian Clough.

Eighty-four calls later – I know because our telephonist had to log them all – success! "Brian," I stammered, "it's Bobby Gould at Bristol Rovers. I'm a young manager and wondered whether there's one piece of advice you could offer me, please, as I start my career." His reply was: "Young man, I'll give you two tips. The first is to call me Mr Clough. The second is to make sure you get your backroom staff right." Then the phone went down. It took me seven years to build my coaching team to my satisfaction, then I won the FA Cup to prove it.

I was somewhat taken aback by Brian's abruptness but not as much as when I rang the same number at the City Ground on behalf of Martin Flook looking for help with one of his charities. The conversation quickly swung to the possibility of a lucrative friendly at Eastville and Cloughie's demands were the most bizarre I've ever heard. They certainly had nothing to do with money. "I'll bring a full first-team down to play your lot as long as your physio will massage my feet," he said.

Roy Dolling, a diamond of a bloke, was a bit nervous about his task and, on the night of the match, we kept sticking our heads round the door to make sure his toe-tweaking was right by the master – a man who was very much a mentor to me.

Cloughie's words of advice came back to haunt me as I struggled to find a coach I was happy with. Garry Pendrey had the briefest of spells as my assistant, then I delved into my past by having John McDowell – a reliable right-back at West Ham well beyond my stay there – after he had had a spell with Norwich. He struggled to get fit, though, and I also had Dario Gradi on board for a couple of weeks without feeling comfortable with his methods.

At the same time, there were player issues. My teething problems with some of the squad I'd inherited from TC, who turned up in no time across the city at Ashton Gate, continued and I weeded some out and won others over. An uneasy peace remained with one or two of the rest and I had cause to fine Geraint Williams a tenner – proof that I'd listened to Ron Saunders. But I must have made some kind of impression. Several of them, like Holloway, Curle, David Williams and Geraint, went into management and I'm sure Mabbutt could have done as well if he had chosen to.

They would inevitably have noted some of my wackier ways and binned many thoughts of copying them. But maybe my passion, will to win and organisation rubbed off on them. We live in a world of leaders and followers and, for a Third Division club like Rovers to produce such a cluster of managers and coaches, was highly unusual.

I groomed Curle as an outside-right and could do nothing to rid him of his tag as the worst crosser of the ball ever. Opposition defenders were under less threat from his centres than the roses behind the goal at Eastville were. We never needed any pruners while he was around. He was forever landing the ball in the flower bed and doing the dead-heading for the groundsman at the same time. What he had, though, was pace in abundance, so I gave him a contract. When he scored in the first 25 seconds of a game at Millwall and then got sent off, it seemed to sum up the fact that we had plenty to work with – and a few things to work on.

'Sammy' went off to Torquay after I left and it was TC who took him back to Bristol and converted him into a defender. I could spot a player in there but, on that occasion, not his best position. The switch was so successful that Keith later joined me at Wimbledon for £750,000.

We lost one of the established players when Mabbutt joined Tottenham for £100,000. He was Bristol-born and a Rovers favourite like his father, so we were sorry to see him go. But the writing had been on the wall. Tony Barton at Aston Villa had already been in for him, so had Bertie Mee at Watford, and it was no surprise. As well as being a good player, Gary was a smashing lad, a bit mischievous, too. He once tied the laces of my two shoes together after I'd kept on at him about the need for discipline and tidiness.

Despite the departures, we couldn't stop scoring when the season kicked off and I'd like to think our pre-season trip to Scotland had something to do with it. I did a recce for the tour by taking the family on holiday there first. Jonathan and Richard saw it as a big adventure but Marge wasn't going to go because she didn't want to leave the cat. So in the end, little Jojo went as well. I don't suppose many managers have taken the family pet along when organising their warm-up programme.

Our kit-man Ray Kendall was in his element when the players set up base in their log cabins on Loch Lomond. As a cost-cutting measure, he made it his business to go round all the chalets and cook the lads' food. He knew exactly what Ollie would ask for. He wanted egg and chips for breakfast, lunch and tea. It's strange. I can't be sure who we played on the trip – it might have been Falkirk and Partick – but I can remember what went on each plate.

Once the serious games started, we clicked big style. Seven times up to Christmas, we won by four goals, with one of the victories coming against the champions-elect Portsmouth. We also put three past another couple of sides. The fact Bristol City were struggling near the foot of Division Four put even bigger smiles on our fans' faces and I dared to think that there wasn't too much to this management lark. How wrong I could be.

I thought we needed another guiding hand and made Mike Channon one of the biggest signings in Rovers' history. Mick, who I'd first met when he was leading out a horse on a night I took Marge to Windsor Races, is still Southampton's all-time leading scorer and had loads of England caps. Our attendances rose considerably after his arrival, although I did surprise him by sometimes leaving him on the bench.

In his short, goal-less stay at Eastville, he was well liked by the other players and the young lads looked up to him, even when he was sitting in the dressing room reading the Racing Post shortly before kick-off or disappearing to watch a race on TV. He wouldn't take any nonsense from what he regarded as junior members of my staff and gave a mouthful to the physio John Higgins, who pulled him up for cutting his toenails on a match-day – one of the wackier rules I brought in.

Mick was sometimes kept out of the side by Ollie, who was open-mouthed when I topped the Channon capture a few months later by landing World Cup winner Alan Ball, once English football's record signing. Ollie just used to sit and stare at him in the dressing room. He was so much in awe.

I rang Bally in the middle of the season to ask what he was doing, he said: "A jigsaw, now leave me in peace, I don't like you." I replied: "I hate you as well, so we're starting off even. Now how about getting your arse up here to listen to what I've got to say?" Within 24 hours, he was in the West Country to sign on a match-to-match basis and we were having the time of our lives together as we posed for the press photographs. As club colleagues, we got on brilliantly and loved each other.

At the age of 37, he said there wasn't much left in the orange – only some juice and a few pips – but his attitude was tremendous. His capture was a terrific coup for a club like ours. Every side we played, people were asking: "What's he doing here?" We went to play Wigan in front of two men and a dog, with the wind howling and the rain pissing down. But Bally produced the finest exhibition of one-touch football I have ever seen. He gave a classic performance and we won five.

Ollie was sat next to me on the bench and had been steaming at the start of the game at being made only substitute. He thought he should have been out there on the pitch and never resisted the temptation to tell me if he thought he had been hard done by. In recent years, though, as he has gone on to become a Premier League manager, I think he has realised that I handled him correctly in those early days. And he has probably never forgotten the exhibition we witnessed at Springfield Park that day.

Bally had a home in the south and often drove to away games, or had someone else take his car, so he didn't have to head back to Bristol afterwards. His red Merc was once parked up by Ray Kendall in a side street near Exeter's ground and had a £25 ticket slapped on it during the game. Our willing kit man didn't realise he had left the vehicle in a 'residents only' area, so I sorted out the financial arrangements. I didn't want such a legend of the English game to be foraging around in his pockets to stump up for something that wasn't his fault.

Life with Rovers rekindled Bally's spirit because he had been at a low ebb following a stint as Blackpool manager and a spell in Hong Kong football with Bobby Moore. He still wanted to play and enjoyed helping bring our youngsters on as well. He was a perfect role model to them as we chased promotion. Unfortunately, the travelling to and from his home in Portsmouth got him down a bit and a good hiding we received at Walsall convinced him he didn't want to be chasing after young bucks any more. But he left his mark and caught everyone's imagination, leaving us with a fitting memory of him when he scored an absolute belter of a winner against Huddersfield just before he departed.

It wasn't just older, established players I was after. Nicky Platnauer worked in a bank when I signed him and was such a success, starting with a goal on his debut in the League Cup at Torquay, that I later took him to Coventry with me as well. Mind you, I had a head start in landing him. The non-League club he came from was Bedford Town, who were managed by my kid brother, Trevor.

Graham Withey also did the rounds with me at Rovers and Highfield Road. I recruited him from Bath City for £5,000 and, like Nicky, he was a terrific lad. I'm told he was the first player ever to score two in a game as a Rovers substitute and the club who copped for that dramatic contribution, Wigan, were on the receiving end from him when he netted another couple in our 5-0 win up there as well.

I had a tip-off about another lad. The trouble was that he was detained at the time at Her Majesty's pleasure. To scout him, I had to make plans to be admitted to Earlstoke Prison in Wiltshire – for the afternoon at any rate – and watch him line up at centre-forward in a game 'inside'. We were given permission to play him in a reserve match but that was a complicated business that needed some diplomatic manoevres.

I asked if he could come out the day before the game so he could train with the lads. Then I drove him to the match and the prison warden stood on the touchline before driving him back afterwards. The lad even stayed overnight at our house. I had Marge and our young boys to think about but I had a gut feeling that they would be in no danger at all and so it proved. In the end, we decided against pursuing the signing but I had a lovely letter from the lad many years later, thanking me for the opportunity and saying it had helped him turn his life around.

I was keeping the papers well supplied with stories. One of the lessons I learned from Jimmy Hill was in how to treat the press. On my first day in charge of Rovers, I had handed one envelope to Ralph Ellis, who worked for the Western Daily Mail, and one to Bruce Perry, who covered our fortunes for the Evening Post. Inside each was the framework of a story. It was my way of showing I understood their needs and appreciated they both needed a decent 'line' from me each day. Being news-hungry journalists, they were still paranoid about what each other had got but they were proper stories, about transfer targets not just a run-down of the groin strains and dodgy hamstrings we had in the camp.

I came to regard them as friends. Not that that arrangement spared them a rocket or two. They also got caught up in the crossfire because they travelled with us to away matches and quickly learned that I took defeat very hard. On the afternoon we were stuffed 5-0 at Walsall – of all days it was when Gordon Bennett, our innovative secretary, had come up with the idea of offering free travel for our fans – I was absolutely steaming. We had a big following at Fellows Park, so I stormed into the dressing room afterwards to announce that the bus would be leaving in five minutes and anyone not aboard should equip themselves with a street map to get them to the nearest railway station.

My sympathies were with the supporters who had made the journey to watch that collapse and I wanted us to be pulling off the car park at the same time as the fans' coaches so the players could gauge the disappointment they had caused. A few of the lads didn't have time to button their shirts, zip their flies up or comb their hair but the person who came closest to not climbing aboard was Ralph Ellis. He was still on the phone to his copytaker, describing Walsall's second or third goal, when he had to make a dash for it from the press box.

The plan to expose the players to the ugly mood of the fans certainly worked. They gave us dogs' abuse, with their noses pressed to the windows. You didn't need a degree in lip-reading to realise we had spoiled their weekend. We were on the M5 in no time, passing or being passed by vehicles in the supporters' convoy. By West Bromwich, I'd had a bellyful of the angry faces and threatening gestures, and changed tack completely. I told the coach driver to put his foot to the floor and warned him that, if he didn't get us to the safety of our cars before the fans spilled out back at Eastville, he wouldn't be driving us to Millwall in the midweek or anywhere else for that matter.

The team bus was an important place. It was where we started to psyche ourselves up for away matches and where we began to reflect on them afterwards. I attached much importance to the journey to a ground from a hotel because it was the time for players to start to concentrate on the task ahead and gather their thoughts.

I banned card games on this leg of journeys and the players reluctantly obeyed. At least I thought I did. I never saw a hand dealt but Ralph Ellis wrote a piece in the Western Daily Press about four years ago and revealed that he'd been sworn to secrecy by the lads about how they played by keeping their cards under the table rather than on it. His phone was ringing by 8.30am on the day the story appeared and he awoke to a volley from me, telling him he'd have been kicked off the bus somewhere in the Cotswolds if I'd found out about the cover-up!

Another time, we were travelling along the M4 – to Swindon, I think – when two police cars were chasing a Reliant Robin (I'm not joking!) that was weaving in and out of the traffic so it couldn't be forced on to the hard shoulder. All the players were on their feet straining for a view and I yelled back from the front: "Sit down, sit down. Focus on the game."

The mood on board would depend almost entirely on results. When we won, the wisecracks flew and we didn't want homeward journeys to end. When we lost, the air could be thick with tension. I was so furious once after we had capitulated at Plymouth that I ordered Ray Kendall not to switch the microwave on or even give the players any cold food. A bit of starvation, I reasoned, might concentrate their minds in reflecting on the drivel they had just served up.

The trouble was that I'd forgotten Gary Mabbutt was diabetic, so Ray had to point out the urgent need for a few biscuits to be sent up to him at the back of the bus to keep his blood-sugar levels up. I had to climb down on that occasion; if one player was to be fed, they all had to be fed.

Funnily enough, I had a letter this summer from one of the fans who were caught out by our quick getaway from Plymouth. He had been hoping to get some autographs after the game but all he saw was the coach disappearing in a cloud of smoke and sent some pictures through the post, 30-odd years later, for me to sign.

After another defeat, the coach driver was told to pull in at McDonalds and I ordered milkshakes for me, Ray and the physio Roy Dolling and left the players on enforced hunger strike. Their stomachs were rumbling all the way home before I got stuck into them in an inquest back at Hambrook.

You'll realise I wasn't a good loser. We played once in the snow at Bradford and I insisted we played with an orange ball. It was 0-0 after 85 minutes, then Trevor Cherry and Terry Yorath had it changed during a stoppage for a white one and we conceded twice. I leapt out of the dug-out to complain and whacked my head on the roof. Despite my hazy memories, I recall accusing the home camp of adopting dirty Don Revie tactics.

On a much happier note, I won my first Bell's Manager of the Month award in 1982 – a 4.5-litre bottle of Scotch with a pennant wrapped round the neck. No-one has ever opened it. I was getting help because Tony Pulis had a useful input into our patterns of play and we provided plenty of ammunition for Punky Randall, who had been re-signed from Stoke, and Archie Stephens. David Williams also got forward well from midfield and had an excellent shot, so the goals really flowed in my second season.

From our total of 58 in 1981-82, the figure rocketed to 84 the following year. We beat Wigan 4-0 at Eastville, as well as thumping them away, and won 5-1 at Orient, hammered Portsmouth 5-1 and drew 4-4 with Exeter. I was attack-minded in those days and thought we could outscore opponents. Not that it always came off. We were mullered at Brentford on the opening day.

You can imagine how up and down my mood was. I slaughtered Micky Barrett for jumping out of a tackle and in another game played a lad called Errington Kelly, who was very poor. I was at home having a family breakfast when the chairman Martin Flook banged on the door at 8.30 on the Sunday morning and demanded that we go for a walk straightaway along the path by the estuary. He battered me and told me never to pick certain players again.

There were costly mistakes along the way. We blooded a 17-year-old midfielder called Steve Bailey early in 1982 and then had two points deducted by the Football League because we hadn't registered him. I was furious about the oversight by the assistant secretary, Larry Lloyd's sister Marge, and had her moved on. But my decision might have backfired. I was later told that my haste would cost us 12 points a season because the referees always used to check in at Marge's office with a spring in their step as they reckoned she wore the lowest-cut tops on the circuit.

I was learning all about the pressures of management, even when I was on the school run with Jonathan and Richard. My white club Toyota had my name down the side in blue lettering and there would be waves and smiles from the other kids if we had just won. If we had just lost, everyone would turn their backs or aim a few insults at me. Thankfully there were more thumbs-up than rude gestures because we were worth watching and well up the table.

We lost only four times in 17 League games and Punky, whose initial signing from non-League football was just the sort of capture I would make a name out of, helped himself to 20 goals or so, with Graham Withey also in double figures.

In my playing days, I broke through by doing well at a club who went up from the Second Division to the top flight, then I had mixed feelings about being sold to Arsenal. A decade and a half on, I was wise enough to know that my scope with Rovers was limited and thought our good showing and final seventh place in 1982-83 was my chance to climb the ladder.

I was highly ambitious and couldn't help but notice that Dave Sexton was having a bad time at Coventry. As my phone quickly became hot, my head was turned but anyone who assumes that I took the issue of walking out on Rovers lightly would be very wrong. The waterworks were switched on again as I packed my bags because I had grown to absolutely love the place.

Enter The Whirlwind

My first meeting with Coventry was virtually in a field half way between Bristol and Oxford. The headlights of Ian Jamieson's waiting car flashed to let me know I was in the right lay-by. It was all very clandestine but, you've guessed it, I didn't quite get it right. I turned up in my Bristol Rovers vehicle, emblazoned with the name Bobby Gould down the side.

After the departure of Jimmy Hill, Ian was the Sky Blues' chairman, a Scot who I had watched as a kid when he was playing for the club as a wing-half. He was a very straight man and made me feel wanted at Highfield Road. And I was comforted to know that George Curtis, an inspirational old Sky Blues team-mate as well as my best man a decade and a half earlier, was not only on the board but about to become a powerful paid director. The trouble was that Dave Sexton was still in the job and one match remained in the League season – for Rovers as well as Coventry. Then someone blabbed about my possible move and the story found its way into the papers.

Dave had been there for two years and would lead the side to a final placing of 19th, only one spot above relegated Manchester City. Although I was being lined up as his replacement, he decided to stay for Coventry's final-day home defeat against West Ham – an option I wasn't given by Martin Flook at Eastville. He let it be known that I was leaving with 17 months left on my contract, so he banned me from the ground while Rovers were playing Cardiff and I went shopping instead with Marge and the boys. Or at least that was the official version.

I actually parked my car, with the window open, just off the M32 and followed proceedings via the crowd noise. It was a sad way for it all to end because it had been a magical time for me and I felt I had turned the club round. The parting was bitter and Martin got his retaliation in first by sending a letter saying he would sue me if I went back to sign any of the Eastville staff.

In one sense, I had a tough act to follow at the Sky Blues, who handed over £30,000 in compensation for my services. And I was soon made aware of it. Dave Sexton had been popular with the players, who didn't relish a proud Coventry boy like me coming home rocking the boat and putting them through the mill. Not to put too fine a point on it, I was walking into a minefield, especially as I would be inheriting John Sillett, with whom I'd had some difficult times at Bristol City, as my no 2.

Iain Jamieson was keen to have another former Sky Blues player as manager, though, and, boy, did I have to manage! Garry Thompson had joined Albion a few weeks earlier, now Danny Thomas wanted to leave and Gary Gillespie, Paul Dyson, Les Sealey, Steve Jacobs, Steve Whitton and Gerry Daly were up for contract renewals. Mark Hateley was safely tied up for another year or two but that was largely irrelevant because he let it be known he was angry at the changeover.

I didn't muck about. The last thing I needed was a poisonous dressing room full of players who didn't want to be there, so I waved goodbye to Hateley to Portsmouth, Sealey to West Ham, Dyson to Stoke, Gillespie to Liverpool, Whitton to West Ham and Jim Melrose to Celtic. Thomas, an England international, went as well, to Tottenham, but not before I fined him two weeks' wages for derogatory comments about the club. He couldn't say I wasn't consistent; I had fined myself £200 at Bristol Rovers the season before for mouthing off at a referee.

Gerry Francis was yet another player to go, although that was more because I thought his legs had gone rather than any desire of his to leave. The one I didn't really want to lose was Gillespie, who was a great character and leader. But how could you hang on to a player when Liverpool came in for him?

I drove Gary to the Post House Hotel at Stoke for talks and was amazed to be met by an Anfield delegation numbering five or six, among them manager Joe Fagan, chairman John Smith, various other directors and secretary Peter Robinson. No wonder they agreed to pay for the tea and biscuits. Doing the deal with them was a daunting proposition for a manager just out of nappies like myself but I was delighted to bump the price up from £250,000 to £375,000. Joe pretended to tuck his trousers into his socks and joked that it was a good job he had brought a push-bike as I had left him without enough money for the petrol home.

With the decks well and truly cleared, I brought in Ashley Grimes from Manchester United for £275,000, Micky Gynn from Peterborough for £60,000, Terry Gibson from Manchester United for £70,000, Micky Adams from Gillingham for £70,000, Sam Allardyce from Millwall on a free, Dave Bamber from Blackpool, Trevor Peake from Lincoln, Raddy Avramovic from Notts County, Dave Bennett from Cardiff and Tommy Langley from Chelsea.

It was a spectacular turnaround and I wasn't finished. Despite the threats, I did go back to Bristol Rovers and signed Nicky Platnauer and Graham Withey. The fact Rovers would show a big profit on the pair obviously persuaded Martin Flook to drop his ban. He was happy to do business. I also took Errington Kelly off their hands. Neville Foulger, from the Coventry Evening Telegraph, and the freelance reporter Mike Dale couldn't believe their luck. They had a scoop a day and I'm told I went on to sign 25 players in 18 months in all. A hurricane was blowing through Highfield Road.

Poor Ralph Ellis probably wasn't as chuffed. After following my Bristol Rovers team for the Western Daily Mail, he moved to the bigger Birmingham Post & Mail group, only to soon have his peace shattered by me descending on his new 'patch'. He covered the Sky Blues as part of his new job – or at least he tried to. I quickly realised we always seemed to lose when he reported on our games, so I banned him for a while on the grounds he was a jinx.

I took some criticism for recruiting so heavily from the Third Division and the bookies made us their favourites for relegation. There were bigger-name players I went for, like Jimmy Rimmer and Kenny Burns, but they proved out of reach. And it was sad that Charlie George departed without playing a game after coming in on trial. I'd love to have seen a few glimpses of the talent he showed us at Arsenal but he just couldn't get over the injuries that were decimating the latter stages of his career.

For me, it was all about acting quickly, even down to seeing through some long-distance travel arrangements that Dave Sexton had set up. In my first couple of weeks, we went to play six games on an end-of-season tour of Zimbabwe, where my workload was increased by the fact Schnoz wouldn't travel because of his fear of flying. But I still made it my business to find out a bit more about the squad I had been left with.

One night, I clocked a few of them breaking my curfew and found a taxi driver to take me to the place I'd been told they were drinking at – an experience in itself as he had lost the ignition key and started the engine by touching two wires together. The players were stunned when I walked in but were impressed with how I handled the matter. I said: "Ten years ago, I was probably trying on what you've just tried and I was probably doing it better. But we're here to do a professional job and that's why I wanted you in bed at a reasonable time. So let's have one drink together, then make our way back."

Steve Whitton was brilliant on that trip and scored a load of goals. He even went out in front of a 40,000 crowd at half-time in one match and gave a fabulous keepy-uppy exhibition. The record books say I scored in a game against a President's XI but what we could have done without, on reflection, was the sight of Robert Mugabe arriving at the ground in a huge car.

There was another strange memory from the trip. I had a knock on my door one day and was shown what I was assured were some 'real' emeralds. I took a good look and was persuaded to buy a hundred pounds' worth. One of the directors also shelled out and we transported them home hidden in a toothpaste tube. Our neighbour in Sutton Coldfield, Albert Raybould, was a jeweller and I went to see him after my return home. He took one look at them, laughed and said: "You've been done." Fortunately, Marge thought it was hilarious.

It wasn't long before we were on our travels again. I set in motion plans for a pre-season friendly away to Benfica, where we had teenager Tim Dalton in goal. Portugal and Zimbabwe were the glamorous bits of our schedule because I brought the players down to earth by taking them for a week in Bridlington, which we used as a base for two or three other warm-up matches.

A problem surfaced when Talbot pulled out as our sponsor but Les Sealey had already pushed us too far by failing to return his club car after joining Luton. George Curtis went with a chauffeur and dozens of spare keys to Kenilworth Road, emptied Les's belongings on to the ground in his parking space and drove himself back to ensure our fleet was back to its right level. I'd love to have seen Les's face!

In my early months back at Coventry, my heart was pumping faster than at any other time in all my years as a manager. I felt I was at the pinnacle of this half of my career. Not only did I have to attend to the players' contracts and the signings and sales, but also draw up training schedules, organise the annual photo call and oversee the reserves and youths. The magnitude of the task was obvious and I wasn't going to shirk. I dared not fail my home city.

Mum and Dad were so proud. They had seen me play for MY club. Now, with the lads settled in school in Bristol, I was back living with them at home because I was in charge of my beloved Sky Blues. Not that my parents saw much of me. I was literally out working every night as well as every day.

I still had a suit case full of old Pinks upstairs and didn't need asking twice when the Evening Telegraph suggested I write a regular piece for them. It was an honour to be handed some of the column space that Nemo had filled in my time as a player.

The Sky Blue Connexion complex at Ryton was a fantastic place to go to work, built well ahead of its time on the vision of Jimmy Hill when he purchased three giant sand pits in the 1960s and converted them into two conventional training pitches and a futuristic all-weather surface with floodlights. I decided I had to base myself there, so I set up office and told my secretary Jenny to gather her belongings and drive herself the seven or eight miles down the A45 to join me. The wind of change, which would result in only three of the players who had appeared in the last match of 1982-83 being selected for the first one the following season, swept even her along with it.

Emotional as I was as an individual, I had to keep a clear head but I was up and running as a top-flight boss, sprinting even. And, despite all the comings and goings, we made a brilliant start. A goal on his debut from Terry Gibson and an own goal by my former Arsenal pal Pat Rice helped us win 3-2 at Watford on the opening day, then we won at Highbury a few weeks later and scored four at Luton and three at Stoke.

It got better still. In early December, we thumped the League champions Liverpool 4-0. Nicky Platnauer scrambled in the first inside 40 seconds, then Gibbo hit a hat-trick and we stood fourth in the table. Joe Fagan said we were title contenders. Not bad considering I had raided the lower leagues for replacements for all the departed stars. Even Gibbo, formerly of Tottenham, had been spotted playing reserve-team football, so he represented another good pick-up – and I loved him. He was a born finisher, always prepared to follow up just in case on saves and shots by getting into the 'honey-pot' position. And he had a nasty streak like myself.

I was particularly thrilled to see Trevor Peake doing so well because my swoop for him nearly ended in utter embarrassment. I went to watch Lincoln, then rang their manager Colin Murphy and told him to send his centre-half down to Highfield Road if he wanted to do a deal. I wet myself when I opened my door to a dark-haired lad when the player I had in mind was a red head.

I needn't have worried. It was only my memory playing tricks. It dawned during our talks that I had after all got the right man in my office and Trevor soon proved his worth in the top flight. He read the game brilliantly and always seemed to anticipate danger. As well as tackling superbly, he seemed to be on hand to make so many clearances off the line. He was the most natural defender I ever had the privilege of working with. All that and he was a lovely lad to boot who came from just down the road at Nuneaton.

I felt then that I was at the top of my game in management terms. I was flying and thought I could do nothing wrong, although I might have known Brian Clough would bring me down a peg or two. I jumped in my club Peugeot to go to a reserve game at Nottingham Forest early on and bumped into him in the corridor. "What they did to Dave Sexton, they will do to you," he said. "Enjoy your time there." It made me think.

My signings gave me great value. Micky Gynn lacked real self-belief and had some injuries but he had reasonable pace, which he put to particularly good use when he played wide. Micky Bennett was brilliant, Platnauer very good and Gibbo performed beyond all expectations. Micky Adams did a very good job at left-back before going on to Leeds after recovering from a broken arm and Graham Withey played ever so well considering where he had come from. Feeling very bullish about my knack for spotting a player, I boasted in the press that I could fill five teams with discoveries like Platnauer and Withey. And I set about proving it.

Towards the end of October, I phoned home and told Marge to be ready late in the afternoon as I was taking her out. When I said we were popping down to Yeovil, she said: "Oh, I don't know any nice restaurants down there." My reply was: "You'll need a warm coat, not a posh dress. We're off to watch a match." It was raining cats and dogs as we motored down the M5 and she was hardly beside herself with excitement.

A couple of years earlier while at Bristol Rovers, I had been alerted to a defender at Wealdstone and done nothing about it. The tip-off had come from my reserve coach Brian Eastick, alias Bostik, who was from London and very strong when it came to knowing players in that area. I thought it was high time I took a look now.

Yeovil's officials noted our presence and treated us like royalty, assuming it was one of their players I was watching. We sat on the front row and the game hadn't been going for ten minutes when the home right-winger landed in Marge's lap after this blond left-back – the object of my attentions – had raced across and tackled him like there was no tomorrow. "Come on, love," I said to her. "I've seen enough."

Wealdstone's manager was a policeman called Hall and I quickly agreed a £22,500 deal with him. I went to meet the player at his parents' house and didn't stand any messing around. I didn't offer big salaries and was mean with the club's money but my usual sales pitch was: "You do want to play in the First Division, don't you?" He said yes and we agreed everything there and then. His name was Stuart Pearce.

He was only 21 and was working as an electrician – something that caused a slight hold-up. He had to serve a week's notice before he joined up with us properly and helped fill the gap by playing for Wealdstone against Basildon. When he did turn up at Highfield Road, George Curtis said I had to play him straightaway against Stoke but I chose to hold him back and allow a little bedding-in time. I threw him in against QPR, mindful of the fact he had been released by them as a kid and would have even more to prove. I have seen some debuts in my career but this surpassed everything. He was absolutely outstanding and we won 1-0.

Pearce was fabulous for the dressing room, so passionate and up for every game and every challenge. He's my best ever signing and doesn't let me forget it. Every time we meet, he ribs me about dining out on the fact that I lifted him from non-League and put him straight on the big First Division stage. Whenever I see Frank Clark, who was Psycho's manager at Forest for a few years, I joke that I only signed his left-back because I was impressed by how high the right-winger had had to jump to avoid Stuart's tackles.

Amid successes like that, there were also one or two question marks. I lost the plot and ripped into Raddy Avramovic after he dropped a cross and gave a bad goal away against Watford. I said in the press conference afterwards that he was a disgrace and would never play for the club again. He didn't. I shouldn't have gone public like that and lost some of the players as a result, although it probably put a few others on their mettle as they knew I meant what I said.

Dave Bamber did okay and I could have sold him to Benfica the time we drew there. He was brilliant. But I should have gone to Reading instead and pipped Chelsea to the signing of Kerry Dixon, who was more prolific. The trouble was that Kerry also had a pelvic problem at the time and I was reluctant to spend decent money on him, so I took the safer option.

Sam Allardyce was one of the first signings I made at Coventry but was one of the last to arrive with us. I negotiated everything with him when he left Millwall but he then went to play for Tampa Bay Rowdies for the summer before we could stick a shirt on him.

Sam did a great job for us. I still shudder at one confrontation he had with Mick Harford when there was blood and bits of nose all over the penalty area. I'm led to believe Sam has been critical of me since and I apologise if he thinks I dumped him too quickly. I obviously knew he had been a tremendous leader at Bolton but I preferred Trevor Peake as my captain – a role the dependable Brian Roberts also filled initially.

It was too much to hope for our flying start to continue. Injuries didn't help and I lost Steve Hunt until the November after he'd had his foot trodden on in an annual bloody pre-season match against a supporters' XI. Dave Bamber had a blood disorder that kept him out for weeks as well and Micky Gynn, a former England youth international, was hurt on his debut.

We drew with Manchester United on Boxing Day but I could see danger signs by the time we lost an FA Cup tie at Sheffield Wednesday. The concern didn't surround the team but me. I felt absolutely shattered and was running on empty. I'd barely had a day off since the summer and had even flown back a couple of times from our summer holiday in Lanzarote to sign or negotiate with players, kicking the doors at the airport one day because I missed out on a target when my flight was re-routed through Spain.

A few months later, all the scouting trips, the early mornings and late nights, and the tension of match-days had taken their toll. At Ipswich on the Saturday after we had lost at Hillsborough, I sought out Ian Jamieson and George Curtis, said I felt a physical and mental wreck and told them I needed a break. My plea fell on deaf ears. All I wanted was about four days to recharge the batteries, clear my head and get ready to go again for what was in danger of becoming a relegation battle. After all, there were no international breaks in those days for you to catch your breath in.

I was making irrational decisions and worried that all the discipline I had instilled in the place was in danger of coming apart. One Friday, I told Micky Adams he was dropped and sent him out on two extra laps of the pitch to help tide him over a free weekend. When he finished, I told him he was in the side and he had a puzzled look as he asked what he had done in the previous few minutes to win his place back. I had no answer for him.

My pop at Raddy Avramovic, which had been preceded by a rant at him after a game against Stoke, was further evidence of the fact my brain had become scrambled. Players can tell when you're not performing at your best and are likely to cut a corner or two. I saw the club doctor, who was pleased I had recognised the symptoms of burn-out and taken my fears to him. He knew I couldn't keep it going.

We went 13 matches without a win and dropped from sixth place to 17th. After the game against Aston Villa, I said to Marge I just had to get away. She was too busy with the lads to think about coming along, so I took myself off to mid-Wales, played a round of golf and slept and slept and slept. It was the sanest thing I could have done.

When I returned, we won two matches on the bounce and I felt great again. The trouble was that the players were washed out by then. We took a fearful pounding at Southampton on what was poor Lloyd McGrath's debut, and I turned to Schnoz near the end and said: "Is that six?" He turned back and said: "No, you've missed a couple. It's eight." Maybe I hadn't recovered as well as I'd thought.

Having been touted as championship challengers when we thrashed Liverpool in December, we went to Anfield for the return as our final away game and were routed 5-0. It was a result Ian Rush rarely failed to remind me of in our time together with Wales because he scored four of them.

I rang his manager Bob Paisley on the Monday morning to ask how he handled his players so late in the season and was interested to hear him suggest a Tuesday training game with no coaches present. So, four days before one of the last-afternoon cliff-hangers that Coventry became famous for, we had tea and biscuits in the Ryton staff room while the players got stuck into each other.

We were at home to Norwich on the final Saturday, knowing that either Birmingham (at home to Southampton), Stoke (at home to Wolves), West Brom (at home to Luton) or ourselves were about to leave the Midlands another club

Goal-den moments with Arsenal. Top: Getting off the mark with an FA Cup effort at Swansea.
Middle: On target on tour in Japan. Bottom: My late equaliser in the 1969 League Cup final.

Operating on both sides of the Black Country divide......Above left: I'm celebrating with Kenny Hibbitt and Manny Bailey after scoring against Manchester City in a hot spell for Wolves. Molineux was a great place to be in 1970-71, when we were busy reeling off a run of six consecutive First Division victories. Top right: I was in Albion colours less than a year later and on the prowl here against Sheffield United. Below: Lunging in on Ray Clemence and Chris Lawler in my last Baggies game - a 1-1 home draw with Liverpool in December, 1972. Hawthorns legend Tony Brown, the 'roomie' who was prepared to offer me butler duties, is backing up.

Getting back to my feet (above) after scoring the only goal of the game for Bristol City against Bolton on the opening day of the 1973-74 campaign. Sam Allardyce is the defender behind me, hands on hips. Below: Blackpool are the opponents in another of my outings at Ashton Gate, from where I was on my way again fairly quickly. A volatile midweek trip to Hull saw to that.

My non-playing role in the 1975 FA Cup final later reduced me to tears but this is a happy memory of the afternoon (above) as I join our two-goal Wembley hero Alan Taylor in showing off the spoils of our success. In my left hand is a small policeman's helmet that had been thrown from among our supporters. I still have it at home. Right: A goal for Hammers fans to remember me by - the far-post finish that helped us to victory at home to Manchester United in October, 1975, just before my return to Wolves.

Above: Much of my second stint at Wolves was spent in the no 10 shirt and Norman Bell was happy to see me score twice in it in this game in 1976 at another of my future clubs, QPR. Below: One of the goals in my debut hat-trick for Bristol Rovers against Blackburn - something that gave me the chance to quench my thirst soon enough (left).

Above: A fond memory of two lovely summers in Norway as I line up with the Ålesund players I worked with as an introduction to my post-playing career. Such were the friendships we formed that Marge and I were invited back there to a highly emotional reunion, some three decades on. Pictured are (back row from left): Reidar Vagnes, Borjne Hotler, Helge Nostdahl, ?, Arne Gronvik, ?. Front: Bjorn Andersen, ?, Kjell Midtgaard, Torgeir Skauvik, Terje Eriksen. I'm sure the unidentified players will have a smile and realise it's my memory I'm having trouble with!

Right: Proud as punch to be able to link up at Chelsea with World Cup final star Geoff Hurst, one of my all-time heroes. We had one tremendous season at the Bridge before the wheels came off.

Whatever the weather and whatever the circumstances, we made life fun at Bristol Rovers - and there was some success as well. The players who helped me to a Manager of the Month award (left) were good at seeing the sunny side of things but soon realised I wasn't above a good pelting when the weather permitted it. Among my tormentors are Gary Mabbutt (in the lighter top towards the left), Keith Curle (behind my hands) and the current Blackpool manager Ian Holloway (far right).

Happy moments for me during my first spell in charge of my beloved Coventry City. Above: Dad was always a proud and frequent visitor to Highfield Road, although his blindness meant he never actually saw me play for the club. Mum never had the chance to witness my Sky Blues goals - I banned her! Below: Joining Dave Bamber to salute our fans after an opening-day win at Watford.

lighter in the top division by going down with the already doomed Wolves and Notts County.

In an effort to reverse the slide in the nick of time, I varied my pre-match routine. My team talk was virtually confined to the message: "Where do you want to be playing next season lads? Arsenal and Liverpool or Barnsley and Carlisle? Now get out there and do it." With that, I closed the door behind me, renewed acquaintances in the corridor with Mike Channon, who was an unused member of Norwich's squad, and invited him into my office. "Don't ever become a manager," I warned him, then I reached for the drinks cabinet and a couple of glasses, one for a lager for him and one for my favourite tipple, Southern Comfort with lemonade.

Mick was surprised I didn't want to be with my players but, at the end of a long, hard season, they didn't need me standing over them any more. We each had a re-fill, then I took my usual place on the bench – and quickly wished I hadn't poured myself such generous helpings. A few minutes after kick-off, I'm sitting cross-legged in the dug-out, absolutely bursting. I longed for the ball to go out, then, when it did, I told the physio George Dalton I had left something in my office and ran down the tunnel to the toilet. I relieved myself and couldn't stop. I was peeing for England.

Fortune smiled on us big-time that day. After trailing to a penalty late in the first half, we were leading 2-1 in the dying moments when Robert Rosario climbed at the Spion Kop End and pinged a header against our bar. The woodwork was still shaking when the ball dropped into the grateful arms of Perry Suckling. Almost straightaway, the referee blew the final whistle and we were safe. A picture in a Coventry book shows me yelling and clenching my fists while Iain Jamieson is thumping me on the back. The relief was massive.

I looked up to the stand, from where Marge had been watching with our best friends Pat and Bill, and so wanted to give her a hug. We had been apart for much of the season as important exams were looming for the lads and we didn't want to uproot them again from Portishead. I longed to take her for a good night out but wasn't much company during our celebratory meal. I was absolutely knackered again and almost fell asleep into my soup.

My mood was better, though, than that of Ron Saunders. The two of us had got on well when I nearly went to play for him at Norwich but here I was helping relegate his Birmingham side. And one of our goals had come from none other than Mick Ferguson, a man who was already a big favourite from his first spell at the club. I took him on loan from Birmingham, of all places, for the final few weeks and he showed he still had that scoring knack. Poor Ron. Ferguson came up with our equaliser and Dave Bennett hit the winner.

Birmingham, who drew at home to Southampton, had a much better goal difference than us and we would have been relegated had Rosario's effort been an inch or two lower. We were all elated after the game but that didn't stop me having Ian Butterworth up the wall in the dressing room, laying into him for not preventing the header. Again, I proved I didn't let such flare-ups fester. I appointed Butts to my backroom team at Cardiff many years later.

We played some great football at times that season with players whose careers hadn't been anywhere but you have to accept sometimes that fatigue just sets in. Thankfully, the club were renowned escapologists. It was probably around that time that someone suggested the Titanic would never have gone down if it had been painted sky blue. However often Coventry teetered on the brink of a return to the Second Division, they found something extra in order to stay afloat.

I should nevertheless have been looking more closely at the staff I had at Highfield Road. I didn't have the back-up team I wanted and had some problems with Schnoz. The trouble was that I was too inexperienced to know who I could trust. I thought back to what Cloughie had told me in my early days at Bristol Rovers and decided he was right. You have to be surrounded by those you are comfortable with.

It was back to the transfer market in the summer of 1984. Fortified by the fact Nicky Platnauer had been named our Player of the Year, I went off in search of more bargains. I signed Steve Ogrizovic from Shrewsbury for £72,500, Brian Kilcline for £60,000 from Notts County, Kirk Stephens from Luton and Bob Latchford and Kenny Hibbitt on frees from NAC Breda and Wolves respectively.

I also brought Martin Jol in for nothing from Albion. He had his passport out and was ready to return to Holland when I suggested he drop his bags off at Coventry instead to see how it went. There was a bit of a gap in our midfield department because I knocked out Ashley Grimes, who didn't do as well as I hoped, to Luton, and Gerry Daly also left, along with Bamber and Allardyce.

I had built one team 12 months earlier but didn't feel as powerful now as I went a long way to building another. And I felt I'd lost a bit of my fire. My budget had been cut and the board were playing a more hands-on role. They told me we needed more experience but I was unhappy that I couldn't seem to get the balance right. It didn't help either that I was living apart from my family.

Ian Jamieson had been replaced as chairman by a Jersey-based businessman called John Poynton, who told me I should look for a new no 2 if my relationship with Schnoz wasn't working. I interviewed my old Arsenal mate George Armstrong, who was by now at Leicester, then I was encouraged to talk to Don Mackay, who I knew as the youth coach at Bristol City in my time there. Shortly afterwards, I rang Don to tell him he'd got the job and his mother answered and said: "He's not in. He has gone to Coventry to become their assistant manager." So much for the decision being totally mine.

Before we knew it, we went five League matches without a win. I left Don in charge for the draw at Sunderland because I went instead to scout Peter Nicholas at Crystal Palace. I felt we needed a midfield engine and always favoured the young ones with legs and enthusiasm. That's not to say I didn't get good value from the older lads, although I once took Hibby off at half-time after I caught him smiling as he came off the pitch when we were losing. I couldn't handle that, even if we were old mates from Wolves.

The board realised I was in a mess and stumped up some money to help me out, so I splashed out £300,000 on Cyrille Regis, who was an absolute diamond, and £250,000 on another former Albion forward, Peter Barnes. Results picked up for a while, although all our victories seemed to be by the odd goal. We still struggled to score.

When we did start to click by netting a couple in a Milk Cup victory at Walsall, we were spectacularly turned over at our place in the second leg. I wasn't at my best and felt I was being found out over my inexperience at that level. I was also starting to lose it. When the referee gave a bad penalty against us at Leicester, I encroached so far on the pitch to voice my protests that I was almost in the 18-yard box. The crowd were yelling at me to get off but somehow the officials let play go on while I retreated again.

Before I was done good and proper by the FA, I was sacked. Following a Boxing Day defeat at Luton that left us one place off the bottom of the table, John Poynton rang me from Jersey and asked me to see him in his office the next morning. I told him to sack me there and then if he wanted to but he insisted on doing things face-to-face and flew in to administer the last rites after I'd festered all night.

He was sat behind his big desk and I threw the keys to my club car at him and said: "There they are. Speak to my solicitor when you're ready." I wasn't strong enough to handle my departure well and was angry with myself for the way I reacted. Embarrassingly, I had no way of getting home to Bristol and it was December 27.

I rang Pat's husband Bill to explain my predicament and found out again what good friends they are. Despite recovering from his own Christmas excesses and having to put up with my dark mood, he agreed to drive me the hour and a half down the M5. It was when I walked in the house and saw the family again that I suddenly felt I'd let down everyone, including Mum and Dad back in Coventry, by losing my cherished job. And I sobbed once more.

A Rovers Return

What do football managers do when they get the sack? Easy: They become normal human beings again. As the shell-shock of being discarded by my home-city club eased, I did what other people do. I took on some window cleaning for Pat's Bill, cleaned out some stables for a local racehorse trainer called Pat Murphy and started playing football for Backwell, a village team near Portishead.

As winter turned to early summer, I also took up cricket for the first time since my Coventry Ramblers days in my mid-teens and was delighted to make it into Portishead first team via a few games up the road for Gordano. With the ball occasionally coming off the middle of my bat, I cleared my head in my time off. I had gone home to roost and to rest following so many years on the football treadmill, many of them spent commuting, and I was happy enough.

There was an enjoyable trip as well to Vancouver, where I linked up with The Reverend while I investigated the possibility of setting up some soccer schools with Dennis Roach and some Canadian backers. I found it an interesting possibility but not half as interesting as the customs officers found me. Did they give me the third degree or what? I was shaking when I finally made it into their country, well aware by then that they didn't easily give up work to foreigners.

The horse racing connection had interesting spin-offs. Marge and I had always wondered what we could do together as an escape from football and a four-year-old filly called Homemaker provided us with the outlet we were looking for. I bought a share of her and recouped some of my outlay when I put £50 on her at Warwick and she won at 20-1 – a victory that brought me plenty of abuse from the Coventry bookies who recognised me.

I was only putting a toe in the water in the sport – not making the sort of major hoof prints Fergie has – but there was more success in a hurdles race at

Ludlow, where she won again. Not all days were like that, though. Homemaker showed her temperamental side by refusing to leave the parade ring on a snowy afternoon at Taunton. She was eventually persuaded to go down to the start but then threw another tantrum by digging her heels in at the third fence and making it abundantly clear she was going no further. Talk about dropping anchor! It wasn't just the embarrassment.......I had also put a right few bob on her.

Like many footballers, I'd always enjoyed a day at the races and felt I was doing it for Granddad Bob Morton when I developed an interest. He had loved having a shilling-each-way yankee every Saturday and taught me a bit about placing a bet. But my involvement was to go quite a bit further. When I managed Wales, my participation in syndicates increased through a link-up with a trainer called Derek Hayden-Jones just north of Cardiff. I bought into a two-year-old called Petite Futie, who, God bless her, soon romped home at Newmarket.

That wasn't quite the end of the story because I decided I wanted a piece of a two-year-old called Solicitude that Derek also trained. She won at 66-1 at Southwell, would you believe, but I must have been getting used to the idea by now that racehorses were a bit like cars and couldn't always be relied on. I only had a fiver on her that day and could have cleaned up if I'd been bolder.

I had always loved Cheltenham and came to love going there with Marge for the festival. I went seven or eight years on the trot and eventually had it written in my contract that I had Gold Cup day off. I didn't want my chairman telling me I should be scouting players or coaching the under-18s when Desert Orchid or Forgive 'n Forget were being saddled up.

With two lads at private school and a sizeable mortgage, though, I couldn't afford just to be swanning from racecourse to racecourse. I needed to work as well and started a media job at HTV, reporting mainly to a studio in Bristol and sitting alongside a lovely gentleman called Bruce Hockin, who helped me so much. I was doing what in-between-jobs football people do; keeping my face in the public domain and offering my opinion on various issues in the game. Then the phone rang and I almost dropped it when the caller identified himself. It was Martin Flook.

Martin was still in the chair at Bristol Rovers and was looking for a new manager following the departure to Norwich of David Williams, who had been appointed as my successor when everyone expected the job to go to Alan Ball. Bizarrely, David, who was still playing, sold himself to the Canaries for £40,000 and then resigned as manager. And I thought I'd done some crazy things in my career.

Martin had made his money selling air conditioning systems to the Middle East and had obviously forgiven me to a large extent following our stormy parting a couple of years earlier. In that respect, we were alike. I was quite capable of flipping my lid with somebody one minute and then putting my arm round them and having a laugh the next.

We lived close by in Portishead, had seen each other around in the meantime and got on well enough for him to offer me the job at a club who were now used to finishing well up the Third Division. Within weeks, I was installed in the hot seat, on my way to France for a youth tournament in the summer of 1985 and throwing up over the side of the Plymouth-to-Roscoff ferry. It was great to be back!

I am always sick on boats if I'm below level and can sense the vibration of the engine, so I sat outside in the rain on my own under an umbrella, occasionally rushing to the side to release more of my breakfast. One thing you can't rely on from football folk in these circumstances is any sympathy, so my floor show drew much laughter from those around me, though no-one wanted to risk getting too close.

Leeds' lads were on the same trip, David Batty included, and their coach Tony Forthrop asked if we'd be interested in a defender called John Scales, who they were about to release. It was a real stroke of luck. John went on to play for me at Wimbledon in the FA Cup final and had a big-money move to Liverpool shortly afterwards. But his emergence at Rovers wasn't all plain sailing.

He made his debut against West Ham at Eastville and we lost five, with Alan Devonshire tearing him apart. Some of the directors told me never to play him again and I must admit I wondered what I had taken on. He was so poor that I had to hide him away for six weeks and then reintroduce him. This time he started to show promise and matured into a fine player.

I was lucky to be surrounded by good staff. Martin Flook, who had been running the show with Barry Bradshaw, soon sold up to Geoff Dunford and Roy Redman after becoming frustrated in the search for a new ground but we had one of the best secretaries in the game in Gordon Bennett, who doubled up as chief executive and was a Rovers fan who once cycled round every ground in the country to raise money for the club.

And Ray Kendall was the finest kit man I ever worked with. He was the only person I know who was accepted as readily into the boardroom as the dressing room and physio's room. He needed to be popular as well because he did everything from load the skip, organise the laundry and cook the players' food to serving drinks for visiting directors.

I admitted I had probably jumped ship too soon when I quit for the first time as the Pirates manager. And time was of the essence now because plenty needed doing. Before I knew it, I was embarking on another signing frenzy. I had a local boy called Phil 'Percy' Purnell as well as striker Steve White, who had come back from Charlton and who later went and did well at Swindon. But, with money so scarce, I was going to have to dig deep in my efforts to build another new side. None of my jobs were easy.

As competition for Tim Carter, the keeper who tragically took his own life a few years ago, I signed Ron Green from Walsall. Gary Penrice came in from local football and I captured Trevor Morgan, who arrived from Bristol City of all clubs and did brilliantly. Wide left, I had inherited a lad called Mark O'Connor, who obviously made an impression on Tony Pulis. He has been part of Tony's backroom team at Stoke in recent years.

We desperately needed some experience, though, and I remembered the impact Alan Ball and Micky Channon had made for me first time round. I read with interest that Gerry Francis had been released by Exeter and, knowing that he lived west of London, thought I'd try my luck. He agreed to sign for £100 a week and even did some coaching for that money as well.

One thing the two of us had in common was pigeons. Gerry and his dad had thousands and thousands of pounds' worth of them and I had a bit of an interest from my Granddad and Uncle Harry, so that was always an available subject of discussion.

I liked Gerry but he needed plenty of reassuring. He had this apprehension about him which was surprising in a professional of his experience and quality. I gave him a bollocking once for ringing at 11pm one Friday night and telling me he had a great free-kick idea. You fear the worst when the phone goes so late and I cut him short by telling him not to rabbit on the night before a game but just to put his plan into practice on the training ground on the Monday.

In Gerry, I had also signed the man who would head up the Rovers management team when I departed for Wimbledon a couple of years later. And he was a big success in the role, with Kenny Hibbitt, who had also fancied the job, at his side.

I gave five debuts in our draw at Darlington on the opening day of 1985-86 and two of the newcomers, including Steve Badock, scored. But the season was seven matches old before we managed our first win – spectacularly so by 4-3 at Wolves, where Badock, who combined football with working as a British Rail clerk at Swindon, netted two more. We had gone four games without a goal but Bill McGarry was having an even tougher time of it at the start of his second spell in charge at Molineux. I was flattered to pick up that night's Express & Star and read that he was looking for a Bobby Gould-type leader for his attack.

We didn't score in the League at Eastville until October and knew full well by then that we were in a battle for survival on the field as well as off it. The board certainly had their work cut out to keep us in business. The chairmanship was handed to Dennis Dunford, whose first match in control was at Bournemouth, where I travelled to separately from the squad because Gary Smart – a young midfielder with a great engine – had a job that meant he had to work Saturday mornings. It was another sign of our problems.

I drove Gary down at lunchtime and came back on the coach. It summed up what a lovely man Dennis was that when he got off at Eastville, he turned to me and said: "Thanks, Bobby. It's been a great day, the best of my life." We'd just lost 6-1 and I was mulling over how I would start my bollocking of the players a couple of minutes later. I wondered what he'd be like if we won 6-1, not that there was much chance of us finding out.

Given that we also won only two of our final 19 League games, none of us knew how we stayed up by such a big margin. We were so short of players at times after having to release higher earners like Aiden McCaffery and Brian Williams that I handed Ian Weston his debut at the age of 15 and gave Andy Spring, a lad I'd known at Coventry, a chance that didn't work out. At least Andy had another talent to fall back on. He would sit down and play the piano on the rare occasions our budget stretched to overnight stays in hotels.

What couldn't be questioned was our spirit. We stayed afloat on the back of our terrific camaraderie, which carried us along as our money troubles deepened. It was damned hard work but we managed to keep our heads above water and Lincoln filled the last relegation place, with us five rungs and eight points better off. From mid-October to February, we somehow won ten League games out of 16 and the victory we eked out at Bolton near the end of that run proved crucial. It certainly gave us some insulation for what was to follow.

We didn't win in nine matches in March and continued to take some wallopings, including one by 6-0 at Walsall that caused me to do my nut. We also lost 4-0 at Wigan, York and Luton and were so hard up that I asked my pal Bob Wilson to come over and do some coaching with the goalkeepers. At the age of 44, he didn't expect to be playing again but he was very close to making a dramatic comeback – and a high-profile one at that against Leicester in the FA Cup.

We had another keeper crisis in our penultimate game when Ron Green went off injured and our leading scorer Trevor Morgan had to go in goal. Thankfully, by then, we were safe and had agreed to play that match – at Lincoln – the day before our final reserve match, at Norwich. That way, we could stay over in East Anglia, avoid making two long, expensive trips across country and use a few of the players twice. It clawed back some of the expense we had gone to when our game at Chesterfield was fogged off at half-time earlier in the season and then rearranged.

We drew 2-2 at Lincoln and, for the first and virtually only time in my life, I encouraged the players on the eve of another match to let their hair down, so we could celebrate our survival together. A few over-indulged and weren't well enough to turn out at Carrow Road. Against my better judgement, I named myself at outside-right and was reminded when we won a corner after five minutes what a good time we'd had the night before. I went to take it, missed the ball completely and broke the corner flag. I subbed myself immediately and retreated to the dug-out to give my hangover more time to clear.

Given our financial problems, it was only natural that I should hand our Jonathan a chance when he started to show promise in his later teens. He played initially as a right-back and turned out for the reserves, whose home games were staged at Forest Green. I also took his younger brother Richard on the trip to France the previous summer, attracted as I was to the fact that they wouldn't cost us anything.

There was a rumour at one point that our wages weren't going to be paid, so I dashed to see Grant Walsh, the manager at Barclays, to assure him we were about to sell Gary Penrice to Watford for £100,000. Another crisis averted. Gary had been signed from Mangotsfield and gave us great value. I couldn't fault him, except for his annoying habit of interrupting when you spoke. Each time he butted in, I sent him on a lap of the pitch as punishment, so he didn't half become fit. The other lads loved it because they would get a breather and would be shouting: "Go on, Penny, open your trap."

It was a slice of luck that Grant Walsh was a Sky Blues fan from Coventry. He was a big help to Rovers and he and his wife Molly have become lifelong friends of ours.

Bearing in mind how difficult we were finding it to function as anything like a normal club, it was ironic that we were asked to help an international team prepare for a big match. Scotland were heading towards the West Country before their game against Wales in Cardiff when the management from the hotel they were staying in rang to ask if they could use our training ground at Hambrook.

I was delighted to help, not least because my granddad had played for Blantyne Vics in Glasgow, the same club that their manager Jock Stein played for. I had never met Jock, who had Alex Ferguson as his assistant at that time, but he gave me two Scottish £10 notes for my trouble when he heard of our perilous financial state – a gift I told the chairman about in the event of things taking an even more serious turn and us finding ourselves absolutely on our last legs.

Several hours later, I was completely dumbstruck when the news came through that Jock had collapsed and died at full-time at Ninian Park. It was strange how a true giant of the game like that had used Bristol Rovers' facilities as one of his final callings. Thankfully, the club never did quite have to bank the money, which still sits for posterity in a mounted frame in our hall.

Eastville had by this time become an embarrassment, not least because we couldn't afford the rent on it. At least once, we fulfilled a fixture there only after an injunction to prevent it being used for football was lifted on the Friday evening. Crowds were dropping as well and it became a pitiful existence, especially when we moved out to ground-share with Bath City at Twerton Park.

Although there had been rumblings about us having to leave, we didn't know that the match against Chesterfield in the April was to be the club's last at what had been their home for over 80 years, so barely 3,500 turned up and nobody was digging up clumps of turf as souvenirs or clutching at other keepsakes. We won 1-0, then Gordon Bennett turned up in a furniture van telling us we had an hour to get out.

Our eviction wasn't all bad news for the sporting community in the city, though. It meant a fourth meeting could be added to the weekly greyhound racing schedule there. The dog lovers could obviously pay their way better than we could and the opportunity to save £30,000 a year by moving to Bath was just too good for us to turn down.

Eastville was a huge bowl of a ground, with only one stand – and that a long way from the pitch thanks to the track used by the dogs. In years gone by, speedway had been staged there as well, so there was plenty of room and an unusual sight or two around the pitch. We had a saying: 'Put that no 7 in the daffodils at the first opportunity' or 'I want to see their centre-forward picking the rose thorns out of his arse' because there were flowers growing in the no-man's land between the spectators and the playing surface.

Despite the wisecracks, I shared the supporters' sadness at our leaving. My two previous spells with the club had been spent there, so I had naturally come to associate with it. It wasn't easy to generate a good atmosphere but I said in the press after one of my three departures: "There's more pride and passion among Rovers fans than the supporters of any other club I've been involved with. They will always mean something very special to me and I will continue to follow them closely." And I meant it.

It's ironic that the club, who had seen their other stand burned down in about 1980, were refused permission to develop Eastville. It was apparently because of the concern of local residents over traffic problems on match-days. Ironic because whenever I drive through the area now, I always see huge queues for the Tesco and IKEA stores built on the site of the demolished stadium. We wanted it to be a home fortress. Instead, we got home furnishings.

Ground-sharing was virtually unknown in English football when we were kicked out in 1986. But we wouldn't have survived without it, even if most of our fans now faced a 30-mile round trip just to attend a home game. And our new match-day headquarters definitely weren't part of the tourist trail for the thousands of visitors who poured into the lovely city of Bath every weekend.

Twerton was a good walk out and was built on the side of a hill, with the pitch on a slope. Although Ray Kendall, God bless his soul, ensured the dressing rooms were okay, the stadium was a dive. Nothing had been spent on it for years. I called it the Azteca Twerton and was determined that we should keep smiling through all the difficulties. We mucked in by giving the place a spruce-up, had a laugh where we could and used the adversity to improve the team spirit even further. The important thing was that we still had a club.

Getting my hands dirty never worried me. I'd come through my apprenticeship at Coventry the old-fashioned way and remember arriving for a game at Walsall's former Fellows Park home once as Rovers manager and refusing to let my players in the dressing room. The toilets were filthy after a match played there in the morning and I was seething, so I got to work and cleaned them while the lads waited in the corridor.

On a Rovers home match-day, we had to take down all the Bath City photos in the directors' lounge and replace them with ours. That was okay until the Bath people realised what our game was and fitted their pictures to the wall permanently. That's when we had to find some Rovers flags to drape over them.

And it was a wonder the sandwiches in the guest rooms didn't curl up. They would be buttered and filled in Bristol and then driven the 14 miles to Twerton ready for plating up and consumption. At least our shopping bill for the bread, ham and cucumber wasn't too high. If there was one away game the wives of visiting directors were happy to miss, it was the one at our place.

The pitch could be a nightmare in the winter. Our groundsman Jackie Pitt, who used to be a hard-man in Rovers' midfield, had his work cut out before one FA Cup tie against Brentford because of waterlogging. Someone had the idea of asking if Prince Andrew's helicopter could be scrambled from the RAF base near Wootton Bassett to whirr its blades and act as a big hairdryer. Our plea fell on deaf ears but it made a good story for the papers.

Before home games, I would drive over there to help prepare the playing surface. At least I had the time because Friday was POETS day – Piss Off Early, Tomorrow's Saturday. In other words, training was short and sharp so as not to take too much out of the players. What I could have done with was building some big walls because many a ball disappeared over those small stands and terraces, never to return. Another few red figures on the balance sheet.....

141

There was a real danger of us losing our Hambrook training ground until the directors clubbed together to buy it and rent it back to the club. It really was a hand-to-mouth existence and tensions were known to spill over, especially when I was around.

As if poor Ray Kendall didn't have enough to worry about with trying to make our whites white, I gave him a flea in his ear after he checked Geoff Twentyman, who I had signed from Preston, into accommodation at Clifton Downs. It might only have been a B and B but even a box room and a plate of bacon and egg added up to expenditure we couldn't afford.

We were so skint that I couldn't have my blue club Sierra serviced. The inevitable happened one day on my way into work and it broke down on the outskirts of the city. I walked the rest of the way to the training ground and was absolutely seething. The players probably felt the backlash with some punishing stamina runs.

Dennis Dunford's son Geoff had joined the board and would give the club excellent long service, although I hardly appreciated his suggestion at the time that I could have a milk float to potter around in while my Sierra was off the road. His family owned a dairy.

I felt better when one of the directors sorted me out with a little run-around but the board weren't too impressed with one of my money-raising suggestions. So much were we on our uppers that I suggested we call Stan Flashman and sell our allocation of FA Cup final tickets on the black market. That prompted a serious draining of colour from the faces around the table, I can tell you!

Not surprisingly, we were forced to sell most of the experienced players. I moved Tim Parkin on to Lou Macari at Swindon for £28,500 in June, 1986, and Ron Green departed for £12,500. I even had the task of telling the Rovers veteran Harold Jarman, by now working in my backroom, that we had to part with him and find a replacement who could play as well. It was a case of employing one man to do two jobs.

On top of that outgoing business, I had to release Gerry Francis after already waving goodbye to Mark O'Connor, Byron Stevenson, Punky Randall, Phil Bater and Steve White. I'll never know how we stayed up. Dennis Dunford flatteringly said he thought the club might have folded if I hadn't worked so hard to keep us afloat but there were many others helping in the uphill struggle.

I trawled the market for wise old heads to help bond all the young lads and stumbled on one from the past. I approached my old Wolves mate Kenny Hibbitt and found he bore me no grudges for when I had subbed him at Coventry. He signed on a free and was golden, a true pro; just the sort for the squad to look up to and try to emulate.

The emphasis was very much on youth, so much so that my side became known as Bobby's Babes. But, like Gerry, Hibby was from the other end of the age scale and gave Rovers great service as a player as well as a coach.

The 1986-87 season started with a few questions. The Inland Revenue were launching their investigation into Swindon's tax affairs and wanted to see my files about the Tim Parkin transfer. Some officers came to the house to see me, probably aware that I kept meticulous notes of all my dealings and movements. And if they weren't sufficient, Jonathan and Richard were by now keeping scrapbooks. The Revenue took some of my dossiers away, kept the originals and returned copies.

That visit was nothing compared with the devastating news that hit me at Fellows Park on kick-off day. I was warming up our keeper Tim Carter when the Walsall assistant manager Gerry Sweeney, who had been a team-mate of mine at Bristol City, came rushing over to say the Coventry Ambulance Service wanted to speak to me. I rang them and found out Dad had died.

He had been getting ready to travel to our game when he suffered a massive heart attack. He was 61. I told Mum I was staying to see through my duties at the game because that's what Dad would have wanted. I informed Roy Dolling, my youth development officer and trainer, and Ray Kendall of what had happened and shed a few tears on my own. Then I went and did my job.

The players had no idea about my loss until I told them after the game, although the substitutes suspected something. We won 3-0. My brother Trevor, who was manager of Bedford at the time, had obviously been given the same news and chose to go straight home from his match at Bedworth. When I was looking at the scores on the Grandstand teleprinter at the end of the afternoon, the Bedford and Rovers results were there one above the other. And the fixture computer couldn't have been any kinder in ensuring we were close to home. Another sign from above…….

Roy Redman took me to Coventry in his car. I quickly went to the garage to find Dad's tool box and our kid did the same. We both said: "What are you doing here?" He had left us £500 in fivers and informed us independently (but not Mum) that it was for the funeral arrangements. We had just been to Lanzarote, where Jonathan celebrated his 18th birthday and Dad was spending money like it was going out of fashion. He knew he was dying.

He would have been delighted that our first League game at the Azteca Twerton brought us a win over Bolton despite Nicky Tanner's sending-off and it was fitting Trevor Morgan should score the only goal. He also got two at Walsall as well as hitting the last one ever at Eastville and it really hurt when we had to sell him to Bristol City in the January and replace him with yet another free-transfer signing, Robbie Turner.

I also tempted Paul Bradshaw out of retirement and continued to scour the non-League circuit. I gave an amateur called Mark Johns a chance while tempting David Mehew down from Leeds. David, or Boris as we knew him, had been with John Scales on the trip to France the previous summer and also played junior football with Jonathan in Camberley, so I had a head start. He did well and finished the season as our top scorer. Because of my friendship with Cloughie, I was also able to take a centre-half called Mark Smalley on loan from Nottingham Forest.

Big Geoff Twentyman was surprised with the tlc I showed when his wife went into labour. Their son was born during the night after we had played Newport in a rare Sunday game and I shocked them by finding out the name of the hospital she was in and ringing through to the maternity ward about 11pm and asking how things were. Geoff was a great pro but I thought he could do with some bonding time with the baby, so I excused him for the midweek game by saying: "Listen to me: You've got a groin strain, okay, but we'll see you in good time for next Saturday."

I always made a fuss of the wives and families. From personal experience, I knew that a player who was settled and happy at home would function better for me. I always made sure I knew the names of wives or girlfriends in case they answered when I was ringing for my player and I kept the local florists busy by remembering plenty of their birthdays and anniversaries.

I wasn't fooled when we went top with six points from the first two games and my judgement proved fairly accurate. We proceeded to lose 21 League games, including Notts County (3-0), Gillingham (4-1), Bournemouth (3-0), Blackpool (6-1), Walsall (3-0) and Port Vale (4-1). Avoiding relegation was our only aim even before the cricket season had ended.

We couldn't afford a pre-match meal on the way to play Mansfield, so we parked up at Derby and Ray Kendall, as resourceful as ever, rustled something up for the lads. Unfortunately, the aroma of the scrambled egg on toast he cooked in the microwave wasn't the only thing wafting down the coach after Robbie Turner had suffered an attack of pre-match nerves and paid a visit to the toilet. All the players chose to evacuate and ate their lunch standing up in a car park. We lost 5-0 and I told the directors it was the last time we prepared like that.

If all else is failing for you in Bristol, there's one thing you must do – win the derby. We went to Ashton Gate on New Year's Day and won with a Gary Smart goal when we should have lost 10-1. We drew with them at home and generally found City's ground to our liking, although, when the directors hired it for the day at Easter as an experiment for our match against Swindon, we lost 4-3 after leading 3-1.

It was only when we won at Newport on the last day thanks to a goal by Percy Purnell that we were sure of staying up. Bolton occupied the last of the bottom-four places and went down after losing over two legs to Aldershot when the play-offs were staged for the first time, with three clubs from one division in the mix with one from the division above.

By then, I had puffed my chest out with pride at seeing Coventry lift the FA Cup with six of the players I had signed for them. In addition, I had given a seventh member of their winning side, Lloyd McGrath, his Sky Blues debut. The BBC had me working as a summariser alongside Don Howe and Martin Chivers at the final against Tottenham and I felt emotional about my dad not having the chance to be there. The other sadness was seeing Gary Mabbutt, who I'd had as a youngster at Bristol Rovers, scoring a vital own goal. But I was so pleased for the Sky Blues fans, particularly those in our extended families, and of course for my old mate George Curtis.

After all that, I needed a good holiday, so we headed to Corfu as soon as we could. I touched down in the sun as Bristol Rovers manager and came back, many phone calls later, with my head in a spin, having no idea that the FA Cup defeat Rovers had had against Brentford a few months earlier was to prove my last in the competition for well over two years.

Culture Club 0 Crazy Gang 1

Stanley Reed, Wimbledon's chairman and the front man for their owner Sam Hammam, was the person who asked me if I would be interested in taking over at Plough Lane. Dave Bassett, having taken the club through the divisions, had moved to Watford six years on from giving me a taste of Crazy Gang life, during which I'd obviously made an impression on the powers-that-be.

The call wasn't a total surprise because I had picked up an English paper on holiday and seen myself mentioned as a contender. But the approach put me in a quandary. It wasn't only the education of our two teenage sons that left me feeling awkward about going back to London. I also genuinely liked the people at Bristol Rovers, where the relationship between the Dunfords and vice-chairman Roy Redman was brilliant. And we were all still excited at pulling off what we thought was a miracle by surviving in the Third Division.

David Foot, the well-known Bristol journalist, said there wasn't a more parsimonious club around than ours. I didn't know whether to thank him or sue him until I looked in my dictionary and saw that he just meant we were careful with our money. He was right and I felt so much a part of the fabric at Rovers that I had big reservations about leaving. If the alternative hadn't been a top-flight club, I wouldn't have gone.

It was home from home in a lot of ways. Wimbledon's Plough Lane home was a non-League ground to all intents and purposes and the changing rooms at our training ground were in the same building as a transport café. So I often found myself brushing past taxi drivers and the occasional trucker as I made my way along the corridor to my office. Would you believe it but I even renewed acquaintances with my 'stalker' Ralph Ellis, who was now on the London patch after joining the Daily Star.

A lot of the players I had briefly grown fond of at Wimbledon in 1981 were still there and there were no surprises when I walked in to reintroduce myself after being appointed. They were still a right rum lot, with some new additions to the horror cast, like John Fashanu, a well-spoken former Barnardo's boy who always had lots to say for himself, Vinnie Jones, the one-time hod carrier off a building site who had been signed from Wealdstone, and cheeky chappie Dennis Wise, who had known rejection at Southampton. They all had lots to prove and the hunger to go with it.

The lads called Wisey 'Ratski' or 'Ratso.' As usual, I didn't quite get my pronunciation right and he went by the nickname 'Rat' if I tried to follow their lead. It was a taste of what was to come when I found out he was suspended for the start of the season. He was a fiery character and we had some right rucks in the couple of years we worked together but, deep down, we stayed friends. Not surprising since I doubled his wages almost straightaway. I liked him because he typified the Wimbledon spirit. His enthusiasm was infectious and he was always at the front of the longer training runs, usually alongside Vinnie.

Every day, life at the club would resemble an outing from England's worst school. If they weren't letting each other's tyres down in the car park, they were burning a team-mate's dodgy gear or smearing black shoe polish over the private parts of some poor soul whose birthday it happened to be. But Sam Hammam seemed to thrive on the organised chaos and obviously thought I was cut out to join him.

Under the terms of my contract, I had to have a property in South London, so Sam put me in his flat for a while. Then I moved into one overlooking Plough Lane. Fash would try it on virtually on a daily basis by saying he was late because he had been stuck in heavy traffic but there was no chance of me spinning such a yarn. I could drop out of bed at 8am and be at the ground, on foot, by half past.

Unlike in my previous spell of First Division management at Coventry, I had plenty of players and the sight of a full dressing room made it a different world to the one I had left behind at Bristol. My problem was that I had no senior coaching or recruitment staff around me after Harry had taken his backroom team with him.

My first appointment was Ron Suart – part of Geoff Hurst's backroom team at Chelsea – as chief scout. He was also there to cover my backside because I didn't want anybody stabbing me in the back. Consequently, I started building my empire with what Cloughie thought was the most important bit; the insulation. And Ron was as loyal to me as anyone had ever been.

I worried initially that Syd Neal, the kit-man I was inheriting, might also have been too close to the Bassett regime. But I kept him on and he was brilliant to have on board, as was his match-day assistant, Joe Dillon.

Although I had been left with a lady masseur, Caroline Brouwer, who the players thought the world of, I still needed expert caring hands for the treatment room, so I rang the FA to ask them to recommend the best up-and-coming physio in the game. I was led to a lad called Steve Allen, who was being trained at Colchester United and who I thought could be moulded into the Wimbledon way. I decided he'd get on well enough with the players' mad ways and maybe become one of them.

When it came to finding my no 2, it would have been dangerous to cut corners but I was thrilled to bits at hooking in the man who was no 1 on my list. It was a decade and a half since I had last worked with Don Howe and he had done great things back at Arsenal since we had gone our separate ways from West Brom, for a lot of the time in partnership with George Graham. He was the one I really wanted.

When Don said he would come for four weeks to see how he got on, I felt like I had been told I could have a dance with Miss World. When he agreed to make his stay permanent, it was as though a couple of smooches had led to wedding bells. I knew the players would respect him and, unlikely though the alliance might have seemed, he fell in love with the place. Never mind four weeks, he was won over in four days and stayed for two and a half years.

Dave Kemp was our reserve coach, then Don recommended that we put Terry Burton in charge of the youths to keep the conveyor belt of young talent turning. One position we didn't have to look at was the important one of washer-woman. At our Richardson Evans training ground just off the A3, that task was already in the hands of the lovely mother of our young midfielder Vaughan Ryan. Things were coming together.

With off-the-pitch matters sorted, I turned to the players and brought in my Bristol Rovers capture John Scales for £70,000. With Nigel Winterburn having joined Arsenal before my arrival, I also recruited Clive Goodyear from Plymouth Argyle, fellow full-back Terry Phelan from Swansea and one of Don's recommendations, centre-half Eric Young from Brighton. All managers feel a strong need to put their own mark on a team and I wasn't any different.

Within weeks, Phelan was in my office in tears, fretting that he couldn't handle the power of those strong characters in the dressing room. It was a jungle. The players were ruthless and would severely test a newcomer to see whether he was up to it, physically and mentally.

I knew Terry could catch pigeons, so I had a word with Don, told him to rip up that day's training schedule and instead concentrate just on running. As we expected, he was top dog in that discipline and had no more self-doubts. The players saw how quick he was and took to him from that day on.

Very soon, we felt like an extended family and Don and I learned plenty about the squad when we went to Sweden to prepare for our first season. The first headache was the accommodation, a motel which prompted me to tell the organiser: "Don Howe and me don't do motels. You've got half an hour to sort it out and find us a four-star or five-star hotel, otherwise we're off home."

I told the players not to unpack and Wisey was soon chirping away, asking: "What the fack's goin' on, Gouldy?" We transferred to a four-star hotel and the lads thought it was brilliant. But they insisted on having a big say in what we did. On our opening day in Sweden, I was at the front listening to Don starting his first talk about tactics with a flip chart on either side of him, when suddenly the likes of Lawrie Sanchez, Andy Thorn, Dave 'Lurch' Beasant and Alan Cork decided we needed a refresher on the Wimbledon way and took over. It had been drummed into the players in Harry Bassett's time that they had to get the ball into the attacking third 174 times in a game. And the two wingers, Wisey and Carlton Fairweather, were detailed to put in at least 44 crosses per game. If they fell short in any area, they knew they were all in for training on a Sunday morning.

I remembered from my few weeks at the club in 1981 how much time Harry had spent practising set-pieces with the players. I inherited that philosophy and was happy to carry it on because it was working. As well as being like a whippet on the left wing, Wisey could deliver a mean dead ball by skimming in curling crosses that sometimes needed only the slightest touch to turn them into goals.

There were still potential collisions. Fash voiced the opinion that John Scales was useless and Don wasn't convinced either that he was going to cut it as a top-flight player. In turn, I had to remind Don that he was the coach and it was his job to make John better. Above all, I was the manager and I still had confidence in Scalesy.

I wasn't finished in the transfer market. Although Corky had a great football brain, I thought his pace was going a bit and felt we needed an injection of speed; someone with younger legs to feed off Fash. I scoured the market and came up with Terry Gibson, who had been terrific for me at Coventry but then struggled desperately for goals at Manchester United. I had to work hard to get Sam to release the necessary £250,000 and started to learn of my boss's eccentric ways in the process. Part of the persuasion process required me to agree to join him at a restaurant in Mayfair for a Lebanese meal, at which he delighted in watching me eat sheep's testicles – a Middle East delicacy I somehow got down me by drowning it in vinegar.

After starting the League season with a defeat – at Harry Bassett's Watford of all places – we kicked off our home programme by beating Oxford. I felt happy enough until Sam Hammam called me in to see him on the Monday, kept me waiting for three hours and then lambasted me for referring to them as 'my' players. He told me in no uncertain terms that they were his players.

Life was never dull with Sam. In fact it was never dull at Wimbledon full stop. We had some terrific results in that first season, winning 3-0 at Spurs, drawing home and away with Chelsea and at home to Liverpool, beating Manchester United 2-1 and thrashing Arsenal 3-1. Finishing seventh after the sixth spot the year before was more than satisfactory.

My attitude was that I wouldn't try to fix what wasn't broke. It was obvious that the strength of the club was the unique togetherness and we needed our Army to be at peace with itself so we could be strong enough as a unit to do battle. If ideas were clearly working, I wasn't interested in changing them, however unusual they might have seemed.

All my life, as a player or manager, I had trained on Christmas Day but learned that Harry had given the lads that day off as their homes were spread all over London. Instead, he would have them in early on Boxing Day to stretch their legs. So, against my better judgement, I did the same – and was rewarded when we went and won at West Ham.

I shouldn't have doubted the players because they were such an honest lot. What had struck us straightaway after our appointment was how much they loved training and were prepared to work. The defenders even complained one day a few months later that Don wasn't being hard enough on them, so he got out 50 balls and knocked them over the back four, one straight after another, towards the corner flag.

There was hardly a moment to pause for breath as Lurch pumped them back into the opposition half, with the full-backs and centre-halves sprinting forward to the centre circle ready for Don to send the next one behind them. They were on their hands and knees by the end and never again complained that we were too soft with them.

There was no let-up in the aerial bombardment. It's well known that we didn't over-complicate our build-ups and the planes that had had to take a different route into Heathrow for years would have to keep our training ground off their flight path for a bit longer.

We won six matches in a row around Christmas and were into our FA Cup run before we knew it. We hammered West Brom 4-1 at Plough Lane, partly thanks to a belter from long distance by Wisey, then won in the last minute at Mansfield. There was no chance of us going up there, swanning around like big-time Charlies and being dragged down by the surroundings. Their ground was better than ours.

By the time we went to Newcastle in the fifth round, things were starting to build and the apple pie and ice cream superstition was in place. But other forces were at work and our team coach was threatened on the way into St James' Park. We had Vinnie Jones to thank for that because he had made the Tyneside hero, Paul Gascoigne, squeal only a couple of weeks earlier by putting his famous squeeze on him at Plough Lane.

Whatever the backcloth to the tie, Vincent was brilliant at St James' and played a big part in keeping Gazza quiet as we won 3-1. We had to change in Portakabins because the main stand was being rebuilt but we played out of our skins, as we had to with Gascoigne on fire.

That victory earned us a quarter-final home match against Watford which would have meant another reunion with Harry Bassett had he not already quit and been replaced by Steve Harrison. But this was very much a triumph for the present Dons regime. Watford had beaten us twice in the League that season and had their sights set on another win when they led 1-0 and we had Brian Gayle sent off.

But Don Howe was magnificent in sorting us out at half-time. He said we were sending Eric Young on as a substitute and switching to one up front and I just stood there nodding my head in agreement. He had everything down to a tee – or almost everything. Amid the haste of telling all the players what their roles now were, he omitted to mention that someone had to be taken off. Corky milked the moment by exaggerating the role of the hard-done-by spare part but was as thrilled as the rest of us when Fash's power took over in the second half and we won 2-1, Fash getting the winner after Eric equalised.

Eric couldn't be shifted from then on and gave me the ammunition to spell out some home truths over our poor disciplinary record. We had piled up five sendings-off as well as 50-odd bookings at that point and also conceded 17 penalties, including one Dave Beasant saved in the fourth round at Mansfield. No-one could dispute that we had an abrasive side to our nature but I didn't need players getting themselves into trouble, so I warned them that anyone else ordered off would be banned by me for the next game, even if that next game was the semi-final or Wembley.

They say every side of Cup winners need some luck and we had some at the semi-final stage. We could have been drawn against Liverpool or Brian Clough's Forest but were pulled out of the hat alongside Luton. That said, they were a more than decent side and had already been to Wembley twice that season, beating Arsenal in the Littlewoods Cup final and losing in the Simod Cup against Reading. They were a considerable test.

In fact, our whole 1987-88 run was tougher than it might now look more than 20 years on. Newcastle and Watford were both well-established top-flight sides and my old club Albion, although in the Second Division, were managed by Ron Atkinson. Even so, Wimbledon v Luton didn't stir the senses too much and, apparently, the attendance was the lowest since the war for an FA Cup semi-final.

I was apprehensive in the build-up to the game despite having experience of that sort of occasion. I played in both the original game and the replay when West Ham beat Ipswich to secure a place at Wembley in 1975. Marge said she had never seen me so pale as I was then. I knew semi-final losers were forgotten in the blink of an eye and the thought of going so close and missing out had drained the colour from my cheeks. The FA Cup was that big to me.

I was relieved when I looked round the Wimbledon players and saw that no-one seemed to be affected as I had been 13 years earlier. But we still had headaches because Steve Allen was working overtime to patch up Fash, Laurie Cunningham, Gibbo, Corky and Sanch. Fash had 20 goals for us already that season and we could hardly afford to be without him.

Our decision to get the minibus out for the semi-final caused another headache. The limited car park spaces were largely swallowed up by officials, so the players who were heading individually to White Hart Lane were refused entry through the main gates and had to leave their vehicles on street corners, in multi-storeys or anywhere else they could find room.

As ever, though, they were up for the fight. We showed them a recording of the Simod Cup final beforehand to instil some extra belief into them and pointed out that Luton weren't half the side away from their plastic pitch at Kenilworth Road. The lads were climbing up the walls of the dressing room as kick-off approached and couldn't wait to get out. At ten to three, they were out in the tunnel, shouting and banging against the doors.

Even if things seemed to be going our way, Mick Harford put Luton in front just after half-time and we needed a bit of a break because the challenge by Andy Dibble on Gibbo that brought us our penalty seemed to be borderline. Fash, who had been nursing a hamstring injury, put it away, then Wisey arrived on cue to win it superbly.

Superstitious as I am, I was scared to change anything, on match days or during the week, so I stayed in Sam's flat much longer than I'd planned. We were on the brink of something special and needed to channel all our thoughts properly if we were to have any chance against Liverpool in the final.

Our League progress in the meantime was middle of the road. We found ourselves bogged down in a run of six successive draws, including one at Forest, where there was a post-match kiss on the cheek for me from Brian Clough. Perhaps he appreciated the fact we had six players under the age of 22 in our squad.

We did break the spell with a win at Norwich but that satisfaction was tempered by the fact that Liverpool, by then crowned champions, won 5-1 at Sheffield Wednesday on the same day to stand 11 points clear at the top. Our Wembley task was certainly a daunting one.

We also threw away a lead and lost to two Brian McClair goals at Old Trafford five nights before the final, when I wrapped Wisey in cotton wool and left him out. We just couldn't afford to lose him. I had hoped to name my

Wembley team near the start of the week to put at ease the minds of any lads on the borderline and stop all the guessing. But that plan went out of the window when Gibbo bruised his ankle after netting at United and was left with a race against time.

I was hardly going to spring a surprise with my formation. Despite the misfortune Carlton Fairweather had in missing the game through injury, everyone knew we would go with our usual 4-2-4 formation – how adventurous does that sound now! – with Wisey so important wide on the left. Don Howe reckoned he had been responsible for 75 per cent of our goals in the season.

There was much debate in the papers as to whether we would pair Andy Thorn or Brian Gayle with Eric Young in the centre of our defence. In the end, we opted for Andy, leaving Brian to rue his sending-off against Watford in the quarter-final.

The media afternoon a few days before the final held one or two demons because Eric Hall was involved. He was Wisey's agent and upset the press pack by demanding more money for interviews with his client. I waded in and said: "Eric, stop pissing about. This is our media day and we want it to be fun." Fortunately, Wisey bought into the spirit of it and did the interviews requested of him.

We also followed in the footsteps of The Beatles by going to the Abbey Road studios to record our Cup Final song, though that was where any likenesses ended. It was great fun getting behind the microphone again, as I had with West Ham more than a decade earlier, but the record was never going to go platinum with our tiny gates.

Thursday was the day for our look round Wembley and that's when we were at our cheekiest. Suddenly, a ball appeared and there we were having a serious training game on the hallowed turf, the lads dressed in their tracksuits. The groundsman did what groundsmen do and rushed over to ask what the hell we were doing. I suggested it might be time for him to have a cup of tea and we'd be off in 15 minutes, his pitch none the worse for the escapade.

Of course it was planned. Liverpool went there once or twice a season and we reckoned it would do us no harm to have a quick feel of the surface that we would be stepping on to for the first time. We were massive underdogs as it was. We didn't want to be Wembley virgins as well if we didn't need to be.

There were fears we wouldn't sell out of our ticket allocation for the game.

Happily, such talk proved unfounded but there was no getting away from the fact that we were small-time. We averaged fewer than 8,000 at Plough Lane in 1987-88 and were always being reminded that our highest attendance at that time was still the one the club had had for an FA Amateur Cup tie before the war. For our League game at Forest just before the final, we had taken only 300 fans with us. We almost knew them all by name.

We contemplated revving the minibus up again to take us to the Twin Towers. In fact I told the press straight after the semi-final victory that we would. But the police said they weren't comfortable escorting us up Wembley Way in that. Fair enough. This was going to be the greatest day of our football lives and we were happy to treat it as something very special, so we booked three coaches – one for the players, one for the non-football staff and one for our families – for our trip along Putney High Street. Ours had 'Wimbledon' written length-ways down its roof, perhaps so the police could spot it from their cameras in the sky.

Things became a bit tense on the Friday night at the five-star Cannizaro House Hotel, with the lads lowering the tone considerably by chucking bread rolls at each other during the meal. They were so highly strung. I sensed they were ready to explode, so I turned to Don and said: "We've got to get them out for a while." I tossed Lurch £50 and told him to take them out for a drink at the Fox and Grapes; only halves, though, I didn't want them to be seen sinking pints on the eve of the final. They probably had a pint and a half each. Wisey reckons some of the surplus went on fish and chips.

Wisey, Vinnie and Brian Gayle hadn't waited for the invitation from me and were in the process of sneaking back to the hotel through the pub's garden when they learned that all the others were heading out with my permission and with their drinks to be paid for by the club. I didn't have a pop at them. It wasn't a time for confrontations.

But there was one more problem to confront before bed time. Don and I were having a drink in the bar when we were interrupted by a call from Vinnie Jones. "What is it, Vincent?" I asked. I always called him by his full Christian name. He said: "Gaffer, Fash has just put his fist through the shower door. You'd better come up quick."

A reporter had confronted Fash by phone at the hotel, alleging he had been playing away – and I don't mean at Mansfield and Newcastle. He hadn't taken the intrusion well, lashing out in his temper and now needing treatment. When I got to his room, he still had his fist stuck through the wood panel and was trying to manoeuvre a way out without doing himself further damage. The film of the game shows his hand bandaged.

By then, I had found out what Terry Gibson wears in bed. Just before lights out, I popped into the room he was sharing with Clive 'Winko' Goodyear and saw these studs sticking out from under the sheet. He had done a deal for some new boots and had broken them in by standing in the bath for ten minutes, then left them on because his feet were cold. He was stark bollock naked except for his Wembley boots but at least his ankle was okay.

My match-day started badly with that call from my big pal Bob Wilson, the BBC's football anchor-man. We were well used to criticism and had heard about Johnny Giles calling our playing style a disgrace. His article went up on the dressing room as an extra incentive. The pundits clearly didn't think it was going to be good for the game if we won. But you play to your strengths. Liverpool were the hottest Wembley favourites for decades and surely nobody thought we could take them on at their passing game and beat them.

The biggest headache was achieving a balance between revelling in our excellent team spirit and keeping a lid on the nervous energy. We warned Vinnie and Wisey against being hyperactive and burning themselves out. I told them they had to keep some of it under wraps until kick-off but they still nipped out on the Saturday morning for a haircut and came back saying they had bumped into June Whitfield in the street. They had also bought some flowers for Princess Diana and were badgering me about how they could present them to her. "Lads, just sit down and fuckin' relax," I shouted back.

My chief scout Ron Suart asked me what my gut feeling was and I told him I thought we'd win. It was the way we played in the semi-final that convinced me. We showed so much resilience and Liverpool had one or two fitness worries of their own, with Gary Gillespie and Nigel Spackman doubtful following a serious clash of heads in the League game against Luton. I'd also said publicly and to the players that we should be carefree because there was no pressure on us.

Although Liverpool won the title by nine points and finished the small matter of 33 points and six places ahead of us, we had a decent record against them, drawing at home with them that season and losing 2-1 at Anfield, where the side had won under Harry the previous year. What I found hard to argue with was the theory that we would have to work even harder on harrying and pressing them because Wembley, with its wide-open spaces, certainly wasn't tailored to the game we played.

My mum had entered into the spirit of the occasion by making dolls of the players, all of them kitted out in yellow and blue. I handed them out at the hotel on match-day morning and the resulting laughs lifted the tension again for a while. ITV had some models of their own – those characters that Wimbledon Common is famous for – but I wasn't happy when they brought them to the Cannizaro and told them: "We're not going on TV with those fuckin' wombles."

The journey to the stadium gave us another 45 minutes or so to mull over our task. The BBC's Gerald Sinstadt was on board our coach and raised a laugh when he introduced a clip of Wisey appearing with Roy Castle on Record Breakers as a 12-year-old.

I was almost undone by a prying lens. As we got off the coach, I took out my wallet to hand a tip to the coppers who had provided our escort and one of them said: "Don't do it now, Gouldy. There's a TV camera over there pointing at us." Instead, we thanked them with replica shirts after I asked Syd Neal to sort them out with a couple each.

We got busy almost as soon as we reached the dressing room. While the players were out looking at the pitch, Don called all the staff together to synchronise our watches, then he ordered us to turn them back two minutes. He wasn't finished there. He had Joe Dillon pull the skip to the wall, stand on it and alter the clock. We might as well have ripped up the protocol booklet the FA had sent us several days earlier because the idea was that we were going to be late at every juncture.

Liverpool's players were looking daggers at us when we finally made it out into the tunnel. They seemed irritated and mystified by the hold-up, as did the referee Brian Hill. As we waited to go out, I could see Vinnie baiting their lads. To say the least, there were a few verbals flying around. We were so wound up for a crack at them and Fash was giving it the loud Yidahoi chant – his usual means of psyching himself up and posturing in front of the opposition.

So much had been said and written to put us down and it was typical of the Wimbledon spirit that, in front of a global audience of a billion people, we wanted to see whether we had another shock result in us. It was the biggest betting final in history and we knew we would be the bookies' best friends if we pulled off a win that would rate even higher in the list of upsets than Sunderland's victory over Leeds, or Southampton's over Manchester United.

We put Vinnie on Steve McMahon in midfield and I suppose there was an argument that he might have been sent off in the first half. He clattered into him, was booked and generally didn't give him a moment's peace. And Liverpool realised by then that they had something else to think about.

Don had come back from a lunch on the Friday convinced that we should move Wisey from his usual position on the left wing to the right. The thinking was that he might not only cause them some problems when we had the ball but also help Winko Goodyear (his nickname was adapted from Wingco because the lads reckoned his moustache made him look like a wartime pilot) contain the threat of the newly-crowned Footballer of the Year John Barnes. We erected a double shield to stop the ball getting to him and it worked like a dream. He hardly had a kick.

I admit we had luck on our side at 0-0 when Brian Hill awarded Liverpool a free-kick for a foul by Peter Beardsley on Andy Thorn just before Beardsley put the ball in our net. Lurch deserved that bit of good fortune with the disallowed goal. What a fabulous servant he was to Wimbledon. It's almost impossible to comprehend now but he had been an ever-present for seven seasons in a row and made a wonderful save with his knee from John Aldridge in the first half.

The goal came in the 37th minute. All managers will say that free-kicks that bring goals have been worked on in training – and I'm no different. It was almost identical to one at Newcastle in the sixth round that Gibbo got a great head on to give us the lead. Now Sanch, a Bachelor of Science and our barrack room lawyer, flicked in Wisey's set-piece and had something to shout about.

I would have put my mortgage on big things happening at that South End of the stadium. People wonder why I'm so superstitious but I think there's something in it all, especially in our family's Wembley story. Our kid Trevor played there for England Schoolboys and Sanch's goal came at the same end that Jonathan made a fabulous save at when Bradford City beat Notts County in the Second Division play-off final in 1996. It was also in that goalmouth that I had scored for Arsenal in the League Cup final against Swindon in 1969, when we, like Wimbledon, wore yellow and blue. I'd even stood at the South End on my first visit to the stadium and watched my close pal Geoff Hurst complete his hat-trick in the World Cup final. Oh and we won the FA Cup the day after what would have been my dad's birthday. Don't tell me some things aren't written in the stars.

The lead really gave us something to cling to and we counted off the minutes and seconds to the interval, so we could get some more instructions across to the players. We became a bit cocky towards the end of the first half; 'leery' as I said on camera. Not that Joe Dillon knew it. Long before the lads trudged to the dressing rooms, we sent him on another unusual errand.

It was 84 degrees and concentration was going to be a problem in the heat, so Don and me, having had the players in for training from 3pm to 5pm the previous day to try to replicate the stifling match-day conditions, made sure Joe ran cold baths for half-time to soak the towels. It was an idea Howey brought back from the World Cup in Mexico. When we reached the dressing rooms, we thought we had walked into a scene from Lawrence of Arabia. All the lads had ice-cold towels wrapped round their heads. We stomped round, looking to give out some individual instructions and couldn't tell one player from another. All we could see were eyes. What we couldn't comprehend was how Kenny Dalglish could bear being in his red and grey anorak all afternoon.

In the second half, we threw Laurie Cunningham on for Corky and introduced John Scales in place of Gibbo with orders to run around up front and stop their back four bringing the ball out easily. We reckoned we had a threat on the counter attack if we could get possession out wide to Laurie but generally it was a matter of survival.

Liverpool won a penalty when John Aldridge, who had scored twice in the semi-final against Nottingham Forest, went over under a challenge from Winko. We didn't think it was a penalty and Wisey enjoyed having a dig at Aldridge after Lurch became the first goalkeeper to save a penalty in an FA Cup final. I stood up, clenching my fists and shouting 'You little beauty.' Don grabbed me by the shirt and said: "Sit down you daft young bugger. There are still 25 minutes left."

Lurch had also saved a kick from Brian Rice at Forest a couple of weeks before the final and spent an hour on the training ground on the Friday with Corky and Wisey. They put the famous Aldridge 'stutter' into their run-up to create the feel of what Lurch could face in the biggest match of his life. That was their idea and we had a job getting them in from training. For all their madcap ways, they were ultra-professional. Aldridge had put away 11 penalties that season after all and never previously missed one for Liverpool, so it was a massive feather in our skipper's cap when his shot was saved.

Maybe Liverpool sensed then it wasn't going to be their day and we had the measure of them. I remember the latter stages of the game being incredibly tense but we were equal to everything they could throw at us and defended as though our lives depended on it.

When the final whistle sounded, I just fell into the arms of those around me. I was so ecstatic. It had been a long, difficult journey and I just wanted to share the moment with those who had travelled it with me.......Don, Dave Kemp, Joe, Sid, even our taxi driver Pat. We shook the hands of the Liverpool staff, who couldn't believe they had lost, then I ran on and leaped into Vinnie's arms. I'm an emotional person and was walking a fine line.

This was the proudest and happiest day of my managerial career, probably of my life in football, and I was utterly joyous. But I knew I quickly had to take a grip of my senses and hold everything together. As manager, you also have to keep another two dozen or so blokes on the rein, including other squad and staff members, and I was demanding of them. They were urged to be gentlemanly and humble in victory, do the right things in their celebrations and make sure they clapped the Liverpool players as they went up for their medals. Vincent grabbed me between the legs and yelled: "Just shut it!"

My words obviously didn't get through fully. Vinnie promptly grabbed his own genitals in front of a BBC camera and shook them vigorously – an action that prompted a deluge of complaints among all the messages of congratulation we received; so much so that my secretary Mad Madeleine couldn't cope with all the correspondence and had to take on an assistant to send out replies. I needed eyes everywhere on that pitch, even after the final whistle.

I was so grateful to Don for his advice. He was much more experienced in such protocol and was well ahead of me in recognising the danger signs and reminding the players how they should behave. One thing he didn't have to tell me was to acknowledge my family. I had already looked up to where I knew Marge was sitting and blown her a kiss.

One by one, the players filed wearily up those famous 39 steps to receive their winners' medals from Princess Di and a hug and kiss from Sam Hammam. How they regretted that it couldn't have been the other way round. Managers and coaches weren't given medals in those days – Sam later generously had some miniature FA Cups made for the management staff and directors – but after waving again to Marge and the boys, I ran up the stairs and gave Sam the biggest hug. I didn't want to leave anyone out.

I was so pleased for Lurch when he became the first goalkeeper-captain to be presented with the FA Cup. To be named man of the match was the icing on the cake for him on a very special day. He had played something like 350 successive games for the club and even had his dad watching him that afternoon for the first time. The occasion was something he would be reminded of over and over again because he could see the twin towers from his house.

It wasn't long before I was thinking of another keeper; one sat up in the Gods. After getting my hands on the Cup, I waved the base of it in the direction of Bob Wilson on the TV gantry and gave him a big thumbs-up. It seemed a long time since our agitated telephone chat that morning but I knew he was always there for me. Dave Bassett was also doing some TV work at the final and we picked him out and let him know he hadn't been forgotten. He had done a lot of work on the foundations of this success.

I told the lads to make that lap of honour the slowest walk of their lives. Just as when I'd set out to put a rein on Kenny Dalglish before kick-off, I wanted them to savour and remember every second of it, not have them wake up next day and realise everything had gone by in a flash. That said, while I was carrying the base of the Cup, I turned to Howey and he was nowhere to be seen. He had won it before and decided to head for the dressing room as soon as he could.

You can imagine how gutted Liverpool's players were, especially their captain Alan Hansen, but they had won enough. This was our day. Wembley had witnessed one of its biggest ever upsets and it would take a lot of digesting by the football fraternity.

Don was giving a TV interview to Tony Gubba in a spare room off the tunnel when I butted in to answer what I thought was an unkind question. It had rankled all day that the media wanted Liverpool to win and have their double and I got a bit more anger off my chest there and then in front of the camera. In fact, it was a major rant; no holds barred.

John Motson famously called it a triumph for the Crazy Gang over the Culture Club, and Sam, seeing me in the tunnel afterwards, demonstrated his knack of coming up with a colourful phrase of his own. He had been in football for a few years but said he felt like he'd just lost his virginity. And he still had his eye on business during all the celebrations. In the tunnel, he said he was putting the entire squad on the transfer list, claiming this was the time when their value was at its highest. And he was being deadly serious.

The lads didn't get rich with our famous triumph. There was no win bonus in place for lifting the FA Cup, just the £2,500 appearance money for reaching the final. I had to remind them in Wembley week not to bleat about it because FA regulations meant there was nothing that could be done at that late stage to alter it. And they had, after all, agreed their bonuses at the start of the season.

Lawrie Sanchez, for example, made less out of the day than his brother, who put £100 on him at 33-1 to score the first goal and walked off with £3,400. And my mate Bill Smith won hundreds after backing us at the same price. I trust they had a good family night out with the proceeds.

I grabbed hold of the Cup as we left the stadium and didn't let go until we got back to the Cannizaro House Hotel, raising a cheer from the lads when I spotted my mum almost the moment we departed the ground. I jumped off the bus to have my picture taken with her. Nor did I miss a chance to show our prize off whenever we stopped at traffic lights or saw anyone giving us a wave.

It still rankled a bit that my day at Wembley with West Ham in 1975 hadn't been as special as it should have been, especially for the players' families, and I didn't want us to skimp as well. Hotels can be quiet places, so we arranged for a marquee to be erected on the pitch at Plough Lane on the Saturday night, win or lose, with each player given a table for ten.

On mine were Marge, Richard and Jonathan, Mum and her partner Bernard, Marge's mum and dad, and our good friends Patsy and Gordon Fry. Trevor, his wife Jackie and their sons Robert and Darren were on another table.

Everybody was happy, or almost everybody. During the festivities, I had a tap on my shoulder from a woman who said: "I'm Mrs Gibson, Terry's mother. Why did you take him off?" It was too late for me to explain the intricacies of how our substitute John Scales had got round the pitch so well with his fresher legs but Marge came to my rescue brilliantly. As the band struck up, she intervened by saying: "Oooh, they're playing our tune. Let's dance."

The lads couldn't wait to see the Sunday papers, mainly of course to pore over the coverage of the game. But they soon turned to the front pages when a copy of the News of the World arrived during the early hours. I nipped out to the gents in the dressing room and found a group of them crowding round having a read and a right good laugh at Fash's sexual antics. He was hot on slaughtering his team-mates for any indiscretions and now he was getting it back big-time. All their Christmases had come at once and they made a block order of the paper.

It was lovely that Jimmy Hill was at the party to share in my happiest football hours. He presented that night's Match of the Day highlights from the marquee and remained a very special man in my life. But not even his presence could make me resist having another go at the Beeb and reminding them that everyone had suggested we were there just to make up the numbers. It was a watered-down version of the rant I'd had on the same subject at full-time. This theory that Liverpool would stroll it really did get up my nose and I was a bit frosty in the post-match press conference as well.

Every top team in the world have since copied the sort of free-kick that brought Sanch's goal and many have followed our lead with Vinnie's long throw. Can we honestly have been the worst thing ever to hit English football when we have come up with routines that other clubs have been so keen to pick up on?

Having organised the players, looked after their families, picked the team, given countless interviews and been the man at the front of everything for weeks, I now felt shattered as well as elated. This was what I'd dreamed of going back more than 30 years to those days as Matthews or Mortensen in the garden at 40 Forknell Avenue, Wyken, Coventry.

We just had a ball and loved every minute of the Cup Final experience. We drank champagne like it was going out of fashion and kept cuddling that silverware like a new-born baby. Terry Phelan found himself as the man in possession at the end of a very long night and got a lift in a police car to make sure he wasn't mugged walking back to the hotel. We weren't about to go all high and mighty just because we were FA Cup holders and Sam would probably have turned his nose up at reimbursing a taxi fare anyway!

A few days later, before a photo call, Sam was running up and down in a panic saying we had lost the Cup. He didn't know I had put it in a box hidden by two comfortable chairs in the 'bunker' – the name I gave my tiny office in the main corridor at Plough Lane. The Cup went almost everywhere with me. I even had it under the duvet with me at the flat after Marge went back to Portishead to restore some sense of normality in our sons' lives. It wasn't half cold when I rolled over in the night and brushed against it.

When we took it out to functions, which was often, we treated it with the utmost care. It was unthinkable that it might be damaged while in our possession, so some of the ladies in the office sewed 12 yellow dusters together to make a bag for it as protection.

In case I ever forget the feeling of elation, on our wall there's a lovely framed picture of Marge and me, dressed to the nines, holding the silverware. The irony is that the photo was taken at a ball at Coventry in 1989 rather than at Wimbledon 12 months earlier. But it's still a special keepsake.

We couldn't have been happier when we paraded through the streets of Wimbledon to show the trophy off to some 25,000 ecstatic fans and were cheered on to the balcony of the old Town Hall. Our fans had blocked the High Street when we returned the night before and they were out in force again now. Whatever jokes about small crowds that were cracked at our expense, we were kings in our castle that weekend. It was a magical time.

We felt cheated that the European ban meant we couldn't go and play in the Cup Winners' Cup. I would have loved another crack at that and the players deserved the opportunity, even if I would have had my hands full keeping an eye on them on the trips. What the Parisians and Milanese would have made of us is anyone's guess. It was not easy keeping a lid on things and I never opened a newspaper without having my heart in my mouth, a point that was underlined only two or three days after Wembley.

That's when Alan Cork, lucky man, had his testimonial match against Chelsea, and Vinnie Jones mooned the crowd. Then, with some encouragement from certain supporters, the rest of them did the same at half-time. I saw what was about to happen as they formed a semi circle and raced from my seat next to Marge in the stand to try to stop them. But a French photographer was already flashing away in a more acceptable manner and sold his picture to the Daily Mirror. I had a right go at the players as police milled round the corridor asking awkward questions. It was one incident I couldn't prevent and it cost us a £10,000 fine.

A good friend of ours, a councillor called Patsy Fry, suggested there should be a second tour with the Cup – this time for me in Portishead. It was by car rather than bus but there I was holding it aloft through the sun roof as we cruised round the local streets. They surprised me by throwing in a get-together at the workingmen's club and the presentation of a plaque that now hangs on our wall and reads: "Congratulations, Bobby, on taking Wimbledon to an outstanding victory in the FA Cup Final. From all your Portishead friends and supporters." We also have a pottery ball showing the magical scoreline: Liverpool 0 Wimbledon 1.

Our kid and his family were among the guests Patsy lined up, so were Bob and Megs Wilson. Bob and me had a good laugh as we washed the dishes back at our house, with the FA Cup sparkling at our side on the draining board. And I'll come clean at last and admit that we did do the trophy a bit of harm. Marge was handing it to Willo when the lid fell and bounced on the kitchen surface, then the floor. The spill broke the band sealing the lid to the main pot but the matter went unreported at Lancaster Gate. I'd had enough trouble there already with my players.

What a memorable few weeks it had been – a victory against massive odds, a saved penalty and a never-to-be-forgotten meeting with Lady Di. We felt like royalty ourselves. In an effort to cement relations, we duly sent the Princes, Harry and William, replica Wimbledon shirts after our victory. Not that I ever remember them popping in at Plough Lane.

A Spirited Follow-Up

The second year is always difficult and there was a massive overhaul in the summer of 1988 as Andy Thorn and our skipper Dave Beasant went to Newcastle and we worked hard to fill the big holes. John Scales, one of our substitutes at Wembley, was given his head and played almost 300 games for the club before eventually going to Liverpool for £3.5m and later to Tottenham. Someone obviously agreed with me that he could play.

There would have been another big-name departure as well if Wisey had had his way. He knew from Eric Hall that Tottenham and Terry Venables were sniffing round after him but I was digging my heels in for more money and things came to a head when we were away on another pre-season trip to Sweden.

I was sat quietly in my room one night, preparing the next day's training, when I heard these fireworks going off. I looked out of my door to see a rocket roar down the corridor, past my nose and smash into the wall. Wisey was seriously overstepping the mark and taunted me by saying: "Gouldy, you'll have to send me home now." To which I replied: "You're going nowhere, Dennis, and by the way, you're fined two weeks wages." I understood the lure of a big club to him but Tottenham weren't coming up with enough, so he never went there.

After we returned home, he handed a transfer request in every morning and was a right pain in the arse. Day after day, I just laughed, screwed them up and threw them in the bin. We needed the Biffa lorry round seven days a week. Eventually, he got an improved contract out of us but his big break came the following summer when I rang him to say Chelsea had offered £1.6m and ask if he wanted to go. He was off in a flash.

In the months following Wembley, I signed Hans Segers from Nottingham Forest, Keith Curle from Reading for £500,000 and Roger Joseph from

Brentford. I also went to Burton Albion to check on big John Gayle and came back with him and another forward, Steve Cotterill. But my rebuilding was still in its early stages when we returned to the twin towers for the Charity Shield against Liverpool.

I feared we might get a right tanking with them in the mood for revenge, so to lose only 2-1 was a decent effort. I wore all my lucky gear again and was not displeased with our performance. Sanch was captain and we had Simon Tracey in goal but he was unable to take a leaf out of Lurch's book. John Aldridge put two past him.

I was so busy with the overhaul of my squad that when my Nan Gould passed away and we had her cremated, I carried her ashes round in the car for a couple of weeks. It took me longer than I thought it would to find time to pop up to Coventry, as arranged with the family, to scatter them in a rose garden. I didn't beat myself up over it. She would have had a right chuckle that she was being driven round by 'Our Bob,' especially as the FA Cup was sometimes in the car as well.

There were other additions to the squad on top of the major signings. I brought in Gary Brooke from Spurs, Detzi Kruszynski from Poland, Paul McGee from Colchester and Steve Anthrobus from Millwall. I still loved an uncut diamond. But I also had a decent idea by then of what I was worth and had gone to see Sam about a pay increase. He accused me of blackmail and then put my salary up from £30,000 to £50,000.

I insisted Don Howe was paid the same, so he had a handy rise as well, although he had other things on his mind. Don was also senior coach for Bobby Robson in the England set-up and went off to the European Championships finals in West Germany before having a triple heart bypass operation.

Don missed the first few weeks of 1988-89 and I had Dave Kemp at my side. Don's first session back was on a school field by the motorway when we were preparing for a League Cup game at Barnsley. He could easily have had more time off because there was nothing glamorous about that trip but it was typical of him that he wanted to be back at work as soon as possible. He was a true pro. He even became frustrated that afternoon because the lads were struggling with their set-pieces, so he went to show them how it was done. To a man, they shouted: "Don't run, think of your heart!" He just shook his head, smiled and realised how much he had missed the banter.

We were proud that things didn't tail off after the Cup success. We finished 12th in 1988-89, when our reign as holders ended with a Stuart McCall goal at Everton in the quarter-final. Then we came in eighth in 1989-90 and in the process repaid Liverpool for some of the pain we had caused them at Wembley. Aston Villa were looking a good bet for the title under Graham Taylor when we went there in the March, beat them 3-0 and cost them momentum they were never able to regain. Liverpool came through and were crowned champions yet again.

Not that my media profile was as big as it might have been. Sam never let me do newspaper, radio or TV work, arguing that I worked for him and Wimbledon rather than big news organisations. The only time I was allowed to comment was before and after games and he didn't shy away from making the point in black and white. I once had to send a copy of my contract to my solicitor, who rang in mid-transmission to say: "My fax machine is on fire. We're up to page 45 and it's still spewing out. How much more of this is there?"

One particular clause in there never failed to astound my managerial counterparts. Sam insisted that he should have the option to change my selected team 45 minutes before kick-off if he chose. Sparks always flew between us anyway but the balloon went up when I left out Terry Phelan, Wisey, Fash, Fairweather, Gibbo and Vaughan Ryan after we lost in the Cup at West Brom in January, 1990.

I accused the players of coasting and behaving like fat cats and brought in Micky Bennett, who I'd just signed from Charlton, Paul McGee, John Gayle and Brian 'Sweaty' McAllister for the home game against Arsenal. Sam was steaming. The directors were ringing me on the Friday telling me to change my line-up but I dug in my heels, saying if Sam wanted to alter it, he should see me on match-day afternoon in the bunker. There was no sight of him.

During the game, Gayley battered Tony Adams and Steve Bould into waving the white flag after a quarter of an hour, then Bennett came in off the right wing to score the winner three minutes from the end. Sam ran into the bunker at the end and we were nose-to-nose, snarling for a few seconds, before a grin broke across his face and he said: "I no do that again. You manager, I owner." And we're there thumping the air in delight instead of punching each others' lights out.

Restraint wasn't always the order of the day and a headache I didn't foresee was deciding whether or not to adopt a Southpaw style after stepping into a makeshift ring to resolve what would today be called some 'issues.' At Wimbledon, disputes were sorted out with a good old-fashioned scrap while everyone else crowded around, egging the participants on.

It all started when a session I was taking at the training ground was interrupted by the shout 'circle.' I realised that two of the lads were having what Mrs Merton might describe as a heated debate. The other players knew what was coming and were preparing for a few minutes' break and entertainment as spectators in someone else's dispute.

I was bewildered because I had never seen or known anything like it before. But I took my place in the circle as the two of them grappled and wrestled in front of us. Then, after a couple of minutes of untidy brawling, they got up, shook hands and we all resumed our work, the air having been cleared.

A few weeks later, I had a pop, in the verbal sense, at Wisey and up went the familiar shout from one of the lads. Wisey was soon at me, mauling and rolling around to great cheers. He was popular in the dressing room and there are no prizes for guessing who his team-mates wanted to see get the bloody nose. It was all about self-protection. No punching was allowed but, as he pulled me over, I landed on his fist and felt this excruciating pain in my side.

Wisey was hailed as the winner and I clambered to my feet, determined to keep a smile on my face and some dignity. It was difficult not to show the pain I was in and the session was over for me. Don Howe saw it through and, as I walked off with our physio Steve Allen, I said to him: "Don't let those bastards know how much I'm hurting." I'd cracked a rib and needed strapping up.

Fash and Sanch had a big go once, then there was an episode involving young Vaughan Ryan. We had beaten Charlton 3-1 at our place one Boxing Day morning but he was still moaning about everyone and everything as he came off, so I clipped him round the head and said: "Shut up, we've got three points, enjoy your Christmas." It leaked out to the newspapers I'd clipped him and they went for me big time.

When we went back into training a couple of days later, the squad were all agitating for a circle and I was in there again. The strange part is that the press were milling all over the training ground that day, sniffing around for a possible follow-up to the story, so I insisted we went as far away from the buildings as we could, hopefully out of their sight. I took my place in the middle of the mob and heard Vaughan say he wasn't up for it. Wisey grabbed him, pushed him in and said 'Yes, you are' before he leapt in as well and the two of them gave me a right good hiding. I was tending to a slow trickle of blood from my face afterwards when Fash and John Gayle leaned over and said: "We want a piece of you next time as well."

Never had the Crazy Gang been more crazy. This code of conduct was already in place from Dave Bassett's time and such was the unique team spirit we had that I thought I had better go along with it. I'm sure they would have rebelled if I had called a halt to it, barmy though it was. We all thrived on it; owner, manager, players and obviously the media.

As West Brom manager a couple of years later, I hung a couple of pairs of boxing gloves on the back of my office door as a reminder. I didn't really expect to use them but Colin West was having problems with my coach Stuart Pearson and, having heard how the Wimbledon lads used to like involving their manager when settling scores, he invited me into 'the ring' in one of the buildings we used as a training base near The Hawthorns.

I suppose the gloves made it slightly more sophisticated than the wrestling of my Plough Lane days but, no sooner had I got them laced on and I'd drawn breath to say 'go' than he caught me a beauty on the nose with a right hook. I was bleeding again and Westy's got his hands up, hailing himself as the winner, with the lads all cheering around us. Every time I see him now, he pretends to be winding up a hay-maker for me and shouts 'bop!"

It was probably inevitable that the practice would spill over into my time with Wales. It was towards the end of my reign when we were training at the Spitty Stadium in Newport before a home game that I noticed a particularly sour atmosphere during the warm-up. I decided that John Hartson was at the centre of it and said to Neville Southall: "Hold my watch." He replied: "You're not having a circle with him, are you?" Too right I was.

John was a big ox of a lad and I could definitely have chosen an easier opponent but I wanted to get rid of the bad feeling hanging in the air. "Come on, if you want a piece of me," I said to him. "Let's get it out of your system." He started with great gusto and didn't let up, giving me the biggest hiding of my life. I'd taken the lid off the pressure pot, all right. I was on the ground with Hartson pounding seven lumps of shit out of me and Giggsy and Sparky

Hughes laughing their socks off, probably thinking how unlikely it was that they would ever see Sir Alex or Gianluca Vialli in this predicament.

I've been asked whether I compromised my authority by being left lying in the dust like that but I don't regret it for one moment. The players could see I would have a go even if I had no chance of winning. I would fight to the last and wanted them to do the same for me on a match-day. It was a way of breaking down any adhesions in a squad.

My 'circle' career ended there with the record of 4 bouts, 0 wins, 4 defeats. But my biggest fight was still a few hours away. Marge always came to stay at the team hotel on the night before Wales home matches and, as I undressed ready for bed, the questions started. My back was covered in scratches following my grapple with Big John, as well as one or two bruises, and I had a hell of a job convincing her where they had come from. I survived to take that decision on points but it could easily have been the knock-out blow.

Sam – A Class Apart

Sam Hammam loved to create a great atmosphere. Once, when the going was tough, I said the players needed a day out to lift their spirits and asked if the club would finance a trip to Sandown Races. There was no money as usual but Sam said "I have idea" and came back with £3,000 in one hand and £5,000 in the other before placing it on the goal-line at Plough Lane while lining all the lads up at the other end.

He announced that the squad could have their day out if they beat him in a race down the pitch. He had a huge start but Terry Phelan pissed it, so did Keith Curle and the players were whooping around as they got their hands on their betting money. Sam didn't do it by halves at the meeting either. He hired a hospitality area and invited the wives and girlfriends along as well.

In the last race, Sam and Wisey picked a no-hoper at hundreds to one and, fuck me, it won! That was him all over. Larger than life and up for a laugh. The players loved him to death because he was fun. He would join in their card games when the stakes were often forfeits rather than money. More than once, he got off the coach with his tie cut in half, the sleeve ripped off his jacket or with a trouser leg missing. And he lapped it up and always came back for more. He was astute enough to realise the value of tremendous team spirit.

I had a very volatile relationship with him but we respected and loved each other and still do. He brought out the best in me and I'd like to think I extracted something good from him. We had some great years together, although he could have looked after me better financially.

Stanley Reed was a wonderful front man for him. He was well liked by everybody, including the fans, who recall him kicking an imaginary ball when he went over to give them a wave. He was such a jolly soul who loved being part of the Crazy Gang as well, even approaching 80. He would come in the dressing room after we had won and start the sing-along, usually with: "Here we are again, happy as can be, all good friends and jolly good company." He also went on every tour with us and, when the time was right for a night out, he would settle the bill with his own credit card. He could put the fear of God into you as well with his strong opinions and I knew I was in trouble if he said to me: "Let's go for a walk in God's fresh air." But he was a very generous man, who included me in his will when he passed away a few years ago.

Things were a bit tight in the Gould household after I'd finally left Sam's flat and bought an apartment in Earlsfield, half a mile from Plough Lane. I had a £70,000 mortgage there and one of £25,000 in Portishead, with a repayment rate of 16 per cent. I was left with £20 a week after bills and Marge and me often went with my staff for a tuna and banana pizza (known as A Pregnant Lady) on a Saturday night, so that was that taken care of as well.

Jonathan was living with me at the time while he worked in the city at Barclays Bank. The arrangement was good for father-son bonding. I had long since told him he wouldn't make an outfield player because he couldn't run, although I had given him some games as a right-back in my Football Combination side at Bristol Rovers. He had really wanted to be a striker and had a decent enough technique and shot. It was just lack of pace that let him down. As an alternative, he had a try-out in goal for Clevedon Town and now, on my free nights in South West London, I worked hard on converting him into a keeper. He also had a few weeks' training at Derby and found Peter Shilton and Arthur Cox outstanding tutors.

Wimbledon's results were still terrific considering we were struggling along on pitiful gates of below 8,000. As well as winning handsomely at Villa, we caned Chelsea 5-2 at Stamford Bridge, dumped Arsenal again and did the double over Tottenham. And we were still doing things off the cuff. Although I prided myself on being organised, we never booked training facilities when we went on overnight stays. All we did was ask the hotel staff where the nearest park was because we didn't want our opponents spying on our set-pieces.

On one trip to Everton, we got pissed off with Wisey and Fairweather taking ages over a set-piece from the left near the end of our training session. Wisey eventually whipped one in and Eric Young headed the ball smack on and then recoiled when he realised he had dog shit splattered all over his bandana. Unfortunately for Lurch, the ball hit the bar and rebounded into his face, so he had a dollop on him as well. It was like a Benny Hill sketch when the players set off in pursuit of the culprits. The pair would have suffered the normal punishment if they had been caught – to have their shorts whipped off and be left half naked in a public park – but I think they were quick enough that time to get away because they had 40 yards start. The session was obviously over, though. It was mayhem.

I had the players on my case when we went for a mid-season break in Spain early in my reign and I flew Marge out independently for a few days in a nearby hotel. As chance would have it, I was running a high temperature and was confined to my room, so Don took training and Marge came round to nurse me. The players hadn't met her at that point and I knew they would slaughter me if they spotted her, so I got up at five o'clock to smuggle her into a taxi the day I felt better. But Wisey and Corky just happened to be on their way home from a long night out as we were saying our goodbyes.

"Fack me, Gouldy, good pull!" Wisey shouted when he saw us in mid-kiss. Marge was well used to hearing industrial language, often from me, and just laughed. She took the comment as quite a compliment. I had stayed in bed the first couple of days but no-one in the dressing room was going to believe any more that it was because I'd been ill. With Marge gone, I waited for the backlash.......and it came sure enough. I opened my bedroom door one day to find all my clothes either floating upside down in a full bath or hung off the balcony, with even my shoes on there, tied together. As if that carnage wasn't enough, the windows and mirrors were smeared in my shaving cream. Another challenging day in charge of the monsters of St Trinian's.....

Eric Young was one of the quieter lads and had his eyes opened soon after joining us from Brighton. He arrived each morning carrying a bag from his former club, with a seagull motif on it, and would pick up anything the other players discarded. Programmes, shin pads, plasters, you name it.....in it would go for safe keeping. He was a kleptomaniac.

This strange behaviour hadn't escaped the others' attention and, when he went in for treatment one day, they set fire to his bag and personal keepsakes while doing a Red Indian war dance round it. The flames climbed so high that they set off the fire alarm and within five minutes, the Fire Brigade were on the scene, hoses at the ready. There was never a dull moment.

The players saw me pissed for the first time on a trip to Sweden. Correction: For the only time. Don was brilliant as a go-between and, when he was absent after his heart surgery, I was guilty of trying too hard to be one of the lads. Unusually, because I don't drink much, I got absolutely larruped and threw up on the training ground next morning while we were warming up. Sympathy was in short supply. The lads told me they had a way of waking me up, then grabbed me by the arms and legs and chucked me in the lake. Their parting words were: "Dry yourself off, sober up and we'll see you tomorrow." They organised training themselves and I left them to their nights out after that.

Detzi Kruszynski received the same treatment when our Richard fixed the squad up with a visit to Army HQ at Sandhurst. The lads were doing some bonding exercises involving carrying telegraph poles when Vinnie ordered his team to put theirs down. He thought Detzi wasn't pulling his weight and took it upon himself to organise a different routine – dumping our Polish midfielder in the water.

Vincent was the highest-maintenance footballer I ever handled. Controversy was never far away with him and, when the storm-clouds gathered, so did the press. Paul Gascoigne was playing out of his skin when we were due to face Newcastle at Plough Lane early in 1988 and I decided the best way to deal with him was through a rigid man-marking job. There was only one candidate for the role. We staged a practice match between the first team and youth team and detailed one of the talented young lads to masquerade as Gazza, with Vinnie told to follow him everywhere.

Suddenly, Vinnie was strolling and I had a go at him. He yelled at Don and me: "I'll do what I want." I shouted back: "If you want to play tomorrow, do your job. Otherwise, you're dropped." He calmed down sufficiently to ask us what he should do if Gazza tried to run past him. I said: "Oh, I don't know… ….grab his bollocks."

I didn't realise how literally he had taken my orders until I picked up a paper on the Monday after our 0-0 draw and my eyes popped out at my first sight of that iconic picture. A photographer had perfectly captured the moment he put his painful squeeze on and he hadn't even waited until Gazza was taking him on. He took an eye-watering handful as they waited in a crowded area for a set-piece to be delivered.

I had known Italian players grab the hairs on my legs but this was something else. Much though you try to stretch the rules, it was obviously going too far and we were lambasted all over again. Keeping Vincent on a tight leash was always a challenge and it was inevitable the football fraternity would look down their noses even more at us after that.

We could have done without being sent to St James' Park only two weeks later in the FA Cup fifth round. Vinnie wanted to douse the bad feeling that was hanging around by flying to Tyneside and posing with Gazza before the tie for a friendly picture. I wasn't too keen and Newcastle's manager Willie McFaul buried the idea altogether by saying he wanted nothing to do with it.

Vinnie was a complex character. He spoke to us about having had family issues as a youngster and you didn't need to be Hercule Poirot to work out that the rest of the world was against him, united in its belief that he had no place in the First Division. I tried to be tolerant and kind towards him and wanted to make a better person as well as a better footballer of him. But I had to spell out the need for us all to be aware of our responsibilities.

I went mad when Vinnie clashed with Kenny Dalglish and did his infamous piece in the paper threatening to rip his ear off and spit in the hole; and I'm not even sure he said 'spit.' Another time, we popped over for a game on the Isle of Wight, which I thought was a sleepy enough place to guarantee that the players would stay out of trouble, but Vinnie got himself sent off. When we climbed off the ferry on the mainland, I told him I was banning him from the club indefinitely.

After missing the start of the season, he returned and was soon in more hot water for a tackle on Gary Stevens that went unpunished by the referee but so incensed the Tottenham fans that Don Howe had to throw a coat over him as he drove him away from White Hart Lane in his car.

The straw that broke the camel's back came when Vinnie was sent off at Everton for an alleged butt on Kevin Ratcliffe that sparked a right set-to among the players. A camera crew from London Weekend Television arrived at the training ground on the Monday morning and upset Vinnie by stepping out of their campervan and calling him the most hated footballer in England. I accused them of trespassing and let down the tyres on one of their vehicles while the police were called . It's no good me denying it because it's on bloody Youtube!

Don had his say afterwards and raged in the dressing room: "What am I doing here with you thugs? You are barbarians." Sam was bitterly upset as well and enough was enough. We couldn't handle it anymore. Vinnie was bringing the club too many bad headlines and had to go.

There had long been a need to treat him as a special case to the detriment of the squad and we were used to having to administer some tlc. For all the problems he caused, he was also loveable. He relished the dressing-room camaraderie, was a fantastic worker and had great feet. He was a ferocious tackler and his stamina meant he was always in the top five in the long runs. On top of that, he took a few set-pieces, had a huge throw and became keen to improve. At times, it was as if he didn't want the hard-man image anymore.

Unfortunately, he and Fash loved their reputation at the same time because it brought them attention and they looked after each other. The critics could see only the thuggish side of their game – and that was something they rarely missed a chance to play up to, like when we had Manchester United at our place. Viv Anderson was knocked spark out by Fash in the tunnel and Alex Ferguson flew into our dressing room in a rage to apprehend the culprit himself. Unfortunately, he picked on Eric instead.

The mistaken identity didn't keep the heat off. Fash was charged by the FA and had the committee – and me – in a state of amazement by producing a huge cardboard plan showing the location of the tunnel, the dressing rooms and all the key people. It didn't do him much good. He was fined £2,000 and banned for three matches. We'd seen it coming.

I was always at FA HQ with our lot. I had a season ticket on the tube to Lancaster Gate. After one hearing, when we were no doubt smarting over another fine, Sam said to the gentlemen in suits as we left: "In my country, camels are very valuable. How many do you want as payment?" I grabbed him by the lapels and dragged him out before our punishment was increased for contempt of court.

We weren't the only club who thought Vinnie was worth persevering with. Howard Wilkinson obviously felt he had something as well because he eventually took him to Leeds for £650,000 and saw to it that he had several more years as a top-flight footballer after he helped them win promotion from the Second Division. He was lucky to play for the right people and certainly couldn't have had a better tutor at Wimbledon than Don.

Fash was not as good technically but was almost as big a challenge. I had inherited him and very quickly worked out that I was happier with him in our side than having him playing against us. Every day, he would see how far he could push us and he stepped closer and closer to that line, usually by turning up late. Eventually, as the fines became more and more regular, I told him to just leave a few signed cheques to save us all time and we would fill in the amounts and dates as necessary.

He used to intimidate the opposition by wrapping a towel around himself and positioning himself in the corridor, all brawn and torso, just as they were arriving. Then he would eyeball them. He was a big wind-up merchant but the odd-ball characters we had in there like him – and myself for that matter – helped keep that infamous team spirit topped up. The struggle was maintaining discipline while keeping alive the Crazy Gang culture.

When that team eventually moved on from Wimbledon, they went for a total of £12m-£13m and they were all big successes because they were so strong-minded. Lurch, Wisey and Vinnie were the three big sales but, from around the same period, Curley, John Scales, Andy Thorn, Eric and Terry Phelan all went on to have good careers elsewhere. And, a couple of years after the Cup win, I signed Warren Barton from Maidstone for £300,000 and he later joined Newcastle for £4m.

My problem wasn't putting money in the coffers. It was identifying the right kind of players. They had to be young, quick and of the right character. I wanted our naughty teenager of a club to become a mature adult and it still upsets me that Sam left me driving round in a Fiat Croma. I asked him for a Merc. Perhaps he was cautious because of the episode when I'd persuaded him to replace the painted concrete floor at Plough Lane with some tiles. We were playing Manchester United soon after when we noticed one or two of the tiles had risen slightly. Sid Neal, a lovely fella, had always been against the idea of a spruce-up and said: "Told you, look! I bet there's a sewer overflow."

I also thought the referee's room needed a makeover. In my first year at the club, we hadn't had a single penalty at home and I thought a little buttering-up wouldn't go amiss, so we had their spartan facilities smartened up and left the officials some sandwiches, a bowl of fruit, dressing gowns, luxury towels and an after-match beer. Coincidence or not, we were awarded six penalties there in my second season.

In other ways, we were still keen to make a trip to Plough Lane a one-off experience. I had read somewhere that Liverpool had a superstition whereby Kenny Dalglish or Bruce Grobbelaar would always leave their dressing room last and turn the light off. I ordered the electrician to doctor the switch so they couldn't do it but Kenny told me over a drink in the bunker afterwards that it was something they only did at Anfield. Oh well, we did them with the clocks at Wembley.......you can't win them all.

Vinnie had his own ideas on bringing Liverpool down a peg or two. Underneath the famous 'This is Anfield' sign, he scribbled a message to the effect 'like we're bovvered' and, when they came to play us in South London, he stuck up a handwritten note announcing: 'This is Plough Lane.'

Considering how pokey our ground was, it was amazing the press didn't pick up on one story after Brian Clough was arrested there during a match. It was just before Forest played Luton in the 1989 League Cup final at Wembley and came while Cloughie was banned from the touchline, word having come back to us about how a week earlier he shouted messages down to the coaches in the dug-out from his seat in the directors' box.

At our place, the police seemed primed for when he started bellowing instructions. An officer was even positioned near the directors box. I disagreed with what was going on because Cloughie was a mentor to me. In an effort to prevent an altercation, I had rung Forest's no 2 Alan Hill, suggesting he came and saw me at the ground on the Friday and I would point out a seat his gaffer could have just behind the dug-out.

I made it clear Cloughie would be in trouble if he shouted from up there but he still opted for the VIP area and Marge, who used to sit right behind our dug-out, tapped me on the shoulder when we were one or two up and really getting at them, to let me know that things were kicking off behind us. I turned round and was dismayed to see Brian being escorted from his seat.

I raced down the tunnel to see what was going on and the police were in the away dressing room. I reminded them that this was one of the game's greatest-ever managers they were messing with. But Sam shouted at me: "Get back out there and do your job." Cloughie was then escorted from the ground to a police observation box 50 yards away, where he could watch the rest of our victory but have no influence on it.

He must have been saddened at the incident but what happened the following season was vintage Cloughie. When we played at Forest, he sent a coach down to collect all the officers, including the one who had arrested him, and paid for their seats in the stand. He even sorted out their food and drinks. That was him all over and I loved him.

Soon after Don Howe had returned following his major heart surgery, the two of us went to the City Ground to watch a game and, like scouts and visiting coaches do, got up to leave ten minutes before the end to avoid the traffic. But Cloughie's secretary Carole intercepted us on the way out and was holding a presentation box containing a beautiful cut-glass vase. She handed it to Don and said it was from Mr and Mrs Clough to wish him a full recovery.

With Richard off by this time doing his two years' training as an Army cadet, Marge was free to live with me and I needed her moral support as tensions mounted. Sam was the cleverest man I had ever met and taught me, among many other things, to always read a contract from the back. He was also one of the hardest-working colleagues I ever had and hated taking holidays as much as he hated you going off on yours.

Our relationship was showing signs of strain, not helped by the fact Marge and me were about to fly off for a break in Kenya. Sam and me had an argument one summer's day and he said: "I sack you." I told my solicitor and, because there wasn't much else to do while the players were off, he advised me to go and do a job around the club that I enjoyed. So I mowed the pitch. The next day, I cut it cross-ways. Then I trimmed it again the morning after that. I'd seen more grass on a snooker table by the end of my labours.

News of these unusual goings-on were being relayed by the secretary Adrian Cook to the Middle East, where Sam was away on business. But there was a complication. Sam was busy at the time trying to install his brother Ned on the board and I still found it in me to intervene when Ned got into difficulty while addressing the families of a year's intake of youngsters. I was at the meeting and helped him out.

When Sam returned to London, he called a meeting at the training ground and it was like the shoot-out at the OK Corral as I got out of my car and we stood facing each other for a few seconds, each considering our next move. Then he greeted me with the words: "I no sack you." I taunted him by saying he didn't have the bottle. We hugged each other and he said: "You good man."

He came round to my place in Earlsfield one night with the chairman Stanley Reed and I convinced myself some serious espionage was being planned. Once Marge had put the kettle on, I ushered her into the toilet and flushed it to drown the sound of me saying to her: "Keep your eyes peeled. I think they've come to bug the flat." I was so melodramatic.

I may not have left but Don Howe did. He went off to work for Trevor Francis at QPR in the summer of 1989. I was desperate to keep him and begged Sam to push his pay up from £50,000 a year to £75,000. With some reluctance, he agreed to it, knowing that I'd have to be paid the same because the two of us were always on equal money at the club. But Don said he'd agreed to go and was happy because it was much closer to his home.

So Don banked the bigger money Rangers were offering and left me lagging behind him. Brian Clough would have been pleased with me, though. I showed I now knew how to assemble an excellent backroom team by bringing in Ray Harford as replacement, having already taken on Joe Kinnear as reserve-team coach, with Dave Kemp still there as well.

I told Ray he was everything I needed and wanted – and I loved working with him. He was right up there, as he proved with what he helped Kenny Dalglish to achieve at Blackburn. The players initially had some doubts and Eric Young started belly-aching about how things were sliding since Don had left. I gave him a choice: He could either get his arse back on the training ground and shut his trap or walk in and return two weeks of his wages. He was as good as gold from then on.

My relationship with Sam was close to breaking point and, when I had a go at him, we exchanged more words. I carried on for a while but things came to a head and he put me on six months' gardening leave, telling Marge and me: "Go and sun your arses."

My eventful reign effectively ended on a beach in Lanzarote, with Ray appointed as my successor, but I was still sent on some scouting assignments in the meantime and received all my win bonuses. I told Don I'd be with him at QPR as his assistant on January 1, 1991, but I was still to do Wimbledon one last good turn. After Ray had quickly joined Blackburn and Peter Withe had bombed as his replacement, I recommended Joe Kinnear to Sam – and the Crazy Gang spirit and top-flight football were secure for quite a bit longer. I was delighted to do that after my three and a half years there.

Life After The Dons

The first thing I did at QPR was get to work on building Don Howe a back four. He said he wanted two centre-halves and a left-back, so I found him Darren Peacock at Hereford for £200,000, Andy Tillson at Grimsby for £400,000 and Rufus Brevett at Doncaster for £250,000. They went into a side who were staring relegation in the face after hurtling down the table and played their part in a spectacular transformation.

Peacock eventually went to Newcastle for £2.7m, Brevett played around 170 matches for Rangers before making even more appearances for Fulham and Tillson impressed sufficiently, mainly as a sweeper, to go on and stack up about 300 matches for Bristol Rovers. I'd like to think I'd done my old club a favour with a tip-off but can claim no credit for that. It was through none of my doing that he headed for the West Country and spent so long there.

Peacock and Tillson signed at the same time and were represented by the same agent, who I wiped the floor with. Darren came in first and Andy was worrying how their man, who was already in bits, was going to pick himself up to put forward a good case for him. But I was fair with the two lads and they appreciated that.

All three of the signings must have been good ones because I was at a cricket match not long ago when a Rangers fan came up and planted a kiss on my cheek as he said: "Many thanks for buying them."

That said, we had a scare with Peacock in a session at our Bank of England training ground. The boot was now on the other foot, with Don as my boss, and he came over to me scowling one day, pointing out that Darren was limping badly and suggesting I'd dropped a right clanger. I went over to ask Darren what his problem was and was shocked by his reply: "It's all right, I've just forgotten the in-fill for my boot." Apparently, he had one leg an inch shorter than the other after a bad break and had that day not put the necessary padding in his boot. You wouldn't have spotted the problem, though, if you watched him week in week out. The only thing that stood out with him was his ponytail. He was a good athlete and a good player.

I saw Tillson at a charity match at Clevedon Town a year or so ago, when he was playing for a combined Bristol City and Rovers side. He is now part of the coaching team at Exeter City and hopefully has the sort of fun there that he enjoyed with us at Rangers – like being rugby-tackled from behind in training by me and having his nose rubbed in the snow.

I had lined Peacock, Brevett and Tillson up for Wimbledon but any disappointment they might have felt at missing out on the trio was greatly offset by the success they had with Warren Barton. It was strange but I dragged Don off on a scouting assignment to watch Barton play for Maidstone and he said after 20 minutes: "I can't see what you see in him. Can I go now?" I suggested he stayed until half-time, had a cup of tea and then went.

Don's forte was working with players, not spotting them, so I made my move anyway by signing Barton, who Sam eventually sold for well over ten times the amount he had paid for him. Another nice little wedge for Wimbledon Football Club.

One of the conditions of my departure from Plough Lane was that I had to leave behind all my lists of players I had taken to the board as recommended or possible purchases. Robbie Earle's name was high on that and he subsequently joined them as well, so I didn't think I left them in bad shape.

On top of the FA Cup win, a few finishes in the top half of the table and a few million in the bank, there was the satisfaction of seeing a trio of their own players – Keith Curle, John Scales and Dennis Wise – picked for England under-21s. And Curley and Wisey made it to the full side. It was a legacy I was very proud of as my career moved on, this time in West London.

As things turned out, I only did two or three months with the likes of Ray Wilkins, Kenny Sansom and Andy Sinton at QPR, in which we got ourselves in no time out of a bit of bother near the relegation area and up towards the safety of mid-table. Then I was on the move again.

It's amazing how often I returned to former places of work to take up employment and, in the February of 1991, West Brom became the fourth club after Coventry, Wolves and Bristol Rovers to have me back. My move to The Hawthorns almost 20 years after I first signed there meant that I had my

£70,000-a-year salary after all and I no longer had London prices taking a huge bite out of it, so it was easy to be tempted.

Comfortable though I was working at Don Howe's side at QPR, my ego got the better of me and I wanted to be a no 1 again. So much so that I went back on my vow never to take on a job in mid-season, which was something I hadn't done since my first managerial post at Bristol Rovers. I also acted against Don's advice by saying yes. He didn't think Albion were in good enough shape at the time.

The approach came from the son of one of the Baggies' senior directors Trevor Summers, who invited me for talks with the chairman John Silk at the Golden Valley Hotel in Cheltenham. Mr Silk later introduced me at the press conference by saying I wasn't his first choice.......talk about a vote of confidence! Perhaps I should have walked out there and then.

If I thought that leaving the capital meant Sam Hammam was out of my life, I was very wrong. When I arrived at The Hawthorns, the biggest bouquet of flowers I had ever seen was there waiting for Marge and me in the reception area. They were in the blue and yellow of Wimbledon, sent by Sam. I rang to say thank-you but suggested that a new BMW might have been more in keeping with all the quality players I had left behind for him at Plough Lane.

The next day, I was in my car when Dave Bassett, who I hadn't been on the best of terms with after he tried to take some of my players to Sheffield United, rang me and said: "Gouldy, you're magic. Sam has agreed to buy me a BMW and he's going to buy you one as well. And there's another for Stanley Reed." Harry did the deal with a guy in Sheffield and we all had spanking new 320is with leather seats. I also acquired the number plate J88 CUP, which I was chuffed with.

In the event, Marge drove the vehicle more than I did because Albion gave me a new car at the same time. My favour back to Sam was the strong recommendation that he should give Joe Kinnear, who I had added to Wimbledon's backroom team, the manager's job there. I wanted to help because there was still a magnificent bond between us despite the disagreements and I hadn't forgotten that he had, after all, been my boss when I had my proudest day as a manager.

The QPR people had wanted to put me in charge there because things weren't working out for them with Don at the helm but I didn't want to betray him like that. It was my few weeks at Loftus Road, though, that reminded me I still wanted to manage. At the age of 44, plenty of fire remained in my belly.

The first thing I should have done at West Brom was get rid of Stuart Pearson, who had done a decent job holding the fort after Brian Talbot was sacked following an FA Cup defeat at home to Woking. But I decided to keep him and use his knowledge as I found my feet. Or tried to find them. After a draw with West Ham in my opening game, we had a calamitous March with six successive defeats that left us facing a real battle to stay up.

We had a big squad containing the likes of Graham Roberts, Gary Bannister, Bryan Robson's brother Gary and Don Goodman, with a young Ugo Ehiogu on the fringes. Unfortunately, they couldn't stop our nosedive, nor could the gangling Paul Williams, who I signed from Stockport just before the deadline for substantial money. He didn't score in ten matches up to the end of the season, so he didn't represent my finest hour in the transfer market.

A few months later, another capture was easy enough.....our oldest son Jonathan. On my first day at Albion, I had taken a message from the secretary John Evans to say that Jonathan had split his nose badly and been taken to hospital while playing for Halifax. But he recovered fully and I felt we needed goalkeeper cover for Stuart Naylor and Mel Rees in my first full season there, so I brought him in on a free.

He never made it past the reserves at The Hawthorns but our relationship at the club was fine – I treated him like any other player. Any tension between us was down to the fact he was single at the time and living with us in our rented cottage at Feckenham in Worcestershire. I arrived home at the end of one weary day to find him watching Neighbours and barked at him: "Make the most of that because there will be no holiday at the end of the season if I'm out of a job."

I had a centre-forward on my mind when we drew 2-2 at Wolves. One of our fans ran on to hand a carrot to Graham Roberts, apparently to give to Steve Bull to depict him as a donkey. I didn't like a super professional like that being shown such scant respect, so I ran on the pitch as well and made a citizen's arrest.

We were undefeated in the last nine games but, remarkably, went down. We won only two of them and drew the last four, and were pipped to safety by Leicester because Oxford hit their woodwork near the end of the game at

Filbert Street on the final day. What made it even more painful was that our last match was against Bristol Rovers at Twerton Park of all places – and the home fans weren't slow to have a go at me.

Jeff Astle was among the Albion supporters who made the trip by coach and of course I felt as though I had let a lot of people down with our relegation. It was the worst feeling I ever had in the game.

As we lived so close, Marge and I travelled back to Portishead by car and we were just pulling out of Bath when she asked me how I felt. I went absolutely ape. She was totally taken aback and vowed there and then never to again enquire about my mood following a defeat. It was the first time I had been relegated as a manager and, like when I went down as a Wolves player, it was a case of me having gone into a club well into the season and not been able to do enough.

I wasn't really a good fit for Albion and was having to change my culture. I have watched Stoke and Blackburn lose home matches this season and have wondered whether they are falling between two stools by trying to modify their style because of the criticism of it. If they have something that works for them, they should stick to it and not worry about what others are saying.

I sympathise with them because I had to compromise myself at West Brom. The rough and ready approach that had worked for many years at Wimbledon wasn't acceptable at The Hawthorns, so I oversaw training drills based on two touches and the ball being kept below head height. The plan was to play a passing game, which I wasn't really used to.

Things were actually looking up on the pitch in my second season. We put six past Exeter on the first day, reeled off four consecutive wins early on and helped ourselves to a second six-goal haul – this time against Marlow in the FA Cup. I won another Manager of the Month award and we were always in contention for a play-off place without me ever feeling I was winning people over.

The press got into me, especially the Evening Mail in Birmingham, and there was big fall-out. Some of the criticism was severe and left me vulnerable, so I made it known I was refusing to take calls from their correspondent Steve Tudgay. The paper left a big white space at the top of the back page, with the words 'This is where the Albion story should have been' in small letters. The main article on the page was an opinion piece detailing why they felt justified in calling me 'eccentric' – the word they used as the headline in huge letters. I had the page framed and mounted in the bolthole.

With one of the local commercial radio stations piling into me as well, the abuse was awful and the pressure intensified when stories surfaced about me going back to Coventry, where Don Howe had turned up to work with Terry Butcher. It was clear that I'd be on very thin ice if ever our results took a turn for the worse.

My decision to introduce a Roy of the Rovers change strip of red and yellow stripes was seen as another radical move but I don't think we ever lost in it. I was having to run a very tight ship, though, and was less than chuffed when the board told me I couldn't play Don Goodman in an Autoglass Trophy game at Lincoln. They sold him to Sunderland for a big fee a day or two later.

My response to being slated in the press was to allow reporters into the dressing room before and straight after games, starting following a match at Bolton. More than once, Denis Sunley of the Express & Star complained about his glasses steaming up and one or two of his colleagues clearly found it strange leaning over the bath to interview Stuart Naylor or Darren Bradley while the players thrashed around in the suds.

I thought it was progressive – a way of breaking down barriers and having more openness like they do in American sport. But I probably went too far when we lost at Bournemouth in the New Year and invited in a fan who was bellowing outside the dressing room door. The players had a pop at me for exposing them to people whose feelings were obviously running high.

The mood turned really ugly after we managed to concede three times in the last 12 minutes at home to Swansea and turn a comfortable win into a 3-2 defeat. The fans refused to leave the ground and called for the board to go. They did the same following a game against Hartlepool a few weeks later, when I copped for a lot of their anger as well. I went out to address them and they eventually dispersed.

It was a tough time but I've always been resilient. I don't go under easily and was determined to fight on, even if the tide was very much against me. It's no coincidence that, when I was on a Coventry radio station this summer and was asked for two tunes on a desert island discs programme, I chose Home by Simply Red (my favourite band) and I Will Survive by Gloria Gaynor.

When I was in danger of being submerged at Albion, I did what I could usually do – pull off a good signing. My West Country roots had given me chance to clap eyes on Bob Taylor, a tall, dark-haired striker who I managed to hook in from Bristol City for only £300,000. It was only a fraction of what we'd received for Don Goodman but I wished so much I could have had the two of them. Then we'd have been a real force.

Bob scored on his debut at Birmingham and was an immediate success, which didn't surprise me one bit. I believed in him implicitly. I'd watched him in a few games and thought he was such a natural predator, whose style would suit us perfectly. He was a real footballers' man. He could hold the ball up, turn well and, above all, score loads of goals. He had almost everything in his locker except great pace.

Unfortunately, as Bob arrived to help our cause, Gary Robson, who continued to give me everything, saw his goals dry up after a terrific first half of the season. The result was that we had another bad March, being trounced in successive games at Huddersfield and Stockport. This time, we won our final two matches of the season but the six points weren't enough to get us into the play-offs and the writing was on the wall when some of our fans carried a coffin bearing the message RIP Bobby Gould at Shrewsbury on the last day.

An ugly pitch invasion, in which one of the crossbars was snapped, marred the end of the game at the Gay Meadow and I don't ever recall a 3-1 victory feeling so hollow. I wasn't wanted there any more and Albion fans, who had dressed up in Roman togas when we played at Bath on the last day of the previous season, came up with imaginative ways of endorsing the point. I couldn't believe it when I went back to Gay Meadow on Cardiff's behalf a few years ago and the groundsman called me over to show me that the very same coffin was still intact and waiting for me.

There was one other high-profile occasion before I was shown the door by the Baggies. The club's Player of the Year do still lay ahead and it was there at the Kings Theatre in Great Barr that I fell victim to another of the Albion fans in the Black Country media, the local radio personality Malcolm Boyden. He was the compere and took it upon himself to have a dig at a few of us during an address that must have gone on for 20 minutes.

I caught the eye of one or two of the senior players, like Graham Roberts and Stuart Naylor, and in unison we stood up and walked out; players and management and our wives, some of them in tears. The directors' wives stood and applauded us as we went. I apologised to the supporters over the microphone as we left and knew I was signing my death warrant at the club. It was all over for me at The Hawthorns.

There had been problems between the players and me during the season but we were still sufficiently together to head off to a nearby hotel and have our own do, sadly out of the sight of supporters who had paid good money to attend. After we'd made a hasty exit, they took their own revenge on Malcolm Boyden by chasing him out of the place and apparently having him hiding in a dustbin.

I was at Warwick Races the next day, Bank Holiday Monday, when the inevitable call came from John Silk. I was invited to his office and, with £10,000 by way of a pay-off, was on the job market once more.

One For The PM

I hadn't quite heard the last of Albion. A few weeks before my departure early in the summer of 1992, I took legal advice when George Gavin got stuck into me after I failed to show up at a live BRMB fans' forum he was hosting in Smethwick. It was the only time I ever chickened out and I was out of order. It was impolite and discourteous of me not to turn up, besides which an appearance might have helped me win a few of my battles.

Nothing came of my talks with a solicitor but I was in the mood for litigation again the following season when I found myself banned from The Hawthorns. And this time I sought the support of 10 Downing Street to fight my case.

Albion, now managed by Ossie Ardiles and with John Silk succeeded in the chair by Trevor Summers, were drawn away to non-League Wycombe in the FA Cup and I was asked along as summariser by Sky Sports. They were showing the game live and enlisted my help again when a 2-2 draw on the Sunday sent the tie back to the West Midlands for a midweek replay.

A day or two before the second match, Sky – then in their very early stages as a broadcaster – contacted me to say I was not welcome at West Brom. Between them, Albion's directors and the local police had apparently decided that my presence in the ground could be inflammatory, so they ordered me to stay away.

All the papers seized on the story and ran big headlines. My old mate Ralph Ellis on the Daily Star was one of those who spoke up for me and there was exasperation at Sky that I'd been banned, especially as Andy Gray – a former Rangers player and a lifelong fan of the club – had been unchallenged when sent on duty to games at Celtic.

I later had a nice apologetic letter from a senior police officer who admitted that the decision to exclude me had been wrong. The FA chairman Bert

Millichip also replied to me, although he said he would stay out of the matter as he was also Albion's president. But I had gone by then to the Prime Minister John Major and the Sports Minister to ask if my civil liberties had been breached.

I was furious with Trevor Summers, who remarked in the press that the Prime Minister would be an even busier man if all football people with such grievances wrote to him. Mr Major was too preoccupied with matters of state to respond, although I had sympathetic letters from his private secretary on Downing Street-headed paper. And, knowing the PM was a keen Chelsea fan, I cheekily followed up by saying I'd be happy to meet him at Stamford Bridge on Coventry's forthcoming trip there.

Yes, you've guessed it – I was now back in situ at Highfield Road, which was a handy development considering our domestic arrangements. We were very happy living in our rented cottage in Feckenham, Worcestershire, so there was a certain good fortune about the Sky Blues deciding they wanted me back.

Terry Butcher had been sacked early in 1992 and the board put Don Howe in charge. We were appointed joint managers in the summer but Don's wife Pauline had second thoughts almost immediately over him travelling several times a week from their home in Hertfordshire, so I was to sail the ship solo again from the start of the 1992-93 campaign.

My financial adviser John Hazell and my agent Marge (well, she was the closest I ever had to an agent) convinced me I had undervalued myself in previous interviews, so I dug my heels in on their orders and found myself successfully negotiating a £4,000-a-week package. With Don out of reach, I recruited Phil Neal as my assistant and he did a steady enough job, although the players tired at times of hearing about all those bloody medals he had won at Liverpool!

Nine years on from my sacking at the club, I felt wiser and was delighted to be back in my home city, especially as Derrick Robins' son Peter was now chairman in succession to John Poynton. Not everything had changed, though. Jenny Poole was still there and would again be my secretary, this time from her desk in the Sky Blue Lodge building rather than the Sky Blue Connection.

It being the close season, I soon got busy once more in the transfer market because the club had just had yet another of their relegation close escapes. Following a tribunal, I paid £17,500 for our son Jonathan and also captured

Phil Babb on the strength of his performance for Bradford against my Baggies side. In addition, I went to Swansea for Brummie John Williams, who had caused me some pain by setting up a Swansea victory at West Brom a few months earlier.

I was happy with life when we won at home to Middlesbrough and away to Tottenham and Wimbledon in our opening three games to become the first leaders of the new Premier League. After beating my old club at Selhurst Park, I took all the lads to McDonald's in Southgate for milk shakes as we made our way across London. I knew how to celebrate in style.

Williams, nicknamed the Flying Postman because of his previous job and the fact he was so quick, delivered by scoring home and away as we did the double over Spurs. Unfortunately, such heights didn't last but we remained a decent team – without the long-term scoring potential I was looking for.

My search for a cure for that headache took me to Newcastle, where Micky Quinn was falling out with Kevin Keegan. Peter Robins, who I was becoming good friends with, tipped me off that Quinny was available, so I picked up the phone without delay. I told him he was the man to answer our prayers and he came in on loan. We hit it off straightaway but I might have missed out on him. I once let a deal for Ricky Otto fall through because I threw out a blonde he had working as his agent. I'm sorry but I was just too old-fashioned to be negotiating a transfer with a woman. What I didn't realise was that Quinny's agent was Mel Stein, the very guy who happened to employ this lady. Fortunately, Mel didn't hold it against me.

Quinny bounced in and made an immediate impact. He was a revelation, the best natural finisher I ever worked with. I described him as a footballing Polaris, who didn't do a lot outside the area but whose periscope went up whenever the ball went in it. We became much more than ships passing in the night. We remain great pals as work-mates at talkSPORT and he still calls me 'Gaffer,' which I'm very proud of.

In his brilliant book, Who Ate All The Pies?, he joked that Coventry had survived so long against the odds in the top division that, if the Titanic had been painted sky blue, it would never have gone down. He was a funny man and the fans warmed to him by singing: "He's fat, he's round, he's worth a million pounds, Micky Quinn, Micky Quinn."

I told him I'd fine him if I ever saw him back in our half. He was a predator

No-one revelled in Wimbledon's Crazy Gang spirit more than the owner Sam Hammam - even when the joke was on him! He could never get enough of the legendary pranks and practical jokes.

Below: An occasion that put an even bigger smile on Sam's face - the 1988 FA Cup final. Our skipper and penalty-save hero Dave Beasant is the man fitting me out with some appropriate headgear while match winner Lawrie Sanchez and central defender Eric Young hold aloft their medals. On the right is Terry Phelan with John Fashanu behind us, Alan Cork in the no 8 shirt and Terry Gibson just in view on the left.

More memories of Wimbledon's historic day out at Wembley 22 years ago, when we pulled off arguably the biggest upset in FA Cup final history. Right: My loyal coach Don Howe joins in with the post-match celebrations before his surprise disappearing act. I insisted this photograph went in - it's just how I remember Howey from after the game. Below: Proof that we did finally succeed in making Dennis Wise relax on Cup Final morning. Our goal-maker and his team-mate Alan Cork are captured in restful mood at the Cannizaro Hotel a few hours before playing their part in the defeat of Liverpool. Bottom: Yet another of the pictures that adorn my wall. The scene of post-match ecstasy as our victory is savoured by players and staff.

Party time at Plough Lane on Cup Final night. Above: My table contains (clockwise from me) my mum, her friend Bernard, Marge's parents Jenny and George, Patsy Fry, Janine Fry, Gordy Fry, Richard and Marge. Below: From left are Mum, me, Jonathan, Marge, our Trevor, Robert, Richard, Darren and Jackie.

Our lovely chairman Stanley Reed takes to the mic, probably to lead a sing-song, following the open-top bus parade we had in the sunshine round the streets of Wimbledon. On the far left is Vinnie Jones. Below: One of my most treasured photographs from our success - the one with the family and the FA Cup safely back home in Portishead. The silverware looks majestic - and just about survived intact after Bob Wilson and I had it as company while we washed up!

The dos and don'ts of Army life......Above: Family pride at Richard's passing-out parade at Sandhurst. Left and below: A less comfortable approach to life with the services as I take my Coventry City squad along as part of our pre-season build-up. The venture had the saddest of repercussions for one player - and might have had tragic implications for another.

Above: A proud step into international football in the summer of 1995. And the photographers wanted to mark it in suitably patriotic style. Left: Back 'home' in more recent times and very proud to be honoured at Coventry City's new Ricoh Arena headquarters.

Time for cricket - in fun and with the pros. Left: A charity game involving my great pal Bob Wilson finds me unable to smile. I had lost my teeth not long before when hit in the mouth by a ball bowled by a 15-year-old. Below: Caught in conversation with Paul Collingwood on England's latest tour of New Zealand.

The best team of the lot - my home team! Above: At a water park in Hastings, New Zealand, a few years ago are (from left): Marge, me, Matthew, Jess, Libby, Becca, Louise, Jonathan, Emma and Richard. Below: Winter woollies rather than swim suits are called for as we pose for another shot, some of us taller and some of us greyer, this time in Somerset in the spring of 2010. From left are: The author, Matthew, Marge, Louise, Libby, Richard, Jess, Becca, Emma and Jonathan. Considering that the geographical spread of our families could hardly be greater, it would be impossible for us to be any closer.

who I wanted in the opposition's penalty area, not getting in the way of our midfielders and defenders. One journalist called him a 13 and a half stone roly poly but he settled in brilliantly and scored twice on his debut against Manchester City and followed up with goals against Sheffield United and Ipswich before hitting another brace at Southampton.

He netted six times in his first four matches and didn't finish on the winning side in any of them. We put that right by cracking five past Liverpool when he got the last couple, then he hit two more as we beat Aston Villa at Highfield Road. He had scored ten goals in his first six games and was gelling well with the likes of Brian Borrows, Phil Babb, Kevin Gallacher, David Busst, Robert Rosario, Steve Ogrizovic, Peter Atherton and Kenny Sansom.

He was a great character to have round the place. He revelled in the nickname Sumo and played up to the crowd when they taunted him about all those pies. It must be a doddle when the fans think up the title of your autobiography. We were thrilled with him but wouldn't let him rest on his laurels. After he had hit two of our five in a great win at Blackburn, I signed Roy Wegerle, who played against us that day.

We were in the top six, having also had emphatic wins over Oldham and Middlesbrough, but still had our madcap ways. As a throwback to my Leofric Hotel days, I encouraged Phil Neal to take the players down the road to Gosford Park for a warm-up before one game – a drill that meant they were threading their way back into Highfield Road, in their training kit, with startled fans.

Losing 5-0 with a young team at Manchester United, when we had Jonathan in goal, was a low point, then we crumbled by winning only one of our last 11 games. We fell away to a final placing of 15th, only three points above Luton, who went down. It was Quinny's goals that kept us up. He finished his first season at the club with 17 from 25 Premier League games. The irony was that, before he came down from Newcastle, he put £500 on us to be relegated.

I again found myself going flat around Easter and wondered why. It was a problem because it gets through to players if the manager isn't sharp. The Fergusons and Mourinhos, the perennial winners, have the answers. Fergie has his racehorses to take his mind off football and Sam Allardyce has become a great exponent of the mid-season break that clears his head. Clearly, I needed to come up with something.

As ever, I wasn't afraid to chop and change in search of a winning formula.

Peter Ndlovu emerged along with David Busst and I used 30 players in my first season back, including 13 who played fewer than ten times. Pete Robins wasn't chuffed on the last day when, with our Jonathan in goal, we conceded twice in the last couple of minutes of a draw at home to Leeds and dropped a couple of places in the table – something that cost us prize money.

I decided we were too soft. During the following pre-season, I didn't bother with Scandinavia, Holland or Ireland as a tour venue, opting instead for Aldershot Army Barracks and the full boot-camp experience. I had done something similar as Albion manager but the trip I organised with Coventry gave Quinny a chapter-full of material for his book.

It was during our stay under the command of the armed forces that I felt a gun poked into my back one night as I slept under canvas, the officer yelling 'name and rank' after creeping up on me like an SAS sniper. I replied 'Bobby Gould, manager of Coventry City' and was told back: "At ease, Gould. But keep an eye out for those daft footballers."

I congratulated the sergeant at breakfast next day on the authenticity of his staff's night manoeuvres and remarked how the stealthy officer could have slit my throat before I knew it. I was met by a puzzled look, though, and it was only later that I found out it was Babb, encouraged no doubt by Quinny, who had been responsible for the threatening with a 'gun' that was in fact a stick. The bastards had done me like a kipper.

There were serious down-sides to the trip, though. Our Jonathan almost died when the players had to wear masks to negotiate a narrow tunnel that was filled with poisonous gas. He started choking, the gas got into his lungs and he needed resuscitating. I would have had a near death experience as well if Marge had got to hear what happened, so, in the interests of family unity, we decided on a policy of 'What goes on on tour, stays on tour.'

The incident was downright scary but at least Jonathan and me lived to tell the tale and continue our careers. Poor Lee Hurst, a popular young midfielder, badly injured his knee jumping from a high wall on the assault course and did his cruciate ligaments. I can still hear his scream as he fell. He was from just down the road in Nuneaton and was a good player who brought balance to our side in the centre of the field. His misfortune hit me hard and I felt so sorry for him when his long attempt at a comeback ended in failure. When you are in charge of a group of players like that, you are responsible for them, although we all realise there are a hundred other ways he could have sustained a similar injury.

Lee's problems cast a shadow over the club but we set out in 1993-94 to put smiles back on everyone's faces. In the first game, against Arsenal, Stewart Robson was injured but Quinny scored a hat-trick, ran half the length of Highbury in celebration and did his Funky Chicken impression in front of me. He was barking mad. I felt like letting my hair down as well because a lot of planning and thought had gone into that game.

After the fixture computer had handed us that assignment first up, I lay on a beach on holiday in Portugal wondering how I could get one over on my old team-mate George Graham. I never felt he gave me the respect I deserved and he chipped away at me for my reliance on a 4-4-2 formation. I decided on the Algarve that I'd go 3-5-2 against the Gunners, so I played that way throughout the pre-season.

But, knowing George would have a scout at our final warm-up game, at Rotherham, I played five different systems just to throw him off the trail. I even tried to simulate the brilliant pitch conditions I knew would be awaiting us at Highbury by playing on another belter of a surface at Millmoor at the end of our programme of friendlies. Everything just fell into place and Arsenal had no answer to our use of three central midfielders.

We followed up by beating Newcastle at our place when Mick Harford, who I gave the no 9 shirt to, scored. Amazingly, despite spending 13 months at the club, he never played for us again. That shows how many forwards I'd accumulated.

We remained unbeaten until the end of September and beat Liverpool, as we always seemed to do, but the victories turned into draws and then defeats. The only win we had in the next month and a half was against Wycombe in the Coca-Cola League Cup and we almost threw that away by losing the second leg 4-2.

Overall, we didn't have enough players. We were so short once that I had to lace my boots up 12 years after my retirement and line up in the same reserve team as Jonathan in a game against Bolton at Highfield Road. It was September 28, 1993, and I lobbed Aidan Davidson at the Spion Kop end for one of the goals in our 2-1 win. Excuse the personal indulgence but it was the very last time I scored as a professional footballer.

Peter Robins was panicking about the financial situation and I was working hard to reassure him. I told him we had a major asset in Phil Babb, who Liverpool were interested in and who we'd be able to sell for £3m at the end of the season. Then we'd put a big slab of it in the bank and release a million or so to me to go and make another two or three signings from the lower divisions. I thought that pep talk would do the trick but it didn't.

I was driving in one day, ironically with my chief scout Nick Robins in my car, when we heard on the radio that his dad had relinquished the chairmanship and passed it to Bryan Richardson. I couldn't believe it. I had met Bryan's brother Peter, the former England cricketer, on holiday in Florida a few months earlier and now sensed difficult times ahead. I had already stuck on the inside of my briefcase lid, in big type, the letters DTAF (short for Don't Trust Any F***er). There wasn't much danger of that.

Straightaway, the board put pressure on me to raise money and sold Robert Rosario to Nottingham Forest for £400,000 against my wishes. He hadn't been doing much at the club until I converted him to a midfielder and he scored a few goals. The flow certainly slowed down after his departure. The financial restraints were growing, although we'd not long got good money in for Kevin Gallacher as well. And there were also rumours of Peter Ndlovu going. As the holder of 45 shares in the club, I was unhappy enough with what Richardson was doing. As his manager, I knew I couldn't work with him.

It was such a shame because we were playing some good stuff and scoring goals, including some real belters. I can still remember one against West Ham that came at the end of a move featuring about ten passes.

We were 13th after 11 games when we went to QPR towards the end of October and lost 5-1. I said to Phil Neal as we walked in: "That's it. I've had enough." I went to the boardroom, dragged Richardson and Robins out and led them to the toilets. I leaned against the door to make sure no-one could interrupt us and told them I was quitting. They said I'd be paid the £50,000 I was due but I told them I didn't want their money. I just wanted out. I'd resigned in the gents, fed up of Bryan's stringent ways.

I went straight to the press box to find the Coventry Evening Telegraph's Adam Dent so he could get the news on the front page of that night's Pink. He wasn't sure I was being serious, so he made me stand over him while he dictated the story to his office. Then I went and repeated my remarks to the other reporters in the press room. By catching the Pink, I had saved myself a phone call because Mum was an avid reader and I wanted her to know quickly of my dramatic decision.

Wimbledon were playing at Tottenham that day and, as the news got out, Sam Hammam raced across to Loftus Road to make sure I was okay. That was his lovely caring side. Marge was driving home from Bromsgrove through the lanes of Worcestershire when the announcement came on the radio – she didn't have a mobile then – and almost crashed the car in her shock; the same BMW that Sam gave me well after I left Wimbledon.

Quinny sat next to me on the coach home and tried to talk me out of quitting but I said: "Managing Coventry is like racing in Formula One in a Mini Metro." This time, I had kept the keys of my car, so at least I had wheels to get me to and from the meeting I had on the Monday to finalise my departure.

Another man feeling less than happy was Ralph Ellis. He lived just down the road from us in Feckenham and came round in search of a story when he heard I'd resigned on match day. At some length, I told him why I had quit but stressed that my comments were off the record and he observed that condition by telling his sports desk that there was nothing from me. He wasn't best pleased when he realised that Martin Samuel of The Sun had pulled on to our drive just after he sped away and I had given him the full story. I was, after all, contracted to the Murdoch newspaper. Next time we met, I was on the end of a rant from Ralph for a change and I could see where he was coming from.

International Manager

It's not just the people in football you know that counts.......sometimes it helps to have friends in the media as well. I was lucky as I arrived back in the 'in between jobs' sector of the market to have a door opened for me by Richard Keys, one of the Sky TV presenters. It helped that he was a big fan of the club I had just left for the third and final time.

Richard invited me to do some summarising at grounds and punditry in the studio while I enjoyed having a break from day-to-day involvement in the game. My batteries certainly needed charging but I'm not sure Andy Gray appreciated my arrival at Sky. I developed a mischievous arrangement with the floor manager to let me know if Andy had popped a sweet or sausage roll into his mouth, then I would link to him by asking a question, sometimes via Richard, and have him choking as he was going on air.

I earned decent money because I also worked for BBC 5Live, often having Alan Green on one side of me in a press box and Ron Jones on the other. I have to say Alan could be obnoxious, although I didn't help myself by getting his name wrong during live broadcasts. I obviously had my former Bristol Rovers keeper Ron Green on my mind, or was it because Ron Jones was there as well? Anyway, I called him Ron more than once.

On top of match-day duties, I did 36 episodes of a Monday night phone-in programme called Talk Back which had previously been hosted by Jonathan Pierce. It was great experience, except when the autocue went haywire and I kept reading out the wrong names of the callers. It was embarrassing having a succession of them correcting me but I thought the episode was behind me until I flew out from Gatwick next day to cover a game abroad. The snooker player Terry Griffiths was staying overnight at the same hotel, bumped into me and said. "I watched you on the TV last night. Shame you got all the names wrong." We were giggling like kids.

Noticing that many of the calls centred on the competence or otherwise of match officials, I put myself to the test. I volunteered as a linesman in a police match at Chigwell, then refereed a couple of their games and reported back on the show about my experiences. I found running the line one of the most boring ways of spending an hour and a half but being in the middle was fun and enlightened me on the problems of referees, even if I did still think they were useless.

My boldness got the better of me when I was on the gantry with Richard Keys at a Monday night match at Swindon. Off air, I suggested a slight tweak to the way we were doing things and immediately had this Scottish voice thundering into my earpiece: "Gouldy, you are there to fuckin' speak. That's what we pay you for. Not to fuckin' think." It was the producer Andy Melvin, the no 2 to Vic Wakeling. It was the last time I spoke up with any ideas.

I also wrote a column for the Pink in Coventry, another for Today newspaper and lectured on a course aimed at teaching international coaches – and caused a bit of a stir by refusing to pass a wannabe from Cyprus. I considered myself well qualified to talk about some of the pitfalls of the profession after my experiences at West Brom and Coventry and wrote out a motto for my 'pupils' which read: "Today's fully qualified manager, it appears, must possess the financial dexterity of a city dealer, the patience of Jobe, the wit of Oscar Wilde and the flamboyancy of Danny La Rue."

I was fully absorbed and occupied by my media work. I earned good money through it and didn't have the worry of trying to win three points at the end of the week. Then I took a call from Andy Melvin and received the bombshell news that Talk Back was being discontinued. Was I becoming a threat to someone higher up?

I didn't find it easy getting back into media work at that level, so I started to think of returning to full-time employment in the game. We were on a beach in Grenada in the summer of 1995 when I received news of a more welcome kind. A member of staff weaved a path among the sun-loungers to tell me I was wanted on the phone. It was my big mate from Coventry, Bill Smith the builder, to tell me he had a job for me. "Do me a favour, Smithy, I'm working on my tan and want to get back to my book and my Southern Comfort & lemonade. And I've got a water skiing session booked in five minutes." Then he told me it was a job in international football and my ears pricked up.

Mike Smith had finished with the Welsh national team and there was a vacancy. The trouble was that Ron Atkinson was strongly linked with it as well and I told Bill I had no chance if Big Ron was interested. Later in the holiday, completely by chance, we were in the jacuzzi when we found ourselves talking to a medical guy called John Fairclough, who said he was a consultant in Cardiff and had the Welsh football team among his clients.

I kept a straight face when he talked about the vacancy but wrote out my application when we got home – and then left it on the mantelpiece for the best part of a week and a half. It was only when Ron made it clear he wasn't interested that I stuck a stamp on an envelope and tried my luck. I didn't have to wait long for notification of an interview in Llangollen.

We look out across South Wales from Evermore but I decided to cross the border a couple of nights early; not to make sure of getting there in time but so I could watch a European game between Afan Lido and the Latvian side Raf Riga, then take in a match between Wrexham and Petrolum Polesti 24 hours later. It was my idea of a recce and some useful research before I met the men in suits.

I knew I'd got the right hotel because I could see all the Zimmer frames outside. There were about 14 members of the 24-man football committee there to grill me but I'm lucky that I've always interviewed well. I'm a 'people' person with belief in my ability, so it was just a matter of speaking honestly and forthrightly and then waiting to see. My Sky Sports profile was a help as well and I felt bold enough to kick off my address to the assembled gentlemen with the phrase: "I have a dream……"

It looked like I was strongly in the running after getting over what I thought was the main obstacle; the fact I wasn't Welsh. Once they could see how passionate and enthusiastic I was, it was as if they didn't mind if I came from Timbuktoo. Soon afterwards, David Collins, the general secretary, invited me across to Cardiff for a second chat about money, so the signals were good.

I didn't regard it as a cut-and-dried thing, though, because Wales had never had a full-time manager and didn't even have an office for one to work from. The nature of the position in the past was reflected in my salary, which, at £52,000, was well down on what I had been earning from writing in Fleet Street and having the make-up girls prepare me for a stint in front of the Sky cameras.

And I admit my coaching and management days would happily have been consigned to the history books had the shutters not fallen on my fingers at Sky. I thought broadcasting would be my bread and butter for the rest of my professional life and I was enjoying throwing myself into the challenge. But I learned football itself didn't have the monopoly for kicking you in the teeth.

Don't get me wrong, after my peace in Grenada was shattered, I was flattered to be offered a job as an international manager and extremely proud to be leading Wales. The first thing I did after shaking on a contract was insist on creating an office in a top-floor storeroom in a building in Westgate Street, Cardiff. It was almost right opposite the Cardiff Arms Park, where we played most of our home matches before the Millennium Stadium was built.

I cleared out all the junk and had some furniture supplied for nothing by a company I had done some advertising with. But that was just the start of it. There was no kit room and we didn't even own any goal posts, nets or corner flags for the training pitch. Wherever we turned up to prepare for matches, we relied on our hosts providing them. I made improving our facilities one of my priorities and created some cupboard space downstairs in Westgate Street so our excellent kit man, Ron Stitfall, could organise the skips better.

Another beef was the car I was given, a Rover. Okay, I love a decent set of wheels but I felt the manager of a nation should have a vehicle more in keeping with the prestige of the job. A bit of extra comfort would have been welcome because I was often travelling. I clocked up 90,000 miles in my first two years; not bad for someone in charge in a country as small as Wales.

Managing in international football was the chance of a lifetime and I was attracted by the prospect of working with players like Ian Rush, Dean Saunders, Mark Hughes, Neville Southall and Ryan Giggs. I had obviously lined up alongside some great players, especially at Arsenal, Wolves and perhaps West Ham, but the stars now under my control represented a big step up from those I had handled at clubs.

I could see a difficult side to the job looming, though. Several of the best players were coming towards the end and it was clearly going to be a period of considerable turnover. I was likely to be the one to put my head in the lion's mouth and end some great careers.

Although we lived just across the estuary, I wanted to be in Wales every day and set out to become a bit Welsh. In no time at all, the car could almost find its own way over the Severn Bridge and then along the northern edge of the river into the capital. And the daily commute allowed me to slide the language tapes into the cassette deck, so I could pick up a few words and phrases of the native tongue and, most importantly, learn the national anthem.

That said, I didn't join in with it at my first few games. I knew the TV cameras would be trained on me and didn't want to appear an imposter, so I just took it all in, feeling very proud and listening to the crowd singing along with great gusto, even when only 5,000 turned up for my first match.

I also wanted Welshmen around me but trying to prise Brian Flynn out of his job as Wrexham manager proved impossible, so I appointed Ernie and Tom Whalley to oversee the under-21s. Jimmy Shoulder was already there working with the age groups below the 21s and I brought in Tim Exeter, Steve Lownes and Ian Cockerill as fitness coach, physio and sports psychologist respectively. Tim and Ian were Midlanders who I'd also worked with at both Coventry and West Brom and I'm proud to look back and think I was a trend-setter in creating positions that are commonplace today. I also insisted on having a specialised masseur and video analyst, John Stanhope.

In the search for a no 2, I tried for Don Howe, who was not comfortable about changing allegiances, thought about Ray Wilkins and went to see Steve McClaren at Derby. But I worked solo for quite a while before eventually installing Graham Williams, a friend and guiding light from my days as a West Brom player. He had won more than 25 caps, still lived in the country near Oswestry and remained a fierce patriot. He became a good ally at my side.

I dipped into my extremely recent past for another piece in the jigsaw. I remembered our meeting in a Caribbean jacuzzi with John Fairclough, who we gave the nickname 'Action Man' to after seeing him and his family taking part in so many of the holiday activities. I increased his duties on the medical side, where he worked with Doc Jones – a lovely soft-natured man I inherited and whose knowledge of the players from many years was to prove invaluable to me. The Doc and his wife still travel extensively as supporters of the team.

Another good appointment was Ceri Stennett, son of the comedian Stan Stennett. I made him press officer on a part-time basis but he became so efficient and trustworthy that he was upgraded and is still serving the national team with great patience and diligence. The press lads think the world of him, even if they didn't always see eye to eye with me.

Becoming an international manager was the pinnacle of my career. I was already in an elite group after lifting the FA Cup at Wimbledon and considered myself even more privileged now to be leading a country. Very few got that far. My dead-end job hadn't worked out too badly for me, had it? John Paul Getty said in his book that the big chair is sometimes placed there for you – and you only – and I quickly plonked myself on it.

I could see international football didn't sit comfortably with everybody, though; not initially at least. You wouldn't believe it from the forceful midfielder Simon Davies has become with Fulham and Everton but he used to be the quietest lad you could ever meet. I remember seeing him play in an under-18 game and he seemed to be looking round at the company he was keeping and asking: "Why me? Why am I here?"

I settled on Spytty Stadium, Newport County's home after they vacated Somerton Park, as my favoured training ground and the town's Stakis Hotel as our base as it was virtually on the M4 on the London side. And we were a contented group after my reign started with a 1-0 victory over Moldova at the Cardiff Arms Park on September 6, 1995. I gave Reading's Lee Nogan his full debut but it was one of the established guys, Gary Speed, who headed the winner in the second half from a free-kick in just the way Lawrie Sanchez had nodded in Wimbledon's Wembley winner. The team hadn't won for a year, so there was something for us all to feel pleased about.

Although old habits died hard and I found it strange not seeing the players more often, I had a lot on my plate. And, boy, did I work hard! If anyone thinks I didn't pull my weight, they should see my diary. I went to Colwyn Bay to watch the under-18s, popped over to Dublin for another of their matches, took in a women's game and then got stuck into a video of Germany thrashing Moldova 6-1. Unfortunately, it didn't stop us losing 2-1 to the Germans in Cardiff three days later in the October but we played really well and had our hearts broken by Jurgen Klinsmann's late winner after Kit Symons scored at the other end.

By the time I took over, the side had already lost five games in their qualifying group for Euro 96 and won only one. That meant we were looking beyond that tournament for improvement. We drew against Albania in my first away fixture but they were the only team to finish beneath us in group seven, so the road ahead was a long uphill one. I was more than happy to put in the time and energy to help us climb it.

In no time, my Rover was pointing towards all points of the principality and beyond. I went to visit Neville Southall at his home in Llandudno and dropped in on Gary Speed near Wrexham, keen as I was to appear more like a club manager than an international one. But there were bigger challenges to be confronted and the biggest of them all was sat behind a desk in Manchester.

Trying to get to grips with Sir Alex Ferguson on the subject of Ryan Giggs' availability was one of the problems I knew I would quickly have to resolve. A few days after my appointment, I requested a meeting with the United manager, who agreed to see me at his office at the club's training ground at The Cliff. I was apprehensive because he's such a formidable figure. It's one thing to have managed for a decade and a half or so, as I then had; something else altogether to try to come to agreement with someone who had ended United's 26-year drought between League Championships and won a clutch of other cups at home and in Europe.

Whatever Ferguson's reputation was for getting what he wanted and not being bossed around by anyone, I was determined to stand my ground and do the best I possibly could for my adopted country. The number of times Ryan had pulled out of internationals before my arrival was getting out of hand, so I was pleased with how the manager-to-manager chat went, also with what the player himself had to say when we spoke afterwards in the restaurant area.

I told Sir Alex that, as a club manager, he had to let Ryan go to play for his country when he was fit and selected. I could understand him occasionally not being made available for friendlies but it was happening too often and I didn't want to see the Welsh supporters conned. I was under pressure to lay down some proper ground rules. Giggsy would put 10,000 on the gate for a start, so you could see why my employers wanted the issue tackled.

During our meeting in the manager's office, I made it clear that there were regulations in place and countries had the right to have players who were considered unfit by their clubs looked at by the international team's doctor and physio for a final decision. It was a case of United falling in line with these rules or being told they had to take on FIFA and UEFA.

As time went on, the situation didn't improve and I felt Fergie was pulling the plug on me by saying Ryan wasn't fit to play for Wales. I responded in a big article in which I said I was not prepared to con the Welsh public by telling them Ryan was going to play for us and then have him pull out. I was driving across the Severn Bridge to Cardiff one day when my mobile rang. It was Fergie in meltdown; the hairdryer at maximum setting. He didn't like how his stance had been portrayed in the media and let me know big-style in a way that made Joe Kinnear's diatribe at Newcastle years later look like child's play.

Our relationship was affected, although I know Sir Alex would have taken the same position as me if he had been an international manager. As a result, we had Ryan down in Cardiff with us before virtually every game but he played only one or two out of 20 friendlies. He would play in the qualifiers by and large but otherwise see a doctor when he reported, be declared unfit and then drive back north via a visit to his nan and granddad in Cardiff. It wasn't the worst arrangement in the world as he was a good family lad.

I felt bullied by Fergie and he never thawed towards me. I was in fear of him after that and he probably knew it. Later, I summoned the courage to pick the phone up to him when I was manager of Cheltenham and ask if I could have his young forward, Danny McIntosh, on loan. I fluffed my lines. I meant Danny Webber. Maybe he still had me on the run from the game at Old Trafford way back in 1988, five nights before Wimbledon played in the FA Cup final. United really got stuck into us and, during a bit of verbals on the touchline, I beat the right side of my chest in the direction of their bench, determined to show we had bottle. Archie Knox looked at me dismissively and said: "Your heart's on the left, you prat!" And to think Sir Alex had been at Jock Stein's side when I did their Scotland team that big favour with the loan of Bristol Rovers' training ground.

I loved Ryan. If you wanted to adopt a son, you couldn't have taken home anyone better. He had such a lovely nature. The day I went to see Sir Alex, I could see on the training ground how long David Beckham and Eric Cantona practised set-pieces for and I used to joke with Ryan that he should take more of them so he was well rehearsed for when he had to whip them in for us.

Giggsy set a trend by being picked early for his country and then retiring a few years ahead of time to spend more time with his club and family. I was at his last game, against New Zealand, when he carried his son out. I was married at 20, had two kids by 23 and was driven on by the need to feed the extra mouths. Later, when I was managing, I had to earn well to pay for a good education for our lads. Players now are so wealthy that they might not want to manage.

It's a pity we couldn't have called on Ryan more. He was so admired and respected by his team-mates and you could see the lift he gave to lads like John Robinson, Steve Jenkins, Andy Legg and Robbie Savage when he was around. But there wasn't much continuity, so they had to get used to him again each time we recalled him to the side if we were striving for World Cup or European Championship points. And it wasn't as though we had that many players to select from in the first place.

We certainly had to do all we could to protect our interests as regards our star men, which is why I went out of my way on the way home from one of my first away matches to make sure Mark Hughes was on-side. As soon as we touched down following a friendly defeat in Switzerland in the spring of 1996, there was a message on my phone from Sparky – by then a Chelsea player – asking to speak to me.

Fortunately, the flight was into Heathrow, so it was only a short detour to pop to see him after he had finished training. He was very upset at not having been picked to travel to Lugano and I saw exactly what people mean when they talk about that fierce desire in him. "I'm Welsh and I love playing for Wales," he said in a tone of controlled aggression, his eyes revealing his amazing passion and intensity. I got the message.

I said I had been happy to experiment with a young side against the Swiss but that he was very much in my thoughts. And we were each true to our word. He played in virtually every game after that and was one of the best players I have ever managed or coached. He was such an impressive character that when I left the Welsh post in the summer of 1999, I recommended him for it.

Another player with Manchester United connections who loomed large in my reign was Robbie Savage. I appreciated the battle he faced to rebuild his career at Crewe after being drummed out of Old Trafford and saw a lot of myself in his fierce will to win. I also think he has been underrated because he has a lot more to him than just a hard-man image.

The first game I saw him play was in the under-21s in the little rugby ground next to the Cardiff Arms Park. He was a forward in those days but impressed me most when he dropped off the centre-halves. He looked talented enough to me with the ball round his feet and his energy and tackling have never been in question, so I thought there was a decent player in there. But I immediately saw him as a midfielder.

I watched him train as well and he was very interested when I told him I didn't think he was in his best position up front. In fact, he was always bobbing around asking questions and seeking feedback. We just seemed to find each other in different places at different times and I became like an uncle to him. I can see why Martin O'Neill revelled in having him in his Leicester side.

He was slaughtered by me and his team-mates when his phone went off in a team meeting in Istanbul and he uttered the words: "Hello Mum." But I loved his enthusiasm and had sent him on for his debut when I needed to make a quick substitution, looked along the bench and noticed he was the one bouncing up and down, shin pads already on. I related to that keenness. I was an impact player as well and it does my head in when a substitution is about to be made and the replacement is fiddling around looking for bits of his gear.

Taking games around the country was a way of showing the people of Wales we cared about them. The hostility between supporters of Cardiff and Swansea is well known but I made sure we played at Wrexham as well and, on occasions when the Arms Park was knocked down to make way for the Millennium Stadium, just over the border at Anfield, where we could pull in big support from the area round Chester and the north coast.

I was a great supporter of the Welsh National League and proved the point by picking Eifion Williams from Caernarvon Town to play for the under-21s. I often watched games in the league and also went to put on coaching sessions at Aberystwyth with Jimmy Shoulder. I look back with pride at the ground I covered to try to make things work and at the relationship with players I was trying to bring through the system.

Jurgen Klinsmann wasn't the only overseas great I had a close encounter with because I once flew to Spain to watch Barcelona train. I wasn't invited, I just turned up and stayed a week. Johann Cruyff looked after me royally. Then the engagements closer to home resumed. In the space of a few days in February, 1996, I went to Wales v Scotland in the rugby stadium, to Anglesey to meet Ernie Whalley and to a Rotary Club dinner engagement in North Wales after that.

March kicked off with a visit to the House of Lords on St David's Day (the first) and contained a question-and-answer night in Newport on the 21st, two Wales v Republic of Ireland schoolboys games on the 23rd, Aston Villa v Leeds in the League Cup final at Wembley on the 24th, a squad get-together on the

25th and 26th, then the clash between Belgium and France in Brussels on the 27th. My diary doesn't record the fact but there might well have been an entry for the 28th saying I was knackered and slept all day.

One of my unenviable early tasks was ending Ian Rush's international career. I steamed into him in one of our first sessions at the Spytty Stadium when I thought he should be showing more aggression around goal. It was a thorny situation. In the sense that I hadn't played international football, yes, I was out of my depth but I couldn't afford to be a shrinking violet. I would have quietly slipped away if I'd lived in awe of these guys and their big reputations.

Making big decisions was difficult but I did what I thought was best and fixed up an appointment to go and see Rushy at his house on The Wirral to tell him I wasn't picking him for the game in Switzerland. He could probably see the writing on the wall because I had taken him off and sent on Crystal Palace's Gareth Taylor in the friendly in Italy on the occasion of his 73rd cap. He was a legend of Welsh football, their highest goalscorer of all time, and I was sensitive to his feelings, so I wanted to do it face-to-face. It was an issue I had to confront – something that just happened to come along on my watch. As we spoke, we both knew he probably wouldn't play for his country again.

The top players were very powerful and I dread to think of the problems managers must have to tackle now with their star men wielding such influence. I may not have had international caps or many medals to show the players under my control and I know some of them have been critical of me. But my preparation and organisation were second to none and I left no stone unturned in my reconnaissance. I tried to give us the best chance of succeeding.

I knew how long journeys would take, where and what we would be eating and what facilities our bases had. When we turned up once in Tunisia for a friendly, one of the press guys said he was in the best hotel room he had ever seen but the lads weren't happy, so I took a taxi half an hour away and had us in alternative accommodation on the coast within an hour.

One of my greatest thrills was flying to Amsterdam for the World Cup draw in 1995-96. My appetite for that tournament was whetted by the staging of Euro 96 in England and another hectic round of assignments......Holland v Scotland, Turkey v Croatia, Switzerland v Holland, Portugal v Turkey and England v Scotland all in the space of a week, with a Welsh FA Council meeting at the Cardiff Post House in between.

Our World Cup qualifying programme started in the summer of 1996, around the time the European Championship finals kicked off in England. We opened with a trip to San Marino, where the under-21s won 3-0 on the Saturday and the seniors went a couple of goals better on the Sunday. Amazingly, Mark Hughes had gone three years without an international goal before scoring twice there. Craig Brown had stressed to me the need for getting points on the board quickly, so I'd made sure we were playing the group minnows early on.

We hit six against San Marino in the return and were flying high, although they gave us such a buffeting that Dean Saunders referred to our opponents as 'savages' in interviews afterwards. We looked like building on our lofty position when we led through Deano's goal going into the last 20 minutes of our game at home to Holland despite Giggsy's absence through suspension. We played really well but were eventually turned over 3-1. No disrespect to Andy Legg but I made a mistake in sending him on. The problem was that Mark Pembridge, who I took off to make way, hadn't played much and I was trying to look after him and keep sweet with his manager at Sheffield Wednesday, David Pleat.

The return against the Dutch came round quickly; too quickly as it turned out. It was just over a month later that we travelled to Eindhoven and I suffered one of the lowest points of my time in the job. It was the night Giggsy was fit to play again after an injury but unfortunately he only turned out for Manchester United's reserves, not for us.

In addition, Barry Horne was absent, so I held a secret ballot among the players to find his replacement as captain. I thought it was a way of giving them some responsibility and bonding them. Although it was only for one game, they could feel part of the decision-making process. The votes came in to me for counting – and who should win by a couple from Deano but Vinnie Jones!

Vinnie probably feared for his fledgling international career when I was appointed as Welsh boss. He and I had gone through some serious ups and downs at Wimbledon, many of them revolving round his ability to court controversy. He had been given his first couple of international caps before I came along and it seemed to sum up his disciplinary problems that he was on a five-match suspension – imposed following a sending-off for alleged stamping – when I moved into the hot seat.

I had him back, though, for the friendly in Switzerland and had no problem handing him the arm band in Holland. It didn't make much difference. We were hammered 7-1 and I felt numb sat a few yards along the touchline from Guus Hiddink as the goals flew past Neville Southall. While this summer's World Cup was on, I read a quote from Gus, who said we gave them a good game for six minutes.

Under my nose was a TV camera which I felt like booting across the other side of the pitch and I sensed the captaincy vote would become a stick to beat me with as the experts went looking for scapegoats. I didn't fancy doing the press conference one bit but I went through with it and made the point that I never wanted a Welsh team of mine to fail like that again. I was quickly reminded that it was the country's heaviest defeat in more than 60 years. Marge, Richard and his wife-to-be Becca were at the game and I just had chance for a hug with them before going back to the hotel for a meal with the players. It wasn't a happy occasion.

Next morning, we went to the airport and the party were to be a man short on the return flight because I was off to Istanbul to watch our next opponents, Turkey, against Belgium. I see the good in people and life and go round for most of the time with a smile on my face but I was very depressed all alone looking out of the window of my seventh-floor room. Mmmmm, would it hurt to jump into the Bosphorus from here?

I went for a long walk and was hassled by a shoe-shine boy trying to make himself a few bob. I agreed to let him loose with his spray and brush and it put the fuckin' tin hat on it when he rubbed brown polish into my black brogues. This was the bottom of the barrel. I walked over the road to McDonald's, bought myself a strawberry milkshake and found it in me to buy a second one, which I handed to the little urchin who had just made my bad weekend even worse. I didn't understand a word he said and he couldn't comprehend any of my attempts at conversation but we sat on the wall, quenched our thirst and had a little giggle.

Fighting Fires And Finding Craig

I only made Vinnie a stand-by player for the next game and felt the humiliation at the hands of Holland had shown he wasn't good enough to play at international level. I also felt there was an inner-sanctum of players who didn't want him there. But I should have gone and seen him to explain my action, or at least given him the courtesy of a phone call. I did neither. I just announced the squad and left him to hear of my selection along with Joe Public. I took the coward's way out and it has become a big issue between us.

His brief international career ended a few months later and it's one of my biggest regrets that I didn't make a better job of handling it. He deserved better than that from me for everything we had been through together at Wimbledon. Afterwards, we didn't speak for a long time and he refused to see me a few years ago when I was in Los Angeles en route to see Jonathan in New Zealand. I phoned Vinnie and wanted to congratulate him on the brilliant success he has had in the film industry but he wasn't prepared to forgive me. I let him down in his other life and he wasn't ready to let me forget it.

Another adversary was lying in wait for me after we played out a couple of goalless draws in Cardiff against Turkey and the Republic of Ireland, the first of them in World Cup qualifying. It was Fergie, giving me a follow-up blast. We were preparing to face Belgium in March, 1997, and had been together all week at the Stakis Hotel in Newport when I took a call from him. "What's going on with Ryan?" he demanded. "He's had people in his room disturbing his sleep."

It was the first I'd heard of the matter and I promised to get to the bottom of it. I sought Giggsy out and it transpired he'd dreamt he'd had intruders in the night. He told his mom about it and the story reached Fergie, who got the wrong end of the stick and criticised me for not having a guard on the door.

That was small beer, though, compared with the storm that erupted around the same time. We were training at the Arms Park before taking on the Belgians and I was sorting out what colour tops the players should have on for a practice game. Some of them had bibs on, some just sweaters and I told Nathan Blake, while I was picking the sides, that he was fine in his black sweater. Nothing was said about it at the time and we carried on working but something obviously niggled with him because a reporter later confronted me, alleging I had made racist remarks to Nathan. I was absolutely flabbergasted.

I thought I had a decent relationship with him. He was by this time playing for Bolton but had been with Cardiff and still had a deep love of his home-city club, whose manager Frank Burrows would occasionally let me pop over there to work with players. When the shit hit the fan and the first of the many headlines appeared, the Welsh FA conducted an internal enquiry and David Collins went for me. I challenged him and said: "You know I'm not a racist and you, as a man of God, should not keep this going."

Nathan alleged I'd also made a racist remark about the Dutch striker Pierre Van Hooijdonk and wouldn't let it lie, although I apologised to him for any offence caused. It was a horrible period in my life but I was encouraged by a card I received from Mickey Bennett, a black winger I had signed for Wimbledon from Charlton. He wrote: "I hope the newspapers and Welsh FA give you the same chance that you gave me – because that was a great chance."

Terry Phelan, a coloured defender who was part of the Cup-winning Wimbledon team, also kindly spoke up for me but I was crucified in most of the papers. For 21 days, the story was news on the back page and sometimes on the front. Then, on the 22nd day, I came down for breakfast and Marge said: "Your name isn't in the paper today." Life started to return to normal at last.

Brian Fear, my chairman at the Welsh FA, was different class. In fact I thank the entire committee, all 24 of them. I couldn't have been given better support. The only people there I had major problems with were David Collins and his predecessor Alun Evans.

They were an ageing group but I liked them despite their unusual ways – and their oddities didn't just relate to the living world. When one of them passed away, Marge and I went to the funeral in the north of the country and were astonished to see the coffin left alone in the church after the service while we all popped over the road for eats and drinks. Then the family members returned and took him to his final resting place.

Results were up and down on the field. We won a friendly in Scotland and led 4-3 after an hour against Turkey, only to lose 6-4. Dennis Bergkamp had put a hat-trick past us in Eindhoven and now Hakan Sukur scored four at our expense.

I sent Paul Jones on for Neville Southall at half-time in Istanbul, where we were on the end of some right rum decisions from the referee. As if it wasn't hard enough against just 11 men in that bear-pit atmosphere. So my scouting trip had helped us gather only one point from two games against the Turks and that had come at the cost of a new pair of shoes and two milkshakes.

The BBC's Ian Gwyn Hughes got stuck into us in his commentary on the game. I caught the flavour of it from Marge when I rang home, so I went marching down the corridor to Ian's room and cleared the air. I copped for plenty of criticism at times and decided to get my own back on the press by holding training sessions at a prison near Usk, where I knew they would struggle to get in.

The Welsh FA had a friend who had done some porridge and he tipped me off about the brilliant pitches there. I was happy to give it a go but less so when the players were outside ready for action and I was still in the dressing room. The bastards had locked me in!

The journalists were looking at their watches, worrying about their deadlines and increasingly impatient to get their press conference under-way, but the warders made them wait in the canteen while the prisoners finished their meal. That was some satisfaction for me but it wasn't the only odd-ball behaviour they saw. I turned up for one 'presser' in a mask – a muppet's head with a big red nose – saying Mr Gould was having a rough time of it from the media so he had sent a friend along to speak to them. It was my way of trying to relieve the pressure because things were getting decidedly bitter.

Another time, at a golf club near Pontypool, I felt they were trying to divide my squad, so I laid out 22 chairs in a big arc and had all my players alongside me for my media conference. The lads normally gave interviews on request to little groups of reporters but I decided we would have everything out in the open for once.

The relationship wasn't always fractious. In Tunisia, we had an invitation to go to a drinks reception with the British Ambassador there and I made it clear the press were welcome as well. A few of them turned up to see Gary

Speed leading a sing-song. We had a good night – and that was after we'd lost 4-0!

Gary had taken over as captain and Giggsy was superb whenever he played but questions were being asked about other big hitters in our squad. John Toshack went public on his thoughts and said it was time we ended the international careers of Mark Hughes, Neville Southall and Dean Saunders. As I'd realised when jettisoning Ian Rush and Vinnie Jones, such decisions don't come easy.

I wasn't ready to write any more 'obituaries' yet but soon had more than the outspoken views of a former Welsh manager to worry about. On the trip to Belgium that followed, I suspected some of the players were trying to nip out of our hotel when they shouldn't have done and thought it was time I stamped out their fun and games. I sat on the landing and earned the nickname The Werewolf.

Their appearance fee was £300 a match and, from some of the further-flung hotels we stayed in, phone calls back home would be so expensive that the lads would virtually be playing for nothing. One of them said to me once with a wry look: "Don't bother sending me a cheque, just settle my room bill."

We lost 3-2 in Brussels and finished fourth out of five in our qualifying group with seven points from eight matches. It was disappointing after our flying start but I suppose it was an outcome that Welsh fans were used to and one to which they have remained accustomed. We shouldn't forget that the country haven't been in the finals of a major tournament since 1958.

It was on the trip to Brussels that I'd asked each of the lads to pair off with someone in the squad they didn't know and to spend a minute revealing to them their good points and their bad points. It took a little while for them to open up, then the tension was broken by the sight of Mark Pembridge rolling on the floor, laughing at something Giggsy had told him. Pembo enlightened us: "He has bought these puppies who keep chewing his furniture. He is moaning that he keeps having to buy new furniture – and he's the richest man in this room!"

When one campaign ended, we looked around for friendlies against teams who had qualified and who would be useful preparation for when we started playing competitively again at the start of the following season a few months later. There was a balancing act to the planning. You wanted some easier looking fixtures in your schedule because any international manager needs a few victories to stem any criticism but you also wanted to get something meaningful from games.

In 2004, when Sanch took over as Northern Ireland manager, I advised him to find the weakest opposition he could find to start with and had a knowing smile when I noticed they were on tour not long after in the West Indies. People will throw the stats at you when the pressure's on, so my suggestion to him was that he might as well put a win or two on the board before many questions were asked.

All that said, I was delighted with the fixture that dropped into our lap late in 1997. David Collins surprised me by saying Brazil wanted us over there for a game and were offering us £25,000 plus expenses. I told him to say we would go for £50,000 plus expenses and we were excited when they coughed up and left us making plans for what was a first visit to South America for virtually all of us.

We were joined on board by what looked like two Mafia hit-men, who turned out to be Brazil's two full-backs, Cafu and Roberto Carlos. They were immaculately dressed in suits and you could tell they shopped in Italy as well as played there. That wasn't the only difference between them and our lads. They went and sat in the posh seats at the front of the plane while we headed for economy.

Considering the splendour of Brazil's football, I couldn't believe the training pitch they saddled us with. It was the worst I had ever seen; not a patch, if you'll pardon the pun, on the one the Italians had done us like a kipper with just outside Rome. I wasn't having it and complained but was told all the facilities were like that. Brazilians worked so hard on their control on dodgy pitches apparently that they were then breathtaking when they played games on a proper surface.

We lost 3-0 in Brasilia but did okay considering we were without Giggs, Savage, Hughes, Horne, Hartson and Symons, and had Coventry reserve striker Simon Haworth making his debut. One of their goals was a screamer from Rivaldo at the end of a brilliant switch-over which left my two centre-halves not knowing whether to shit or shave. It was a great education and one of those occasions when the experience from facing such outstanding players outweighed any inconvenience – or fears that you would get a right pasting.

Naturally, we went souvenir-hunting before we left the pitch at the final whistle. The lads were desperate to get their hands on one of the famous yellow shirts but some were lucky, some weren't. Brazilian players were given only one shirt at a match, rather than the two our lads were issued with, and that taught them not to hand such treasured keepsakes out lightly. I was grateful to my counterpart, Mario Zagallo, for sorting one out for me.

I also had something else in my luggage when I got home. The Brazilians had presented us with a magnificent two-foot high statue of two warriors which I decided would sit nicely in the bolthole, so I told the kit-man to make sure that item was destined for Portishead when we disembarked the coach.

Somebody, somewhere has plenty of footage of Zagallo and me. A camera crew followed us throughout the game and an interviewer asked me at the end: "You shout a lot at your players, Zagallo doesn't. Why is that?" I said: "He has great players. Mine aren't quite as good, so I have to encourage them more and send on regular instructions."

It was difficult not to ask ourselves during the trip why we had been chosen as opponents for the World Cup holders. But, the following month, when the draw was made for the 1998 finals in France, Brazil's name came out alongside that of Scotland – and our conquerors must have been glad they had had a taste of playing against a British side. Coincidence or not? Make your own mind up.

One of the things I loved about international management was the friendships it brought me with the other home country bosses. I didn't particularly click with Glenn Hoddle but Bryan Hamilton and Mick McCarthy became great pals when they were working over in Ireland and we're still mates. And I think the world of Craig Brown, who had a first meeting with me that he and Marge have never forgotten.

I was always keen to go on courses that would expand my knowledge and hopefully improve my effectiveness, and first bumped into 'Broony' on one in Malta. He appeared from round the corner at the supposedly private place we were staying at and copped an eyeful of Marge sunbathing topless. From that day, he sent postcards from wherever he was in the world, all addressed to Marge and headed: "How to murder your husband."

Jonathan became known to him as 'Son of the Mother' when he was part of his Scotland squad and Broony was pure class. In Malta, we had to do some role-play in twos, with one of us taking the part of the manager and the other that of a player who was being dropped. We went on and on, with him telling me why I was being axed and copping for a right strop and a thousand questions in return. It was unrehearsed but so convincing that the other coaches gave us a standing ovation when we finally sat down after 20 minutes.

I also went on a course in Denmark and was lucky enough to qualify as a holder of the UEFA A License at the magnificent Clairfontain academy in France, complete with its Platini Pitch. There wasn't a blade of grass out of place on it. It made my lawns in Portishead, which are my pride and joy in my semi-retirement, look like a piece of scrubby common land.

The home managers were once invited to a photo shoot by Four-Four-Two magazine and Broony set the tone by turning up immaculately, as requested, in collar and tie. I had followed suit, if you pardon the pun, but something got lost in the message to Mick McCarthy because he showed up in an open-necked shirt and had to be strategically positioned behind my outstretched arm so he didn't stand out like a sore thumb.

Mick is as good as gold and I've been delighted to see him doing so well at Wolves in the last few years. He always finds time for a chat with me when I'm covering games his side are involved in and I could see him glowing with pride when I met him in the corridor at Upton Park last season after Wolves had beaten West Ham convincingly in a televised midweek match.

We once drew a friendly against his Republic team in Ireland and then went up a few weeks later to Kilmarnock, where John Hartson's first international goal brought us a 1-0 win over Broony's Scots. For a while at least, I basked in the satisfaction of holding the British bragging rights.

I was always keen on youngsters and gave debuts to a lot of players, such as Bristol Rovers' Marcus Browning against San Marino, Robert Page against Turkey and Wolves defender Ryan Green in Malta. Early in my reign, I had driven to Bisham Abbey to watch Jimmy Shoulder preparing the under-21s for a tournament in Norway and spotted this little lad spinning and knocking it past opponents; an absolute dream.

I couldn't get to Jim quickly enough to ask who he was but was told not to be too enthusiastic because trying to control him would drain all my energy. I wasn't going to be that easily put off and couldn't take my eyes off him. He was a real ants-in-your-pants character, the most talented lad I had ever seen in keep-ball or five-a-side sessions. This was my introduction to Craig Bellamy.

Whatever the age group, I went on every trip I possibly could to see what was coming through and this boy whetted my appetite to keep adding to my air miles. He was absolutely outstanding. I gave him his senior debut at 18 as a substitute against Jamaica at Cardiff early in 1998 – a fixture I pushed hard for with David Collins because I thought their supporters would come in droves and create a great atmosphere. We weren't disappointed. Sav played sweeper and we won 2-1.

Bellers then scored a late winner with a far-post header when I threw him on as a substitute in a European Championship qualifier in Copenhagen and made the dressing room a lovely place to be afterwards. He was very much the new kid on the block and we never clashed, despite Jimmy Shoulder's warning. All he ever wanted was to be up there with the superstars.

He never stopped asking questions and travelled the length and breadth of the country and even Europe watching matches. I'm sure he'll make a great coach. I rang up numerous managers to tip them off about him because he was just a kid at Norwich and clearly wanted to be the best. He could be a pain in the arse and had this impetuous, difficult streak, but it's a shame if people perceive him only as a trouble-maker because there is so much to like and admire about him.

At the end of 1997-98, we fixed ourselves up with a nice end-of-season trip to Malta and Tunisia, the latter game causing particular interest among the media representatives with us because Tunisia were England's first opponents in the World Cup finals in Marseille a couple of weeks later. We broke our long run without a victory by winning well enough in Valetta but crashed 4-0 a few days later and didn't play well.

The Gould family were well represented at the World Cup. I was going to watch the countries like Italy who we would be playing in the next European Championship qualifying group from the following autumn, so Marge and I hired a car – a small Fiesta to save the Welsh FA money – to get around. We had a lovely time, made all the more enjoyable because Jonathan was there with Scotland.

He had gone on to have an excellent career, helped on his way by an old pals' act between Jim McCalliog and me. My early-70s Wolves team-mate gave him his first chance in League football at Halifax and obviously left an impression because Jonathan had a cat he called McCalliog. After playing 20 games or so for me at Coventry, he then moved to Bradford and played under Chris Kamara before a surprise door to the big time opened in 1997.

I took a call at 9am one day from Craig Brown's brother, Jock, who was Celtic's chief executive. He said they needed another keeper as cover for their forthcoming European campaign but required one in a hurry as the deadline was midnight. Jonathan had cleared it with his club that he could go on a free if he could get fixed up but Kamara's mouth dropped open when he realised who was after him. Jock still had to confirm things with the Celtic manager, Wim Jansen, so I told Jonathan to take his mobile out to training with him among his gloves and caps. Confirmation came during the session and he was off to Scotland.

It was while he was at Parkhead that he caught the eye of the Scottish management and I went to see him in one or two of his appearances in finals at Hampden. Playing there was another one-up on me. The nearest I'd got to appearing there was a friendly with Arsenal down the road at Rangers and those trips to Greenock Morton with Wolves and Coventry.

Jonathan was a late inclusion in the 1998 World Cup squad as Scotland's third-choice keeper after Andy Goram pulled out. And he helped us gain privileged access. Broony was very good about allowing us around the team hotel and, as you may imagine, was especially pleased to see Marge. Jonathan didn't play in the tournament and the Scots went out at the group stage but it was a great experience for him.

We hired a villa in the South of France and struck out from there to watch England v Tunisia in Marseille, Scotland v Norway in Bordeaux, Argentina v Japan in Toulouse, Italy v Cameroon in Montpelier and Scotland v Morocco in St Etienne. The highlight was going to see Scotland play but, for Marge, that was rivalled by a breezy day in St Etienne when she discovered what a Scotsman wears under his kilt – or in this case doesn't wear.

By the time Jonathan won his two senior international caps, against Australia and Latvia, I was out of international management. But I'm very proud of a picture of the two of us showing off his Scotland shirt and have hung it on the wall in the bolthole.

A less happy memory is the Robbie Savage shirt incident, which kicked off when we were being looked after by my mate Hamish Ferguson at the terrific

Carden Park Hotel near Chester before a game against Italy at Anfield. I went back to my room after my early morning run, put Sky on and there was Sav being interviewed by Pete Colley, who handed him a shirt with Paolo Maldini's name and no 3 on the back.

The next thing, Sav is throwing it in the bin with some derogatory comment, so I rang Graham Williams in a rage at about 6.30am and said: "Did you see that?" I went ape-shit. He was still wiping the sleep from his eyes, so I told him to get his telly on and cop an eyeful like I just had.

I looked up the number of the room Sav was sharing with Paul Jones, woke them up as well and demanded that he got round to mine straightaway. I asked if he realised what he had done with his stupid action and told him he was dropped. Brian Fear was next on my list of calls and supported my decision, so I told Robbie to pack his bags and clear off to his parents' house in Wrexham, otherwise I was calling the police to have him marched away. He was in tears, very upset.

A deputation of players – Ryan Giggs, Gary Speed, Mark Hughes and Dean Saunders – soon came to see me, asking for a rethink because they thought I had acted too harshly. They were right. I knew I had gone off the radar but I did what I did because I care so much about the game and I'm proud of the brilliant players in it; even when they are in the opposition's colours.

The media were happy to whip things up and paint me as Mr Nasty. It was a role I was still carrying off easily enough because I was incensed and very uptight. After assembling all the squad and checking that they all thought the same way, though, I said I'd meet them half-way and put Sav on the bench.

I suspect the reporter had set him up and I should have closed the matter there but agreed to go in front of the cameras with Sav for the apologies and explanations. I don't know who was squirming the most, him or me. He went on for the last few minutes of the game, we lost 2-0 despite playing well and our relationship cooled for a while. But I soon loved him again.

He is like extended family now and we speak regularly, particularly if I think he's down and needs cheering up. There's respect between us. He hit the book shelves a few weeks before me with his autobiography and I could tell from that that he still has a lot of warmth to me.

The end for me as an international manager came in Bologna. I suppose I could see the signs when I was having a stroll round the city with my coaching staff on the day of the game and was pick-pocketed by this gypsy boy, who appeared from under his mother's long skirt and got busy with his roaming hands as someone else bumped into me and spun me round. It was only when I was back at the hotel that I realised I had lost my wallet. It had a few lira in it but, fortunately, I kept my credit cards separately.

After we lost 4-0 to the Italians that night, I couldn't see a way forward and thought it best if I went there and then. The fans were chanting against me, so I summoned David Collins and Brian Fear and told them I felt it was right now that someone else should have a go. At least the setting was a step up from the gents', the venue for my resignation as Coventry manager. We were now in the drug-testing room.

I informed the players of my decision straight afterwards and then did all the necessary media interviews. It was strange flying home the next day as just another member of the party rather than the one in charge of 18 or so players and almost as many staff and officials. I normally sat at the back of the plane, so I could watch everybody. This time it didn't matter. I was an ex-manager.

We still had a chance of qualifying and had another game four days later, against Denmark at Anfield. I watched it at home on TV and willed them to win. I recommended Mark Hughes and Neville Southall as my successors and told the committee they really had to go for someone Welsh. As much as I didn't want to feel an outsider, the fact you're not from the same country does become a stick to beat you with when results are not good.

I am proud that Wales went close to reaching the European Championships finals two years later when they had their opportunity. I had put some decent foundations in with grooming lads like Sav, Bellers, Simon Davies, Danny Gabbidon, Rob Earnshaw, James Collins and Carl Robinson, and given a first chance to Southampton keeper Paul Jones, who was outstanding. I'd also made Wolves defender Ryan Green the youngest-ever Welsh international at 17.

In the role, though, I had always suffered from carousel syndrome – that strange, almost helpless feeling of waving your players off at the airport and knowing they were under someone else's control until you next called them up a few weeks or months later. You have eight or nine intense days when you are responsible for them, then everyone collects their luggage and evaporates in front of your eyes.

Back On The Club Beat

When you manage a club, you see players several days a week and usually play matches at the weekend and in midweek. It's a nine-month treadmill that's completely different to managing in international football and I'm not alone in having encountered a bit of a void while I was in charge of a country. But leaving the job was even more bizarre than that feeling.

Being in charge of Wales had consumed me totally and then suddenly it wasn't there any more. There was a big emptiness, more so than when I had left my various club positions, and I was in a hurry to get back to work quickly.

Within days, I was interviewed for the Sheffield United post and knew straightaway I wouldn't be going there. They sat me down for a chat in the foyer of a hotel, not in a private room, and I wasn't happy with that. I took it as a signal that they weren't treating me seriously. But I set my sights on the Bolton job when I was called for talks about succeeding Roy McFarland.

I went into the interview with a clear outline of how I would run the club, right down to detailing the budgets. They looked elsewhere in the end but I found out years later that I had made a good impression. I went to cover a Bolton home game for talkSPORT and their chairman Phil Garside invited me into his office and said: "I'll never forget that interview. You really entertained us that day."

I suppose the odds were stacked against me being installed at Bramall Lane or the Reebok Stadium. I never played or managed north of Wolverhampton, although I once had talks with Jim Smith and left him wishing he had signed me. In the end, I joined Bristol Rovers instead and scored a hat-trick against his Blackburn side on my debut.

The only pressure on me to jump straight back into employment in 1999 was self-imposed. The Welsh FA gave me an £18,000 pay-off and, after my initial haste, I decided I would only return to the game for a post I really fancied. So was I ready for a reunion with a man who had played a huge part in my past? Sam Hammam was back on the scene.

Sam had sold Wimbledon to a group of Norwegian businessmen and was on the look-out for a new club. Our families were close, so it was no hardship for him to come to our house, where he fell in love with our back garden. He relished the peace there and called it his heaven. When he wasn't admiring the lines on the lawn and the chrysanthemums in the borders, he wanted my advice on which clubs had the necessary potential to lure him.

West Ham and Tottenham were mentioned and, when his sights were lowered a little, we considered anywhere within a couple of hours of his London base. His search took him to Cardiff, where he was recognised and had fans asking him when he was going to buy the place. A seed was sown. He was flattered by the attention and couldn't get the idea out of his head. In no time, he had taken over.

When you see Cardiff's fans tapping their heads with both hands, that dates back to when he went in there. They thought it depicted homage to the Ayatollah. He loved it because it was fun and because he was back doing something he felt so passionately about.

He wanted me in as manager but I was worried about the baggage I was carrying from my time with Wales. It wasn't that I didn't fancy working with him again. I was smitten with the idea but expressed my reservations before we shook on a deal. He showed he had learned from our past differences by making sure Marge and I were both happy with my money, then he told the chief executive David Temmy to sort me out with a lovely Audi 6. It had always been my ambition to get a nice club car out of him.

Some time later, I left in a rush to drive to a Football Combination match at Bristol City and stopped to fill up with fuel. The trouble was that I put diesel in. The forecourt staff said I'd probably just make it to Ashton Gate, which I did, but the engine gave out as I set off for home, and I had to ring the AA.

While I was waiting, I rang Jonathan in Glasgow and asked how he was. He said: "Better than you." When I asked what he meant, he explained that he was on a Cardiff website as we were speaking and he'd just read about my misfortune at the pumps. A supporter had been filling his car up at the same time, seen what I had done and then written about it on a fans' forum. It was my introduction to the amazing world of Information Technology.

My remit at Cardiff was to draw Wales' best under-21 players to Ninian Park. My track record for finding them was second to none and I was well placed to work the system, having set it up on behalf of the country. Sam trusted my judgement completely. I soon signed Danny Gabbidon from West Brom for £800,000 and helped groom Rob Earnshaw and James Collins as they came through the ranks. They eventually made the club £10m between them, so that little sum paid for my Audi, my salary and left a bit over as petty cash.

I didn't want Sam overspending and I knew I could still find the players. I treated his pound as my pound, so I set strict levels on what I thought players were worth and wouldn't go above those valuations. But I still felt battle-weary from my travels and wasn't at my best. Apart from my job description, there was one other key difference from our time together at Wimbledon. Sam was now full-time and had set himself up in the biggest office at Ninian Park. At Plough Lane, he had had no permanent headquarters and just used to flit in and out. I had a power there which I never felt I acquired at Cardiff.

I knew I probably wasn't going to be able to give him the FA Cup again. The competition still meant a lot to us and we were disappointed when we went out to Crewe after progressing through a couple of rounds. You can imagine my feelings when Sir Alex Ferguson took his players to Brazil a few months earlier instead of entering our Cup. I thought it was very sad, a disgrace even. I would never have done that to 'my' trophy.

I opened the season in the dug-out and we didn't lose any of our first nine League matches, although we drew most of them. But Sam's presence had weakened my authority and I wasn't the same character as a result. My decision-making wasn't as good as it should have been. I suspect he thought I had lost the plot and he took measures. He was fond of recreating the Wimbledon connection and had already brought in Alan Cork as coach.

It was working well enough, with results continuing to be decent, but Corky was ready to take on more power and it wasn't long before he was put in charge of all playing matters and I became director of football on the same money. Of course it hurt – it dented my ego and opened some wounds, although I loved Corky to bits and he had been brilliant for me at Wimbledon. The bottom line was that it was Sam's club and I couldn't really challenge what he decided to do with it.

I spent more time watching forthcoming opponents and looking for players, which was something I was good at and was comfortable doing. I also coached the reserves, who I called the Nearly Dead Squad because they were made up of several players who were on their way out of the club.

Success came with promotion from the bottom division with three matches to spare. We made sure of going up by drawing 3-3 at York thanks largely to a hat-trick by one of my signings, Leo Fortune-West. It was a typical day's work. Rob Earnshaw couldn't stop scoring and our record of 95 League goals was far and away the best in the division, although we finished second well behind the champions Brighton, with Paul Brayson and Jason Bowen also in double figures.

I knew my position and didn't go to by any means all of the first-team games but I felt enough a part of it to join in the celebrations at Bootham Crescent. As a forward, like Corky, I knew I had done my bit to make us a major force at that level. All that said, I resigned that summer because I wasn't enjoying the work as much as I hoped. It wasn't me.

Sam knew there was no point trying to talk me out of my decision. I just wanted him to be successful and we continue to have a brotherly relationship. If I was in trouble anywhere in the world, I know he would be the first person on my doorstep asking what he could do to help. Out of the blue, I'll text him and say: "It's Gouldy. Just thought I'd let you know I'm thinking of you and missing you." I do the same with Willo and Howey.

I hadn't been at my best at Cardiff but I specialised in parting gifts and the one to my latest club was the recommendation that they should sign Neil Alexander, a Scottish keeper who Jonathan spoke well of, and a midfielder called Graham Kavanagh. They went on to total 400 games there between them, so it proved a good tip-off.

I was 55 and took my football pension while resuming my training as a domestic engineer and free spirit. My golf improved and I also took up cricket again, playing for the local side at the Lake Ground in Portishead, where I became known as the Ex Superstar and lapped up the dressing-room banter.

I had a head start after all my years in football and remember hoisting a team-mate's boxer shorts on the sight screen – something for which revenge was carried out while I was batting in the next match! I got it into my head that opposition bowlers found another 10mph when I went in, so I sometimes walked out wearing a pig's mask if I hadn't been spotted beforehand.

It was an appropriate accessory because my family reckoned I snored like one when I arrived home from an exhausting day and fell asleep in my favourite armchair. It was Marge's idea we bought a mask when we saw one in a shop in Torquay. Things changed when I lost several teeth through edging the ball into my mouth a few years ago and I decided I'd better strap a helmet on for proper protection from then on. But I had some great fun in the meantime, taking guard from under my bizarre disguise and whipping it off after two or three balls – if I lasted that long. Someone would shout: "Fuck me, look who it is!" By then, though, I'd hope I'd disarmed their angry fast bowlers with a laugh.

I became involved with Somerset over-50s – not a bad decision as we went on tour with Kent over-50s to St Lucia and played on the new Test ground there. It was one of the ladies on the trip, Marge's close friend Daff, who nicknamed us Punch and Judy because she observed how our marriage could certainly never be described as dull!

Life was more than pleasant. I accepted, out of respect for my dad, an invitation to play in a golf tournament for the blind at Wentworth and saw other offers come in from the celebrity circuit, so I played at Woburn, Gleneagles and in Ireland in a series of events arranged by Steve Redgrave. My garden had never looked so good and my lawns, in particular, became my treasure. Being under Marge's feet was a new experience but converting some loft space to the office that I Christened my bolthole meant she had somewhere to banish me when I stepped out of line.

As happens to all football people, I realised that you could only play so much golf or run the mower up and down so many times a week. I started to miss the game that had been my living for four decades and was hankering for a return. I had sampled the retirement business and failed.

I began applying for jobs again and went for the one at Everton without getting an interview. I also cast an eye back into the international game and made a pitch, at different times, for the manager's jobs with the Republic of Ireland, Northern Ireland and Scotland. I even rang Swindon Town when I heard there might soon be a vacancy and was a little embarrassed when the then incumbent Andy King answered the phone – something that caused bad blood between us.

The call to get back in the dug-out eventually came in January, 2003, from

Cheltenham Town. I was so glad at the prospect of being involved again that I said at my interview: "Gentlemen, football has been good to me, so I'm quite prepared to do this job for expenses only." Not surprisingly, there was a certain attraction to them in my offer.

Much as I loved a battle, this really was one that would take some winning. Under my predecessor Graham Allner, the side hadn't won any of their first eight games of the season, then they suffered a couple of 4-0 spankings shortly before my arrival. On top of that, the popular club captain Chris Banks, who had been holding the fort with Bob Bloomer and Mark Yates after Graham left, announced his retirement before my first match.

They were one place and one point off the bottom in their first ever season in the third tier, so the die was cast in a lot of ways and survival looked a long way off. I obviously threw myself into the role, though, because I was sent from the dug-out at home to Stockport in one of my first games. I had never been dismissed in my career and always prided myself on being able to pull back from the brink when I was jousting with referees and linesmen.

But I couldn't help myself after a dreadful tackle on Tony Naylor by Carlton Palmer, their player-manager, and went catapulting out of the technical area to protest. I was ordered to watch the rest of the game from up in the stand and Palmer followed me after a second diabolical challenge later in the first half. I think it was the first time the managers of both clubs had been sent off in the same game.

I suppose the incident told me I still had fire in my belly. I had taken the job to see what remained in the tank and had partially answered myself, so I was content enough on that score. Nor was it much of a hardship to rev up the silver Mercedes that I had always wanted and finally treated myself to, and drive the 50 miles up the M5. My lads bought me the number plate R88 CUP to commemorate a certain day out at Wembley and I was a happy traveller.

I was pleased to inherit Ian Weston as physio because I had given him his debut as a Bristol Rovers player. I also thought the world of Bob Bloomer, a former Rovers player and a great lad who was my coach in the first year. I liked working there, both at the Zurich sports ground and the stadium at Whaddon Road, where I had a lovely secretary and Marge was made to feel very much at home. A footballer's wife can lead a lonely life but she was happy going to matches there.

We made a decent start by going three games without losing, including a draw at the leaders Wigan, and I was pleased the board backed me with the £50,000, a club record fee, I needed to sign midfielder Grant McCann from West Ham. As usual, though, I turned to youth and gave chances to lads like Shane Duff, who was given a testimonial by Cheltenham this year, and a Bristol City striker called Marvin Brown while also handing pro contracts to youth teamers Luke Buttery and Luke Corbett. I even had a look in practice matches at Cleve Holder and James Clarke, two lads I had seen playing for Portishead.

The Ashton Gate regulars didn't spare me when we lost 3-1 there but we were beaten only twice in the last 12 games of the season and gave ourselves a fighting chance of pulling clear. The 3-0 thrashing we handed our rivals Swindon was well received and we might have been safe if we hadn't twice chucked away 2-0 leads on our travels. We were still in there battling when 3,000 of our fans followed us to Notts County on the last day but we hit the post and bar, and lost 1-0. Chesterfield drew at Blackpool on the same afternoon to stay up at our expense, two points and one place above us. Like when I went down with Albion in 1991, there had been too many draws.

The chocolate feast I had promised the lads if they pulled it off at Meadow Lane had to be shelved but I was heartened by what we had done. We had taken 25 points from my 20 games in charge and I thought we could make a strong challenge in the bottom division. It was my second relegation as a manager and I responded by doing what I'd done after the one at West Brom – I signed Bob Taylor. He was now 36 and had had a decent spell at Bolton in between his two stints with Albion, where he was an absolute legend. I knew he would still score goals.

Thankfully, my flair for being able to spot a good prospect was still there as well and I went to Forest Green and bought a tall striker called Kayode Odejayi for only £5,000. After a slow start, he became a right handful before being sold for a record Cheltenham fee of £200,000 to Barnsley, where he hit a winning goal against Chelsea in the FA Cup two or three years ago.

I was eventually put on a contract and given a Mazda estate. I brought in Graham Williams as scout for my second season because he was a good talent spotter. I squeezed the budget to add a sports psychologist and also draft in as football coordinator David Burnside, who lived just down the motorway in Bristol. No wonder I was hopeful we could build on our first few months.

What I didn't expect was to fall out with the local newspaper. I had a nightmare with them. I had been mullered by some of the reporters at West Brom a decade or so earlier but this was a football backwater by comparison and a club who weren't that long out of non-League football. The expectations and climate should have been altogether different.

It started soon after my sending-off from the dug-out, an indiscretion for which I apologised profusely both to the referee and the FA by saying I was new to technical areas – or cages as I preferred to call them. They accepted my explanations and said no further action was to be taken but the paper's correspondent rang the FA and asked why I wasn't being charged with bringing the game into disrepute.

As someone who wanted to cultivate links with the community through the local media and keep them well stocked with headlines, I was absolutely livid. I went to their offices to meet the reporter and his editor but felt they always had a downer on me from then on.

The board were brilliant but, when we got into a sequence of defeats, the fans turned and the task of stabilising the season became very difficult. We had finished 2002-03 as a side who were very hard to beat but one who drew too many games because we didn't score enough. Although we then lost the prolific Tony Naylor to Telford over the summer, we were exactly the opposite in the new season. We couldn't stop scoring goals, nor, unfortunately, could we prevent them going in at our end.

We lost our first three games, including one in the Carling Cup, then soon won three in a row, with the crowd getting full value for money as Bob Taylor found his feet. It was one thing or the other and, after a couple of uncharacteristic draws, we nosedived by losing six games out of seven around a victory over Yeovil. Only four teams had scored more than us but we had leaked 31 and the natives were restless at our position not far out of the bottom four.

The fans were chanting for my neck in a home defeat against Rochdale in the last of those matches and were singing the name of Steve Cotterill. I had signed him at Wimbledon and he was the manager who had taken Cheltenham to promotion. He was on the market again after an unhappy spell with Sunderland and I thought my position was untenable. I went straight to the directors' box at the end of the game and quit.

I was sorry to go because we felt we could still have made something of the season but the anger I felt the Cheltenham press had stirred up made life very difficult. The board were good to me even as I left, saying in a statement that I had been treated appallingly by the local media.

I was becoming well used to leaving jobs and looking around for what to do next. To fill the gap this time, I coached the village team in Portishead and took a few drives back up the M5 to put the lads at Hartbury College, who were based near Gloucester and played in the Hellenic League, through their paces. I also started scouting for David Pleat at Tottenham and particularly enjoyed an assignment to AC Milan he sent me on. But I didn't find it easy writing up reports afterwards, nor not following up on my findings, as I would have done as a manager.

I was with Marge at a Tottenham v Birmingham game on a ticket provided by Pleaty when Barry Fry bumped into me and asked what I was up to. I was kicking my heels and told him to give me a ring if he needed any help at Peterborough, where he was owner, chairman and manager. I informed him I only wanted to coach, not manage, and before long I was being offered a route back into the game, at a club who were battling against the drop to the bottom division.

Was it my ego that tempted me back – or was I looking for some extra financial insurance? Or maybe I had the thought in the back of my mind that you are a very long time retired. Marge told me I'd be going on my own as she wasn't prepared to uproot again. She would have been quite happy to see me leave the game behind, concentrate on my media work and see more of the family, so I went solo for a long while. I had some nights in a hotel but also did a lot of commuting and often drove to Peterborough and back in a day, leaving home at 5.30am.

Despite our position, it was a fun period and I enjoyed my relationship with Barry, who had been very brave with his money, and the other staff. One of the coaches, a terrific guy called John Morley who is now with the Irish FA, likened the club to a circus because of our barmy ways and gave us all appropriate nicknames. Barry was the Ring Master and I was the Lion Tamer because we had one or two difficult characters who needed a crack of the whip to get them in line.

We were speeding along the dual carriageway going to Colchester for one game and three cars containing our London-based players zipped past the coach. Crazy! We stayed up and Barry organised a pre-season game a few weeks later at Darlington. Geography was obviously never his strong point. He said he didn't remember it being that far up the A1 and the lads could never recall going such a distance for a friendly. In fact, some of them hadn't been that far on holiday.

That was one mistake. The other was me going into a bookies at our ground a couple of days later, after we had won five or six, and putting £400 on us for promotion at 20-1. We started well, then levelled out and, a month and a half into the new season, had a game in the LDV Vans Trophy at Bristol City, so I met the squad in the afternoon at the hotel. We were playing out from the back more than usual, certainly more than I wanted us to, and I did my nut when Andy Legg gave the ball away and they scored. Curtis Woodhouse was very strong in his influence on the squad but I despaired at how things were now changing when my back was turned and I said nothing at half-time.

There were undercurrents between Curtis and me, and when the players went out for the second half, I followed Barry to the toilet and told him I'd had enough. I couldn't have my authority undermined like that. I rang Marge, who was up in the stand with Jonathan and his wife Emma, and told them not to bother going back to their seats. We were off.

I had resigned as Coventry manager in the gents' at QPR, now I was doing something similar with Posh at Ashton Gate, at half-time no less. I was criticised for jumping ship but I didn't do it for effect. I'm my own man and couldn't stand the thought of trying to coach players who didn't want to hear what I said. It was goodbye to the Antigua holiday that I'd had in mind when I placed that bet on us winning promotion but we would soon be travelling even further afield than the Caribbean.

Taking Flight With The Kiwis

The Goulds' landing in New Zealand wasn't an overnight thing. Jonathan was still in his teens when I sent him there in 1987 for six months with a Wimbledon lad called Brian McAllister. The visit was part of a reciprocal arrangement with Napier City Rovers, who had despatched two players to England around the same time under a scheme set up by Colin Stone, who worked in the offices at Wimbledon.

Jon loved the lifestyle but it was the best part of another 20 years before he took the decision to uproot his family and move out there to live and work. It was a giant step and one that kick-started our family's regular travels to that distant part of the world.

Much as Jon longed from a young age to be a footballer, I wanted him to learn the ropes in a safer job first and give himself something to fall back on. Then I'd help him in his efforts to establish a playing career. So he spent two years working for Barclays Bank while I nurtured him as a goalkeeper, both of us trying to make the best of his outstanding hand-to-eye coordination.

He spent six months Down Under in his first stay, playing part-time for Napier and working in a nightclub to supplement his earnings. He was quite successful and stayed in contact with them, with the result that when his playing career in England and Scotland ended, Colin Stone contacted him. A new franchise league had started and he was asked to go and start an academy at one of the clubs, Hawkes Bay United.

He couldn't get on the plane quick enough and played in goal for them at the weekends but not, initially, with much luck. They lost their first six games and the manager Perry Cotton was sacked. Some people might regard that as a case of being in the right place but he was very much in the wrong place for dealing with a crisis back here in Portishead. And it all started when I tried to move a plant pot at home and hurt my back; my L4 and L5 to be precise.

I saw an osteopath but suffered some internal bleeding and all hell broke loose. I was in a mess and it wasn't long before I was bed-ridden and becoming dehydrated. Inevitably, I ended up in hospital and was put on a drip for 24 hours. I was in there for ten days and one of the other chaps in the ward came over and said: "You're Bobby Gould, aren't you? I thought you were dying."

I might have had my mad moments in football dressing rooms but I didn't half get that ward organised. The racing on TV was the highlight of our day and I became Honest Bob The Bookie, surrounded by my friends Richter (because his snoring went off the scale), X-Ray and The Toll Collector. If anyone came in during the afternoons to see us, we told them to clear off and come back after the last race.

My leadership instincts surfaced when we thought the women were getting preferential treatment and we were being left with cold showers. From my bed, I rang the Evening Post anonymously, asked for the medical correspondent and told her I wanted our protests splashed across the front page – with me identified only as Bob The Bookie. In no time, our showers were hot.

I told the sister what I had done and it wasn't long before one of the doctors was saying: "Mr Gould, we think you're well enough to go home." I went back to Portishead and promptly had a relapse. My doctor saw me, tapped me on the knee to get a reaction and I cried out with pain from my back. My ex physio, Ian Weston, fixed me up with a scan in Cheltenham and I had a back spasm while I was in there and had to be yanked out.

Eventually, the guy who reads the scans rang home and told us an ambulance was on its way immediately to take me to Frenchay Hospital. The staff at Southmead Hospital on the other side of Bristol had been trying to thin my blood but I had now been diagnosed with acute blood poisoning. The sirens and blue light were on as the laughing gas was applied to ease the pain. It was nearly Goodnight Vienna – or Goodnight Irene as they sing at Bristol Rovers.

There was no hospital banter this time. I was in a private ward on my own for six weeks. I had an infection in my spine and went into another spasm when they were about to operate. My left leg swelled to the size of a tree trunk and I remember having six doctors at the bottom of my bed at six o'clock in the morning. I had contracted deep-vein thrombosis as a result of my blood thickening through the enforced inactivity.

It was the same leg that Peter Osgood had broken all those years earlier and

I was told the following 24 hours were critical. I was put on a drug to thin the blood and realised that the nurses, who were absolute angels, used different types of needles for the tests. Some hurt and some didn't, so I occasionally reached into my wallet for a note, put it under my pillow and said when I was seen to: "There's a fiver. Make sure you use the kinder needles on me."

I pulled through but I was in there for another eight weeks and the whole saga dragged on for three and a half agonising months. When I was finally allowed home for half a day to see how I got on, I'd never been so frightened in my life; the consequences of another down-turn didn't bear thinking about.

There was an incentive for me to get well. We were intent on going to New Zealand in late 2005 for the winter months to stay with Jonathan and his family but those plans brought their own complications as the doctors would only let me fly when my blood had returned to a certain level. I was so bored when told I had to take it easy that I logged on to the Internet and worked out that we could make the trip across land and sea in four weeks by taking the train to Naples and boarding a boat that would take us through the Suez Canal.

In the end, I was given clearance for take-off and we flew to Napier with Emirates Air via Dubai, Singapore and Brisbane. The return journey gave us the chance to visit our great friends Patsy and Gordie Fry in Australia. They had by now unfortunately separated and were living in Sydney and Melbourne respectively. We also took in Bangkok, where we might well have had an extra few nights. The plane was overbooked and we would probably have stayed behind for a free extension to our trip had it not been for my insurance – a bloody expensive one at that – being on the point of running out.

Throwing my arms round Jonathan, who I had forbidden from coming home to see me during my ordeal, was an amazing, emotional experience. I'm sure I had tears when I hugged him, Emma and their kids. I had by no means been certain that this day would come round again. Another hug was soon on the way…….Terry Phelan, my Wembley left-back at Wimbledon, was head coach of Otago while Jonathan filled the same role down the road at Hawkes Bay.

I gave myself another treat to celebrate my recovery – a new Mercedes (in red to remind me of all the blood I'd given). But I locked it away in the garage for a few months after Jonathan asked me to go back to New Zealand in the autumn of 2006. We went for three years on the trot and I became known as Father Ted to the lads there. It must be something to do with the hair colouring.

The squad were a mixture of Kiwis like David Geary, Ian Hogg, Cole Peverley, Mitch O'Brien, Leon Birnie, Sam Messan, Dean Johnston and Stuart Hogg, Englishmen Chris Davies, Danny Kirkup and Ricky Gillies, Scots Craig Henslee and Graham Fyfe and a South Korean called Woo Joe Kim. Fyfe had been with me at Cheltenham and with Jon at Celtic. They were great to work with. It wasn't exactly high-pressure stuff after some of my jobs but it was Jonathan's livelihood and I did everything in my professional way.

He finished bottom in his first season, then sixth, fourth and fifth, making a big enough impression in front of those 1,500 attendances to be invited to leave the NZ Championship behind and go full-time with Wellington Phoenix in the A League – a much more challenging competition made up mainly of Australian teams.

At Hawkes Bay, as well as coaching the academy lads on a Monday and Wednesday, I worked with the first team on a Tuesday, Thursday and Saturday – all in the evenings because they were amateur and had other jobs. Friday was a day off and we played on a Sunday against sides like Canterbury and Waitako. It is a beautiful country, quite stunning, and I loved my time there.

Jonathan and I had one big fall-out. Graham Fyfe missed a great chance and our son nearly took a chunk out of the dug-out by kicking it so hard. I told him he was out of order, so he glared at me and told me to see him in the gym later. When we reconvened, he called me the biggest hypocrite of all time, pointing out that I had been known to 'flip' once or twice in my career.

That was my point. I remembered letting my temper get the better of me, like when I mullered Raddy Avramovic at Coventry, and feeling that I'd let my emotions cloud my judgement. I was trying to warn him against making the same mistakes but I looked back at him and sensed our relationship was in danger of being damaged. "You're right," I replied. "I am the biggest fuckin' hypocrite of all time." He burst out laughing and gave me another hug. That's how a lot of disputes end in the Gould family.

I'm so proud of what he has achieved. He left me running Hawkes Bay at times because he was also goalkeeper coach with the New Zealand national side. He went with them as their no 2 at the Beijing Olympics, where they played Brazil, and also to Canada with the team they sent to the Under-21 World Cup. And it was Rikki Herbert, the former Wolves defender who was in charge of the Kiwis at this year's World Cup, who appointed him at Wellington.

It was Jonathan's hunt for players that took me back to Wimbledon earlier this year. I've missed a couple of reunions of our Cup Final squad, so I was delighted to accompany him when he went there to look at a transfer target. We had a lovely welcome and were invited to the boardroom when the word went round that we were present. I even had a hug off the womble and was pleased to hear they still played our Wembley song when the team run out.

My time Down Under wasn't confined to football. Despite being a cricket lover, I had never been to a Test Match until I watched England win the last one in New Zealand early in 2008. The game was at McLean Park in Napier and I was thrilled to be interviewed on the BBC's View From The Boundary by Jonathan Agnew, with whom David Pleat had put in a good word about me.

I soon had access to the players and first met Paul Collingwood while the squad underwent a net session outside the stadium. I had my picture taken with him and we got on well, staying in touch by text for the rest of the tour. One thing led to another and I was able to welcome Michael Vaughan (and his family), Colly and Steve Harmison to a barbeque at the cottage we were renting on ten acres of land owned by our good friends Bill and Sarah Calver.

We had a great time. Having spent a lot of my life in hotels, I was aware what a stifling existence they can create and I think the lads appreciated a change of scenery. I have always been fascinated by the science of sport, all sports, so I loved talking to them about their preparation and training.

Around the same time, I got to know the Aussie opening batsman Justin Langer, who lived in the same Somerset village as our other son Richard. With time on my hands back home, I found myself chauffeuring him to Cardiff and Swansea and then further afield to Lord's and Old Trafford. I was delighted to help because Richard is the chief executive of Somerset County Cricket Club and Justin was playing for them at the time.

As a result of this friendship, I was invited in by Somerset's conditioning coach Darren Veness to do some pre-season work with the players. Not that there was a cover drive or googly in sight. The ball I used was a big white one rather than that small red missile they play with and the drills I was involved in were passing and shooting.

Many cricket teams warm up with games of football and that was my brief for the day, so I made sure there were plenty of silly games and opportunities for mickey-taking. It was all light-hearted, lively stuff and the players seemed to enjoy it. I was a different voice, a break from the more serious exercises the coach Andy Hurry put them through.

I'd never want to be seen as an imposter or hanger-on and was pleased when Somerset also asked me into the dressing room before one game to give them a pep talk. Justin Langer is very big on motivational ideas and spends some of his time flying round Australia to address meetings now he has retired from tormenting England's bowlers. I think it's fair to say we are kindred spirits.

Other offers have stemmed from there and I went to Middlesex earlier this year to do some preparation work with them at the request of Richard Johnson, who used to play for Somerset as well as briefly for England.

My cricket links have even enabled me to open the batting with Marcus Trescothick. Okay, it was only in a benefit game but it was a great experience watching him belt the ball to all parts from close up. I looked at the scoreboard when we brought up our century stand and saw that my contribution was 12. And I was out soon after. At the height of my struggles against some very quick bowling, the umpire said he'd buy me a pint if I scored a run in front of the wicket. That was an extra incentive and, with some difficulty, I played one solitary shot off the middle of the bat that earned me a free pear cider.

My other summer sporting pastime is golf and I'm always very happy to support the days Bob Wilson organises for the Willow Foundation in memory of his and Megs' late daughter, Anna. It is a wonderful charity that has raised millions and become a very special part of our lives. I'm rarely seen without the lilac coloured wrist band that bears the foundation's mark.

It's over 40 years since Bob and me became mates at Arsenal. We were away on tour in Germany when our Jon was born, so Megs and Anna took him and Marge back to our home at 1 Vincent Close, New Barnet. Our kids grew up with Anna and her brothers Robert and John and we had two or three family holidays together that we'll never forget.

In between jobs, I worked for Bob at his soccer schools in Cockfosters, where Mega and Anna were part of the organising team, and he once came for nothing to speak at a fund-raising dinner at Bristol Rovers when we were on our uppers. We would do anything for each other but what can you adequately do for or say to a mate who loses a beautiful daughter to cancer at the age of 31? It was just so desperately sad.

A Time For Talk

Not only do I have the perfect face for radio, I've got a mastery of the English language to die for. Try these Gould sayings for starters:

* I wanted to conceive all my energy.
* The chief scout and manager must be in unicism with each other.
* The referee has misinterpretated that.
* The keeper was like a rabbit in the headlines.
* I'm what you call a country pumpkin.
* The papers are portraying Rafa Benitez as a parrot, just like they did when they showed Graham Taylor as an onion.

And these: When I was previewing the Norwich v Bayern Munich game, I said: "The good people of Suffolk will be looking forward to this one." And a website gave me their Uneconomical Nickname of the Week award for calling the Birmingham manager 'McLeishy.' Bob Wilson, who is always so assured at the microphone and in front of the cameras, must have winced.

My ghost-writer thought it was a good idea to list all those quotes and have me go through them one by one to indicate whether I was actually responsible for them. No point. I'm guilty on all charges, m'lord. And there are probably dozens of other crimes against proper vocabulary that I should ask to be taken into consideration. I might even have sounded a bit too much 'o' when I was talking about Michael Ballack before the World Cup this summer. Alan Green was right to repeatedly call me Mrs Malaprop.

My word-clumsiness hasn't just brought chuckles among radio listeners. A journalist once said of a piece I'd written: "The English language has just suffered another multiple collision with Bobby Gould." And, at Wimbledon, I won the British Gas Gobbledegook Award with my programme notes. My predecessor Dave Bassett had used Tony 'Stengun' Stenson to write his but I chose to go solo and dictated them to our secretary, Mad Madeleine. Between us, we hardly put any commars and full stops in, so they made precious little sense. Madeleine was a good sport and had to be. I sent her across London to a big lunch to collect the award.

I don't even have the excuse of putting my awkwardness with words down to lack of practice. As far back as my first spell as Coventry manager, I did a local BBC radio show which went out on a Saturday morning. A presenter called Stuart Linnell would go with me in the week to a school, office or factory, where we would collect interviews that Stuart would knit together in the studio and intersperse with bits of music. I loved it.

Not only was I taking Coventry City's name into the workplace, I was having close, friendly contact with the people of my home city. It was a role that suited my outgoing personality and gave me the taste for the media work that helped pay the bills whenever I was in between jobs in the following years.

The radio is more than a bit of fun for me these days. Working for talkSPORT is the nearest I have to a job and I love the involvement, whether that means offering opinions at the weekends with Andy Goldstein and Jason Cundy on The Sportsbar (produced by 'Jumper'John Chambers), bouncing off Danny Kelly on Kick-Off during the week or reporting to Adrian Durham when working alongside the likes of Dave Rowe, Ian Abrahams, Geoff Peters, Dom McGuinness or Clarkey at matches on a Saturday. Mark Saggers, a well-known voice in radio circles, is another character I look forward to seeing there.

Ask retired footballers what they most miss and the majority will say the camaraderie and banter of the dressing room or team bus. These lads give me some of that and I loved working for them during the World Cup. I was at the mic for most of the first couple of weeks, usually at the side of John Rawling, Graham Beecroft or Nigel Pearson, and hope we kept the home fires burning in between the live commentaries from the guys in South Africa.

I relished being part of such a team effort and there were some farewell hugs when it all came to an end. It's a very happy set-up, headed by the boss Moz Dee, with Liam Fisher and Matt Smith as programme controllers. I have been blessed throughout my life with great secretaries and Kay Townsend and Lauren Webster are the ladies these days who get me to the right game at the right time on the right date.

But the atmosphere is less convivial when we have our annual five-a-side competition with teams selected under such banners as 'the morning lot' and 'the afternoon bunch.' With Alan Brazil, Andy Townsend, Jason Cundy and my old Coventry pal Micky Quinn on the staff, you can understand why some of the tackling is a bit fierce.

My radio appearances haven't been confined to Talk. I've also been a guest four or five times on the Radio 5 Live Saturday morning show Fighting Talk. Jonathan was keen that I went on because he reckoned it had a cult audience in New Zealand. Whether he believes me when I say that I always made sure of not winning is another matter but that final deciding round, Defending the Indefensible, has terrified me ever since I got the wrong end of the stick when Colin Murray explained the idea. I'm better out of it.

The bosses at Talk were very understanding when I took a call in the spring of last year from the well-respected journalist Ian Ridley and was handed a short-term route back into football management. I had met Ian at a Wales game and told him I'd read he had put his neck in the noose by going back in as chairman of Weymouth. I left with my usual parting shot: "Give me a call any time if you are in trouble."

A couple of Saturdays later, we were having a lasagne at home when the phone rang. It was Ian. He reminded me of my remarks at Wimbledon in 1987 relating to Don Howe and Miss World. He said: "How would you like to come and dance with me at Weymouth?"

The club were in a right mess. They had not long lost ten or 11 league games in a row and were having to play their youth players following a walk-out of the first-team squad. Moz Dee at Talk was brilliant. He said his staff didn't often get opportunities like this and told me I was free to take the manager's job for the last five games. Marge, as ever, backed my judgement and gave me a vote of confidence. She also gave me a road map because she made it clear she was staying put and I'd be living the lonely hotel life for a few nights a week.

I drove down the next day to meet the players, then had a walk along the sea front and saw some cards with Punch and Judy on. I bought one, sent it home unsigned and wrote: "Are you missing me yet? Around the same time, I came into possession of a card that I put up in the bolthole and read: "Craziness doesn't run in my family. It practically gallops."

I stopped the rot with a draw in my first game with Weymouth and would love to have kept them up because the staff and players were brilliant. This wasn't my ego getting the better of me. I loved putting my backside in the hot seat again and being in charge. I still had the energy and motivation.

Marcus Browning was player-coach and I rearranged training for the afternoons rather than mornings, thinking the players were fretting over the league table when they went home for lunch. We all enjoyed working together and I like Ian. I'd go as far as saying that the experience taught me why Fergie is so reluctant to turn his back on managament.

But staying in the Blue Square Premier was virtually a hopeless task and I couldn't turn it round. As one defeat led to another, I had some vicious calls from my mates at Talk, asking what I was spending all my win bonus on. They larruped me. Weymouth went down and it wasn't long before I was back on the reporting beat, sticking to the habits I'd had for decades.

I like to prepare for reporting on matches in the same professional manner that I did as a player. If I'm going to games 100 miles or more away that kick off at lunchtime, I book into a hotel overnight, do my research and go for a run next morning before heading for the ground. It's the routine I am used to and it has always served me well. Who knows how many Saturday afternoons I have left in me? That's why I'm determined to do it properly.

My set ways get me some friendly stick from my work colleagues but I've never had a problem with that, nor with having a good laugh at myself. And it normally causes a few titters at the studios when I eat out with Marge or friends. It must be something to do with the fact I tell them I'm just popping out for a lamb shank.

Andy Goldstein must be the only bloke who has had pictures of a steaming plate of food sent to him from Santa Monica, San Diego and New Zealand. He also likes to admire the stripes on my lawn, so I photograph those on my mobile as well and send him the pictures at talkSPORT HQ. By more traditional means, I had some fertiliser and a spreader despatched to him for his garden.

I'm just grateful to be making a living from a profession that keeps me in regular contact with my many friends in the media. I even cover a lot of Wales' home games and have made good mates out of several of the reporters I saw as adversaries when I was the national manager.

I drove out of my way a couple of years ago to go and have a cup of tea and a hug with Joe Kinnear when I was doing a Sunderland home game and he was having a lousy time at Newcastle. Their match was later in the weekend and it seemed the most natural thing in the world to take a detour and check he was okay, even if I turned up on spec rather than by arrangement.

My meticulous match-day organisation starts before I even leave home. I lay my clothes out on the spare bed so I can just put them on next day or place them into holdalls or on to hangers. Shirts, trousers, socks, underpants......all garments colour-coordinate in my world. If the grandkids allow it, that is. When they stop over, they deliberately swap the various accessories over to confuse me.

I'm so lucky that my life has panned out as it has. There is very little that I would have changed. We've even been so successful in bridging all the miles separating us from Jonathan's family that I was climbing up the wall a few months ago when that bloody ash cloud spewed out and they had to stay with us for another few days before flying back to New Zealand! Don't get me wrong: I love 'em to bits but I value my space as well.

We speak to them a couple of times a week and rely so heavily on Skype. The computer pictures mean we can see how Matthew and Louise are growing as well as talk to them regularly.

Meeting up with Richard, Becca and their two, Jessica and Libby, is nothing like as difficult. They are based a few junctions down the M5 within striking distance of his enviable office at Taunton – overlooking the square at Somerset County Cricket Club. But he, too, has worked in football.

Following his 12 years in the Army, who made him a Major and deployed him in Bosnia and Northern Ireland as well as putting him on stand-by for the first Iraq conflict, he got on well enough with the chief executive at Bristol City, a former RAF man called Colin Sexton, to be appointed there in the role of commercial manager.

He then moved on to county cricket and opened doors for me, both in terms of new friendships with players from another sport and with my bits of training work. He himself has not played sport for a living, nor looked like following me and his older brother. He was Army mad when he was growing up and is a red-hot operator. Where he and Jonathan got their brains from I don't know, because they're brighter cookies than I ever was.

When Matthew arrived 16 years ago, Marge decided she was too young to be known as Grandma, so he was brought up to call us by our Christian names. We followed suit with Louise, Jessica and Libby but the four of them had a vote last year as to whether, now we're in our mid-60s, we should be known as Grandma and Grandpa. It went unanimously against, so we're still Marge and Bob to them all.

I'm still very close to our kid, Trevor, and we were all together in the summer for the wedding of his and Jackie's youngest son Darren to Lorna. A wonderful day was had by all. Trevor played at Wembley before I did when he lined up on the wing for England Schoolboys against Scotland in front of 100,000 in the 1960s and also went for England Youth squad training with the likes of Peter Shilton, Alun Evans of Wolves, Alan Whittle and Archie Styles.

There was more subtlety about him than me and he was very quick, albeit not with my aggression. When he made his Coventry debut against Albion at Highfield Road, I didn't want to put added pressure on him by making it known I was there, so I drove up from London and stood proudly and quietly on the Spion Kop. It was a happy night. All nine of his League games for the club came in 1969-70 but he was actually with them for 18 years as a player or youth coach, having first signed in 1965. He was golden with me when I was manager, his long list of discoveries having included Chris Kirkland, Gary McSheffrey, John Eustace, Willie Boland, Barry Quinn and Marcus Hall.

He went on to play more than 100 games for Northampton – the home town of his wife-to-be Jackie Enfield, a former Olympic swimmer – before joining Bedford. He was thrilled when Bobby Robson took England to play his Aylesbury side some years later and when I put him back on the Highfield Road staff in 1992. He has had spells working as a brickie but has done well in non-League management and is back in the game full time these days with the academy at Northampton, where he made another of his four England Schoolboys appearances. There's a further football link in the story because his other son, Robert, manages a club called Wellington Town just off the M1.

Mum now lives less than a mile from us in Portishead. We brought her down here about five years ago, so we could offer her the sort of care she gave Dad for so long. Although she is the person I get much of my determination from, she was so, so good to him, administering his two insulin injections a day for 24 years and learning to drive when he no longer could. She never ever shied away from her responsibilities.

One member of the extended family doesn't mingle in sporting circles but still commands several pages in my scrapbooks. Mary Morgan, nee Gould, is a sister of my dad's and has made us all proud with her exploits in the theatrical world, including the Belgrave in Coventry, where she has worked in production and administration. She lived in Toronto for decades but is much closer to home again now, in Swindon, although the travel bug hasn't left her. She has been out to see Jonathan's family in New Zealand, where she revelled in the nickname 'Mad Mary' she was given by the kids.

Which brings me to Marge, no doubt the love of my life and my rock of great support in good times and bad. Our first six years of marriage brought us two wonderful sons, four different homes and six top-class football clubs. Beat that if you can! And never once did The Good Lady of The House give me an ear-bashing. She just quietly uprooted and moved on to build another loving home for the three men in her life.

She always trusted me in my belief that I would become a successful professional footballer and our needs would be answered by my roving spirit; we would eventually find the keys to 'Evermore.'

Don't ever think our married life has been a bed of roses. It hasn't been, especially when I went into club management and my personality started to change under the pressure of that must-win business. But Punch and Judy have survived and all the kids have grown to love our nicknames.

We both realise that football has given us so much – lovely homes, wonderful holidays, great education for the boys and now security to enjoy the latter stages of our married life. Looking back to Sunday, February 3, 1964, I must say how lucky I was to have spotted that attractive red-head on the Locarno dance floor in the Coventry city centre precinct. The rest is history.......

As the daughter of a lady who ran a string of thriving hair salons in Warwickshire, it couldn't have been easy for Marge leaving her home patch for the first time, pregnant and just turned 21. But she has always kept a beautiful house, put some lovely food on the table and, above all, been a brilliant mother to Jonathan and Richard. Oh, yes, and the ladies of Portishead tell me she still gives them a super blow wave at the Jean May salon.

The Final Knock-Ins

How do you properly end a book? I'm happy with the 188 League and cup goals I scored for my various clubs, thrilled to have played for a team who won the FA Cup and so, so proud to have managed an unfancied club to Wembley glory and to have found myself in charge of a country.

I'm also honoured that there is a Bobby Gould Wall at Coventry City's ground because that's where it all started for me – and tickled pink that one of my cricket pals down in the West Country has created a Bobby Gould The Man The Legend group on Facebook. It's Somerset over-60s that I play my county cricket for these days, by the way.

But the question of how to round this project off is something that crossed my mind many a time in recent months on my training runs. There's plenty of thinking time because, every other day, I do four miles, my chest strap connected to my Polar watch so I can check my heart beat and calculate how many calories I've burned off. And I need to burn a few because, every day at four o'clock, our special china come out and I sit down with Marge for a nice slice of her home-made cake and a cup of tea.

The run is more than a period of contemplation and a means of staying fit. It has taken me to parts I wouldn't otherwise have reached. I go out wherever I am in the world and have pounded the tarmac on the Great Ocean Road in Australia, on some of the lanes around Havelock North on New Zealand's North Island, past the comedian Eddie Large's place here in Portishead, along the promenade at Puerto Del Carmen in our beloved Lanzarote, even down the sea front in Beirut. And not too many people can say that!

It is also a way of meeting friends, new and old. On holiday in Barbados earlier this year, a car pulled up alongside me and I was checked in my stride by a big grin from Winston White, a player Manny Bailey signed at Hereford all those years ago and who later followed me to Albion. In Portishead, four guys on a boat in the marina yelled one morning to say they had just heard me on Radio Bristol. Another day, Ken Knighton – a player and former Sunderland manager who I faced several times in my career – was going the opposite way on his power walk and we realised after all these years that we live just round the corner from each other.

For weeks on the run, I mulled over this closing section and realised it was one for me to decide on; not Marge, or the boys, the grandkids or any of the chairmen, managers, players, reporters or fans I've served, signed, selected, sued or saluted. But I trust that, if they have gone the full distance and made it to towards page 272, they will think I have lived up to my promise that this book wouldn't be boring.

Right, so to my epitaph – in other words, something that might go on my headstone. I've looked beyond my scrapbooks and pictures and come up with: "Please Lord, let us reach 51 points, so I can relax." It was a phrase that used to spin round my head endlessly in my days as manager of Bristol Rovers (twice), Coventry City (twice), West Bromwich Albion and Cheltenham Town and was, unfortunately, much more relevant than: "If I get to 84 points and win promotion, I'll be ecstatic."

There are some things in life, though, that transcend even football – hard though we sometimes find that to believe – so I'm going to sign off with a quote I borrowed and used in my manager's programme notes at Eastville in 1985-86: "If you have lived well, laughed often and loved much; if you have gained the respect of intelligent men and the love of children; if you could leave this world better than you found it; if you never lacked appreciation of the earth's beauty or never failed to express it; if you can look for the best in others and you gave the best you had, I think that would be success."

And if you can win the FA Cup as well, that's even better.

The Gould Rush

THE PLAYER

Coventry City	(July, 1962 - February, 1968)
Arsenal	(February, 1968 - June, 1970)
Wolverhampton Wanderers	(June, 1970 - September, 1971)
West Bromwich Albion	(September, 1971 - December, 1972)
Bristol City	(December, 1972 - November, 1973)
West Ham United	(November, 1973 - December, 1975)
Wolverhampton Wanderers	(December, 1975 - October, 1977)
Bristol Rovers	(October, 1977 - September, 1978)
Hereford United	(September, 1978 - October, 1979)
Wimbledon	(July, 1981 - August, 1981)

THE IN-BETWEEN

Ålesund	(Summers of 1978 and 1979)
Chelsea	(October, 1979 - May, 1981)
Aldershot (player-coach)	(August, 1981 - October, 1981)

THE MANAGER

Bristol Rovers	(October, 1981 - May, 1983)
Coventry City	(May, 1983 - December, 1984)
Bristol Rovers	(July, 1985 - July, 1987)
Wimbledon	(July, 1987 - December, 1990)
Queens Park Rangers	(December, 1990 - February, 1991)
West Bromwich Albion	(February, 1991 - May, 1992)
Coventry City	(July, 1992 - October, 1993)
Wales	(June, 1995 - June, 1999)
Cardiff City	(August, 2000 - July, 2001)
Cheltenham Town	(January, 2003 - November, 2003)
Peterborough United	(April, 2004 - September, 2004)
Hawkes Bay	(winters of 2005-06, 2006-07, 2007-08)
Weymouth	(April, 2009 - May, 2009)

ID Of Supporting Cast

Bantams - Coventry City
Bellers - Craig Bellamy
Big Jeff - Jeff Astle
Bomber - Tony Brown
Boogaloo - Trevor Brooking
Bonzo - Billy Bonds
Broony - Craig Brown
Colly - Paul Collingwood
Corky - Alan Cork
Daffy - Ron Greenwood
Dicksy - Alan Dicks
Doog - Derek Dougan
Fash - John Fashanu
Fester - Bobby Ferguson
Flying Postman - John Williams
Geordie - George Armstrong
Gibbo - Terry Gibson
Harry - Dave Bassett
Hibby - Kenny Hibbitt
Hopey - Bobby Hope
Howey - Don Howe
Jilly - Billy Jennings
JR/Richie - John Richards
Kindo - Steve Kindon
Lofty - Phil Parkes (Wolves)
Lurch - Dave Beasant
Manny - Mike Bailey
Mary - Ian Ure
Mooro - Bobby Moore
Nabbers - Bob McNab
Nemo - Derek Henderson
Ollie - Ian Holloway
Ossie - Peter Osgood
Pilgers - Norman Pilgrim

Punky - Paul Randall
Quinny, Polaris, Sumo - Micky Quinn
Radders - John Radford
Sammy - Keith Curle
Sanch - Lawrie Sanchez
Sav - Robbie Savage
Schnoz - John Sillett
Snout - Peter Storey
Sparky - Mark Hughes
Sparrow - Alan Taylor
Squeak - Derek Parkin
Stan - Peter Simpson
Sundy - Alan Sunderland
Tate & Lyall - John Lyall
TC - Terry Cooper
The Beard/Bearded Wonder/JH
- Jimmy Hill
The Hud - George Hudson
The Reverend - Les Wilson
Vincent - Vinnie Jones
Waggy - Dave Wagstaffe
Willo - Bob Wilson
Winko - Clive Goodyear
Wisey/Rat - Dennis Wise
Wuzzy Woo - Trevor Tainton
Yorky - John Kaye

The Gouldfather, Mrs Malaprop, Snip, The Ex-Superstar, Gouldy, Gaffer, Moroccan Mule, Bunter, Father Ted, BG - Me